2.50

C000301558

A MISCELLANY
OF WRITINGS

of

Michael Clark

Grosvenor House
Publishing Limited

This book is published by
Grosvenor House Publishing Ltd
Link House
140 The Broadway, Tolworth, Surrey, KT6 7HT.
www.grosvenorhousepublishing.co.uk

A CIP record for this book
is available from the British Library

ISBN 978-1-78623-543-5

On honeymoon at Ilfracombe in June 1958

CONTENTS

AN INTRODUCTION

I have always enjoyed writing and when I was quite young, I decided that I should learn every word in the dictionary; needless to say, an ambition that was never achieved. I also quickly realised that using those words 'in the right order' was of paramount importance. After school, my writing was mostly in the form of letters of the more formal kind. In this I have always been grateful for the guidance I received during my early years in the Inland Revenue.

During our near sixty years of married life, Margaret gave me great encouragement and was always willing to read what I had written, often making constructive comments, such as, "that's lovely," or "I wouldn't have said that," or "you haven't mentioned…" Since the end of the 1970s we have made many, many journeys in France and Margaret maintained detailed daily records. It was her wish and hope that I would prepare a narrative record – a 'personal commentary, journal, guide' based on her records and present it in the form of a book.

We received encouragement for such a project from a number of people we met in France who, when hearing of places we had visited, often said, "you know France better than we do – you should write a book". Although I have now compiled a record of quite a number of our journeys, there is more I wish to do to complete my *'France – A Journey'*. However, during recent years I have also written a number of pieces on varying topics relating to visits, experiences and history and I have gathered these together with a narrative of six of our France journeys and a condensed autobiography, to offer as a *'Miscellany of Writings'*. I hope you will find these pieces interesting and enjoyable reading.

A VERY ORDINARY LIFE

It seems inappropriate to begin an autobiography by expressing a regret, but I do have one particular regret. During her long life of nearly 94 years my mother had an excellent memory and for her last 37 years she lived next door to us. Naturally we made many and frequent, but necessarily brief, visits to her. Sometimes she would say, "I have been thinking…" and then proceed to tell myself, or perhaps Margaret, her recollections of family history or events. Invariably it would not be a convenient time for us to absorb what she had to tell us. I often suggested that she might like to "write it down," but she never did. Consequently, much of what she held in her memory was never recorded.

My mother was born, Ada Stevens, on 21 February 1901 and died on 4 February 1995. Her mother was Sara Ann (Chivers) born in 1867 and died 28 May 1957 and her father was Henry Stevens born on 17 July 1874 and died 3 December 1943. When I was born in 1930, Mum's parents lived at Camerton Farm Cottage at the top of Skinner's Hill opposite Camerton Farm on the southern side of the village of Camerton. Her father was a shepherd on the farm and Mum had been a domestic worker at the farm, which was in the ownership of the Miles family.

Mum had a brother, Arthur, who was born in 1898, married Alice Durbin in February 1922 and died in 1965; a sister Nora born in 1906, married Albert Vere in 1933 and died 20 June 1995; a sister Ivy Grace born in 1910 at Camerton, married Norman Gilbert Ashman (died 30 December 1951) in 1939 and died in 1964.

My father, Reginald Samuel Clark, was born on 11 June 1898 and died on 2 December 1967. His father, Richard, was born on 2 June 1873 and died in 1936; his mother Selina (Webber) was born in about 1875 and died in 1935. These grandparents lived at Tunley on the top of the hill on the northern side of the village of Camerton. Sadly, they both died when I was quite young.

Dad had a sister, Beatrice Louise, born in 1900, married Frederick Hampshire and died at the Royal United Hospital, Bath on 8 August 1926; a brother, George Henry born in 1902 and died in 1963; a sister, Amy Nora born in 1905, married George Williams on 14 January 1928 and died on 28 March 1988.

Mum and Dad were married in Camerton Church on 22 December 1923, by the Rev M.C. Dickenson. A wedding present, a clock, is still chiming regularly in our sitting room.

My family had a presence in Camerton for, at least, two centuries, until 1997. My great-great-grandfather, Edward Clark, was an Inn-keeper. He was a contemporary of the famous diarist and Rector of Camerton from 1800 until 1839, the Reverend John

Skinner; as such, he may well have been one of the Rector's antagonists!

I was born on Saturday, 7 June 1930 at Bridge Place, Camerton, a terrace of cottages, since demolished, close to Bridge Place Farm, which is now a privately occupied residence. It was in the valley, close to the Cam Brook over which a wooden bridge provided access to the road leading to Wick Lane. On the other side of the road was situated Camerton Station.

I was christened in Camerton Church by the Reverend Llewellyn Thomas on Saint Peter's Day, 29 June 1930. The Rev Thomas is buried close to the entrance to the church.

Camerton is a village of about six to seven hundred inhabitants, situated about six miles south west of Bath and, until local government reorganisation, was in the historic County of Somerset and then, from 1974 to 1996 in the County of Avon; since 1996 it has been within the unitary authority of Bath and North East Somerset. Camerton has a long history; its ancient church of Saint Peter and the Camerton Court, with its beautiful and interesting gardens, are features of which the village is proud. On the southern edge of the village lies the route of the Fosse Way and the site of a Roman settlement. Coal mining became an established industry in Camerton with the construction of the coal canal towards the end of the 18th century, followed by the building of the railway. It continued for some 200 years until Camerton New Pit finally closed in 1950. The railway was then redundant and that too closed, in 1951.

A memorable event occurred in Camerton, at the station, in 1931. It was the filming of scenes for the film *'The Ghost Train'*. Many well-known stars of the day took part, including; Jack Hulbert and Cicely Courtneidge (his wife for 62 years), his brother Claude Hulbert and Arnold Ridley – Private Godfrey in the BBC television show *Dad's Army* and the author of the play. I have been told that I was taken for a journey on the train by my aunt, but I was not old enough to remember the experience.

The main sources of employment in the village were agriculture and mining and my father, Reginald Samuel, worked at the nearby Camerton New Pit, where he was the 'saw-man'. He served in the Machine Gun Corps of the 51st Highland Division in France towards the end of the Great War.

When I was about four years old, we moved from Bridge Place just a few hundred yards up the hill to a semi-detached cottage, 10 Camerton Hill, which was accessed from the lane by the school and which was the original entrance to Camerton Court. The property was on the side of the hill and afforded excellent views over the valley and towards Tunley and the village of Timsbury, as well as all the activity of the colliery and the railway in the valley below. Of course, at both homes we had extensive gardens and Dad, and Mum, ensured that, so far as vegetables were concerned, we were self-sufficient. However, we had no mains water supply until the early 1940s – our water had to be lifted from a well, and we were not connected to the electricity supply until after the Second World War. Until then we had to light oil lamps every evening and use candles for occasional use. In 1948, Mum and Dad purchased 10 Camerton Hill from the Woodborough and Camerton Estates for, I believe, £350. It was a happy home and, in fact, 10 Camerton Hill became, with the benefit of three extensions, our family home for the next sixty years.

We were then about one hundred yards from Camerton School, which I attended. Unfortunately, I do not have strong memories of my years at junior school. Perhaps the teaching was not particularly inspiring; I don't even remember such occasions as plays and entertainment, but I do remember 'nature walks'. Without memorable achievements, I duly proceeded to senior school where I found the specific subjects, such as, English, arithmetic, geography and history so much more stimulating. My parents were anxious that I should have a good education and arranged for me to transfer to the Bath Technical College. Here, in addition to the subjects that I had liked, I was introduced to French, as well as shorthand and typewriting! However, after perhaps three years I decided to leave, partly because some of my friends were leaving and partly because I felt that I should not continue to be wholly supported by my parents, although they had wished me to continue. My father's wages were about £10 per week! Certainly my 'education' did not cease at that point and I followed it with a correspondence course; later, I attended evening classes. I have always been keen to learn and as the late Tony Benn commented when asked about his education, he described it as 'work in progress'. I do not know how it came about, but I found myself with an appointment for an interview at the office of H M Inspector of Taxes, in 1/3 Southgate Street, Bath. I was surprised to be offered a job and invited to start work, I think, the following week.

I have never regretted my decision, for it set the course of my entire working life. My ten years in the Inland Revenue, mostly in the Bath Office, formed a good foundation, as high standards of work were expected, particularly by the District Inspector, Mr. T.H. Hore. As an example – it was his practice to read letters before they left the office. One day, I was called to his office and he referred to a letter I had written to a firm of lawyers. He said, "you have addressed this letter 'Dear Sirs'" and he added, "These partners were colleagues of mine at university, please address them, Gentlemen". There was an atmosphere in that office of respect, conscientiousness, responsibility and efficiency, but at the same time, it held an air of amicability. I was taught the basis of good letter writing and given a mnemonic – seven words all beginning with the letter 'c' – to aid the memory! Those important words are:- correct, clear, coherent, concise, comprehensive, courteous, and complete.

I only left the Inland Revenue on being ordered to transfer to an office in the centre of London. After a short while I answered an advertisement by a Bristol firm of chartered accountants, C.J. Ryland & Co., for an assistant in their tax department for a period of six weeks. I was offered the post, started work on the following Monday, and stayed for eleven years. In time, C.J. Ryland & Co merged with another firm, Grace, Derbyshire and Todd; the joint practice subsequently being acquired by Thomson, McLintock, which later became part of KPMG. I did not feel particularly comfortable within such a large organisation. I then took a position as 'manager' of the small team of the tax department of the National Provincial Bank in Corn Street, Bristol. It was a very amicable situation and we virtually had independent control and responsibility for our activities. However, it was not long before the National Provincial Bank was swallowed up by the Westminster Bank to become National Westminster Bank. We were transferred to a large new Trustee Branch in Bath. The new bank was proposing to extend their services to include, not only personal clients, but also small businesses. One by one our small team departed. I felt the bank was not sufficiently equipped and prepared to offer this additional service. Once again, I felt that I should head in a different direction.

In 1973 Value Added Tax was introduced. It was a new tax to all of us and I felt that it was an opportunity where I could offer a service to small businesses who were then required to keep appropriate records and to complete the quarterly returns to H M Customs and Excise. Moreover, I could also handle related matters such as preparing accounts and tax returns. I advertised and received an encouraging response. With the wholehearted agreement and support of my wife, Margaret, I became self-employed. Together we spent time acquainting ourselves with the new tax. Indeed, Margaret happily and enthusiastically engaged herself in learning new skills and for nearly forty years she undertook a considerable portion of the workload, until the onset of dementia at the beginning of 2012. I am pleased that I have since been able to continue to act for a small and diminishing number of clients; indeed, I still have one remaining client. Providing a direct personal service to many and varied clients over many years has been a fulfilling experience for both of us. Therefore, since that surprising interview at 1/3 Southgate Street in the 1940s I have never strayed from the field of taxation, a period of more than 70 years.

Returning now to my early years.

Home entertainment in the 1930s and 1940s was provided by a gramophone, a radio and, of course, the piano. The radio was powered by an accumulator, which had to be exchanged every week. I remember enjoying playing records of such singers as Frank Titterton – tenor and Anne Zeigler and Webster Booth – duettists. Radio artists I recall are – Tommy Handley (ITMA and Mr Murgatroyd and Mr Winterbottom), Jewell and Warris, Rob Wilton and Donald Peers – whose signature song was *'In a Shady Nook by a Babbling Brook'*. Programmes I remember listening to were *'In Town Tonight'*, *'Happidrome'*, *'Workers Playtime'*, *'Albert Sandler and his Palm Court Orchestra'*, and *'Bird Songs from the Surrey Woods'*. I particularly liked listening to orchestral concerts by the BBC Symphony Orchestra conducted by Sir Adrian Boult – I bought a copy of his book, *'The Art of Conducting'*. Newsreaders became very familiar, particularly during the war years. I remember Stuart Hibberd who had a very distinctive voice and was BBC Radio's chief announcer, Frank Philips, Bruce Belfrage, Alvar Lidell and John Snagge. Whenever we heard John Snagge's voice we knew it was to be significant news.

The War Years, from 1939 to 1945, made an indelible impression on my memory – National Registration Identity Cards (my number was WPEQ 117 3), gas masks, blackout, rationing, a searchlight on nearby Tunley hill, air-raid sirens, ARP wardens, Camerton Court became a hospital, and from time to time, bombs dropping nearby. I have an acute memory of the night of Sunday, 24 November 1940. We had been to church in the afternoon and in the early evening we heard the constant fearful drone of enemy aircraft. Soon a strong glow appeared in the sky in the direction of Bristol, about 12 to 13 miles away. This frightening sight and sound continued for hours. It was the night on which much of the centre of the city of Bristol was destroyed. Officially, the raid lasted from 18.21 until 00.08; 200 people were killed that night, including members of Mum's family in an air-raid shelter. Despite our limited facilities – we had no electricity – we gave shelter to a Mr and Mrs Tucker. Mr Tucker was the advertising manager of Fry's, the chocolate factory in Keynsham and he had access to luxury items which were not readily available to us in those days, such as toys and books!

In 1942 came the Bath Blitz. On the weekend of 25–27 April, Bath suffered three air raids during which 417 people were killed. After which Dad's sister, Amy, Uncle George and their daughter, Louise came to stay with us.

Yes, the War transformed our lives.

Childhood holidays were rare, but enjoyable. One of the first, in the 1930s, was spent with Mum, in High

Wycombe, at 'Camerton' 247 West Wycombe Road. This was the home of Mum's sister Nora and Uncle Albert (Vere), as well as their fox terrier, Tiger. I recall outings and, particularly, sitting on the banks of the Thames at Maidenhead and sailing a toy boat on the water. Other 'holidays' I spent with Mum's sister Ivy and Uncle Norman (Ashman) at Hope Cottage, Holcombe; that too was before the Second World War. I remember their neighbour – the jovial Fred Langley. As I recall it, the mother and stepfather of Uncle Norman had experience of a Guest House in Ilfracombe and one year, in the late 1930s, I suspect, they took Auntie Ivy and me there for a holiday. The Guest House was 'Glendower' in Wilder Road and the proprietors were the Misses Brooks. What an exciting experience that was. In a later year Mum, Dad and myself spent a holiday there, travelling by train from Radstock, with the inevitable 'change at Templecombe', to the station on the hill at Ilfracombe. Prominent memories of my stays in Ilfracombe are of Sunday morning services at St James Church on the right-hand side of the road leading to the harbour. I believe that Mum, Dad and me only spent two holidays together, the first being at Glendower and the other was in Bournemouth, where, I recall that we stayed in 'bed and breakfast' accommodation; we certainly travelled by train, again from Radstock.

My social life in the period up to National Service was, it seems, quite limited. From time to time there would be some amateur entertainment events in the Church Room at Camerton. There was a cinema in Radstock – The Palace – which I do not remember entering. At Midsomer Norton there was The Palladium and I did go to see one or two films there. I did attend ballroom dancing classes at Paulton, which were well conducted by a Mr Bidwell. He was employed at the Bristol Aeroplane Company works at Filton, Bristol, I believe, and from time to time he would arrange for a coach to take a group of his pupils to dances which were held in the large canteen. These were very popular as music was provided by well-known bands of the day. Following my National Service, in the early 1950s, the cinema did attract me a little more – the Forum, the Odeon and the Beau Nash in Bath. However, I liked to go to orchestral concerts in the Pavilion, and the Forum and to organ recitals in the Abbey in Bath. I am fortunate to have seen Sir Thomas Beacham and Sir John Barbirolli conducting. I used to attend the Saturday night dances held at Bob's Palais at Midsomer Norton and I became part of a group of friends which included Brian Willcox and Don Dando. These dances were well controlled, Bob Purnell saw to that, and the music was provided by Arthur Marshall and his excellent band. I used to have to walk back to Camerton after midnight and, at Radstock, I would sometimes encounter activity on the railway which served the local coal industry. Other occasions of that period which I recall are travelling to London to see Tommy Cooper, Jimmy Edwards and The Crazy Gang. I also went to see 'King's Rhapsody' by Ivor Novello, which opened in September 1949.

Undoubtedly, the church was a great influence in my life, its ceremonies and, particularly, its music. I grew up during the twelve years incumbency of the Rev Edward Stephens, an imposing and inspiring man, both in stature and in speech. He had suffered the loss of an eye while serving as a chaplain during the Great War. As soon as it was practical, I joined the choir. I have a special memory of one young choir member who used to attend, when he was available, in naval uniform; his name was Philip Baker and he still had an excellent treble voice – at Christmas, his solo verse of, *'Sire, the night is darker now'* was moving and predictive. I had piano lessons from the late Mrs B.G. Stone, who lived at Radford, in the valley at the western end of the village. She was an excellent teacher and I enjoyed those Saturday morning lessons. Sometimes I was fortunate to have a lift home with the horse-drawn Radstock Co-op delivery baker. I took a series of Trinity College of Music examinations which were held in the premises of Milsom's music store in Northgate Street, Bath. I have never forgotten my reward for success in my first examination; it was a prized copy of *Hymns Ancient and Modern*. However, my ultimate aim was to play that king of instruments, the organ. I was directed to an organist and teacher, Mr Stanley Pearce, who was the assistant organist at St Mary's Church, Bathwick, Bath. Lessons took place on the St Mary's organ, on which I was allowed to practice. I was also able to practice on the organ at Camerton Church, but I needed the assistance of Dad to pump the organ! Stanley Pearce was an inspirational teacher and always encouraged his pupils into organist posts. He became a personal friend and, indeed, played for our wedding in 1958.

Having been organist at St Peter's, Camerton, my next position was as organist at the church of St Philip and St James at Norton St Philip, following which I was appointed organist and choirmaster at the Parish Church of Peasedown St John, after which I served at the Church of St James, Southstoke, where the Vicar was the charming Charles George Hamilton Dicker. My next appointment was at the church of the Holy Trinity, Frome. Here, there was a lively congregation led by the Rev C.G. Shipley. There was an enthusiastic and competent choir of men, with one lady alto and about fifteen boys from whom I received much support and loyalty, enabling us to achieve excellent results. A particularly memorable occasion was on 21 August 1966 when we took part in a BBC televised celebration of the Eucharist at St John's Church, the parish church, in Frome. During my time at Holy Trinity, from 1963 until 1968, I attended a residential course at The Royal School of Church Music (RSCM) at Addington Palace and with much pleasure I arranged for a number of the choir boys to attend RSCM residential courses also. A notable occasion was a Whitsunday Evensong; we had a visit from a RSCM Commissioner, Christopher Dearnley, who was Organist at Salisbury Cathedral and subsequently, for 22 years, Organist at St Paul's Cathedral. His report and comments were very complimentary. Holy Trinity was a demanding yet most rewarding experience – the high-point of my career as an organist. It was when my work took me to the National Provincial Bank in Bristol, that I realised that I could no longer give Holy Trinity the time and attention which I wished. After a short period at All Saints' Church, Dunkerton I spent three years at St Nicholas Church, Radstock. It was the end of my career as an organist.

I already had a number of private piano pupils and teaching the young people and preparing them for examinations was so rewarding. Nevertheless, it was choir training which I found particularly inspiring. Early in the 1970s, together with my piano pupils, our two sons and some of their school friends, we formed a choir. Soon we were joined by a number of enthusiastic adults to create a four-part choir – The Camerton Choir. Margaret gave the choir her unstinting participation and support. We enjoyed performing at various venues, churches, chapels, a hospital, residential homes and the local Cheshire Home. Eventually, sadly it was its success that brought about its demise. With the increased membership we mostly had to rehearse in our sitting room as two groups, there being no suitable venue available in the village. We were then not able to continue to maintain the standard which we had been pleased to achieve. Since we came to Trowbridge in 1997, we have been able to attend many of the wonderful recitals and concerts held at the excellent Wiltshire Music Centre in Bradford-on-Avon, including concerts by the Trowbridge Symphony Orchestra. In recent years our enjoyment of music has been found in our own large collection of CDs and in the valued Classic FM.

From my younger days, although I have never participated in any formal games, I have had an interest in sport, particularly football and cricket. Groups of us used to gather in a nearby field called Hurdles to play football, that is until Farmer Matthews chased us off. On one occasion he confiscated the ball, my ball, and I had to go to the local police station to recover it – a formality! We would also meet in a field, not a pitch, at Hopyard, Wick Lane, to play cricket, where one of the lads loved to emulate the stroke play of the great Denis

Compton. I would often watch our local football teams in the 1930s and 1940s, such as Clandown, Peasedown, Paulton Rovers, Welton Rovers. During the period of my National Service, in the Royal Air Force, from October 1948 to May 1950 I was stationed at RAF Warton in Lancashire. This was relatively near Blackpool to which there was a bus service from the camp. I was fortunate, therefore, to be able to see many of the games of Blackpool Football Club at Bloomfield Road during the 1949–50 season. Blackpool were one of the top teams at that time and their squad included such great players as Stanley Matthews and Stanley Mortensen. I can still name nine of the regular players of that season. I regret that I do not have any match programmes – no doubt they only cost a few pence, but my pay was only four shillings a day! In the 1950s I often watched Bristol City play at Ashton Gate; their international forward, John Atyeo, played for the club from 1951 to 1966 scoring 351 goals. In fact, I saw Atyeo play in two international matches at Wembley – on 30 November 1955 when England beat Spain 4–1 and on 9 May 1956 when England defeated Brazil 4–2. The programmes cost 'one shilling'! Nowadays, I can watch football on television, and I look forward to the results of Bristol City, Bristol Rovers and, as my cousin Derek and his son Richard are ardent supporters, Wycombe Wanderers' games.

I have mentioned my period of National Service; in fact. I have some fond memories of that period. I did not resent having to serve and I considered it a valuable experience. The greater part of my service was spent at No 90 Maintenance Unit, RAF Warton. It was not particularly stimulating, working in the stores, but we did have the facility for visiting Blackpool where there was a great variety of entertainment, etc., available. We often headed for the Silver Grill Café for a welcome meal of steak pie and chips. I went regularly to evening classes at the college. I often listened to the great Reginald Dixon at the Tower Ballroom organ and sometimes to Horace Finch at the organ of the Winter Gardens Pavilion. Also, for the first time, I had the opportunity of seeing operas, performed by the Carl Rosa Opera Company and the D'Oyly Carte Opera Company. Less appealing, of course, were the regular nightly guard duties. Fortunately, my duty was normally with a good friend, Jack Coyle from Glasgow. Like me, Jack was fond of classical music and history. Often, on the bleak deserted airfield (I don't know what we were guarding) alongside the estuary of the River Ribble, in the middle of a bitter winter's night, Jack would tell me stories of Scottish clans and battles.

During my school years and certainly until my period of National Service my means of transport was the bicycle. It was a means of getting to school and to work and it gave me much pleasure. I fondly remember one sunny Sunday afternoon in the 1940s, with two friends, Neil Lowe and Ian Clark (a second cousin), cycling from Camerton, up and over the Mendips, through Burrington Combe and on to Weston-Super-Mare. On the road leading into Weston we all collided – I think we were dawdling, but we all casually recovered and continued. Remarkably, I have no recollection of any other traffic! After a couple of hours in Weston we returned along the A368 on the north side of the Mendip

Hills and I particularly recall a pervasive smell – perhaps it was of garlic – as we rode along a section of road in a sort of bowl near Rickford in the still, quiet and calm of the late evening. I don't know what time we reached home but it must have been quite late. It was, indeed, a wholly enjoyable and, obviously, memorable journey.

However, soon after returning from the RAF I sought an easier means of travel. I purchased an Excelsior two-stroke, 125, motorcycle with the registration of BGL 774; it was soon followed by a more powerful machine – an Excelsior 250cc bike – CFB 901. I then acquired all the special weather protection clothing I needed as advised by my organ teacher, Stanley Pearce – greatcoat, waders, helmet (not a hard one) and goggles. After three or four years I realised that there was an easier, a more comfortable means of travel – by car. I bought my first car from a lady in Stratton-on-the-Fosse with the guidance, and a loan, from Mr Jack (Sonny) Coombs, a friend, and garage proprietor in Timsbury – a black and red Morris 8 – DHT 193 and I think it cost £100. That vehicle was followed by another Morris 8, a black Series E model of 1939 – DOR 695. This was one of our favourite cars – the one which I owned when Margaret and I met in 1956. Next came a black Hillman Minx – FGL 987 – followed in August 1969 by a black Hillman Super Minx – FHW 11D. In 1979 we entered the world of Swedish cars and we bought a white Volvo 144 – NHR 391M (£1,750). In 1982 we replaced the Volvo 144 with a blue Volvo 244 – BAE 980V (£4,400). In 1994 we bought a white Saab 9000 – G213 XMG (£7,995). During the years 1977 to 1994 we had a second car for my occasional and business use – Margaret never drove!

They were an Austin 1100 – HYD 923K (£625); a Renault 12TL – KTC 322P (£1,580); a Morris Mini – OYD 773L (£500); another Mini – MYC 455V (£1,300); a Vauxhall Nova – E268 SYD (£5,295). All are fondly remembered. Not least our final vehicle, a Blue SAAB 9-5 SE AUTO ESTATE – Y304 UGF, (Margaret suggested that this was an abbreviation for Useful for Going to France) which we purchased in June 2004 for £13,200 and which has given us so much pleasure, particularly in safely and comfortably taking us over many thousands of miles in France and is still parked on our drive.

During the early 1970s I took an increasing interest in local affairs and was elected to the Parish Council, serving for some 27 years. I was Chairman for six years and, with the support of the very competent Parish Clerk, the late Terry Webber, I found this experience very rewarding. For my service, I was awarded a framed Certificate of Commendation. For several years I served as the Parish Council representative Manager of Camerton School.

France has interested and attracted me for much of my life. From being taught French by Monsieur Fred Emonnet, to learning of day visits to France by my aunt and uncle in High Wycombe in the 1930s, to enjoying Sunday school or choir outings to Weymouth and speculating on that foreign land beyond the horizon. My own father had served in France in 1918 and cometh 1939 and the Second World War, France was constantly in the news and in our thoughts. My Uncle Norman did not escape from Dunkerque in 1940 but, fortunately, later returned to England by another route. Life was frequently interrupted by air raids by enemy aircraft based in Normandy. Then, in 1944, we had the exhilarating news that Allied Forces had landed on the coast on Normandy – after four years of brutal repression the liberation of France had begun.

I had to visit that country. My first opportunity came in the early 1950s, with a visit by ferry to Boulogne and, particularly, to the Flying Bomb sites nearby. Then, in 1952 I participated in a two-week guided tour of Paris arranged by a civil service travel agency – Whitehall Travel. In 1956, together with four friends, I planned a journey across France to the Mediterranean, then continuing into Italy, Switzerland, Germany and Belgium before returning to France. We were well prepared and equipped with a detailed route plan prepared by the AA we set off, with Don Dando with me in my car and with Neil Lowe and Cliff Menhinnitt with Brian Willcox in his car. We set off on Sunday 29 July and reached Dover at about 10.30; the weather had made it a very unpleasant journey and we realised that there were severe storms in the Channel. After a very long delay, at about 18.30, the ship – Saint Germain – sailed. However, on reaching the open sea it began to roll and as it did so many standing passengers were thrown to the floor. I grabbed the frame of a sliding door and immediately the door closed, temporarily trapping my leg. I was in some pain and, although I did not realise it, I had broken my leg. It was the end of my adventure and I have written a detailed account of my experiences elsewhere. It was not until July 1970 that I next set foot in France when, during a family camping holiday in Kent, we crossed to Boulogne by hovercraft – the Princess Anne – in very pleasant conditions. In 1979, when Paul and Ian were 19 and 15, we enjoyed our first family holiday in France, which was followed by several more. In fact, for Margaret and myself, it marked the beginning of 35 successive years during which we visited the Hexagon, once, twice or perhaps three times. We developed a great interest in and love of the country and its people and came to regard it as our 'second home'. I am in the process of preparing a 'personal commentary, journal, guide', of our experiences entitled, *'France – A Journey'*.

Whilst tracing the various threads of my life during the past 88 years, I have barely referred to my personal and family life, which was, of course, the backbone of all that lies before.

I had a very happy and secure childhood and parents from whom I received love, support, encouragement and understanding. I suppose I would have to say that my mother had the greatest influence being the one who was, seemingly, always there – Dad providing the means on which we lived. During the course of my 20s I began to think more of the future than the present. I began to think of the kind of person I would like to spend, perhaps, the rest of my life with. Someone who would be compatible with my established life, someone who would share my Christian faith, preferably of the Anglican tradition, someone who would share my love of music, my interest in France and more, someone who, in short, would succeed my mother. It seems rather a lot to expect!

During the 1950s many young people would attend Sunday evening church services, perhaps it was because there was often boys and young men in the choir; it was so at Camerton. I liked to attend services at Bath Abbey; the music, under Ernest Maynard, was so inspiring and Archdeacon Cook and then Prebendary Geoffrey Lester were uplifting personalities. I sometimes went with Don Dando and there was one particular Sunday evening in the summer of 1956 which I shall never forget. We were sitting towards the rear of the nave and at the end of the service we remained seated, while others around us left and while the main congregation made its way towards the west door. I suppose we were rather conspicuous and as they passed, two girls looked in our direction as we looked towards them. They then disappeared into the Abbey Churchyard and we made our way back to my car, which was the Morris 8 Series E – DOR 695 which I have already referred to, with the intention of returning home. I think we had parked in Manvers Street and after passing the railway station we drove along Dorchester Street towards the Old Bridge when, suddenly, Don said, "that's those two girls we saw in the Abbey"; they were walking in the same direction. I instinctively stopped and as they reached us, we opened a window and asked if we could give them a lift and they, perhaps surprisingly, accepted. We must have sat there for a while introducing ourselves – their names were Margaret and Brenda. We asked where we could take them and we learned that Margaret lived in Oldfield Park, Bath and, so far as I recall, that is where we took them, in fact, to Faulkland Road. We had a very friendly conversation and we all agreed that we would like to meet again. It must have been that, there and then, I suggested a visit to Ilfracombe, a place that held happy memories for me. They were pleased to agree. We decided on a date and must have exchanged some contact details, although none of us had a telephone – I expect I had learned that Margaret worked in the Appointments Office of the Royal United Hospital in Bath. We said goodbye and Don and myself continued home. What a memorable evening it had been!

When the appointed day arrived, I collected Don – he did not drive – from his home in Midsomer Norton and we continued into Bath to meet our new friends. I have no idea which route we took to reach Ilfracombe but reach it we did – I'm sure we had been consumed in conversation. We had a very enjoyable day in Ilfracombe; I am certain that I pointed out the large guesthouse facing the Capstan – Glendower. On our return journey, the floodlit tower of Wells Cathedral is a striking memory. We had had a splendid day and I found that I had established a good relationship with Margaret – that eye contact in the Abbey had contained a message. From that day onwards each of us were never far from the minds of the other. I so wish that I had a record of the dates of those two meetings. We soon discovered a mutual love of great music and on 2 June 1956 we were at the Colston Hall, Bristol for a concert by the Liverpool Philharmonic Orchestra, conducted by Hugo Rignold. The programme included the *Tone Poem: Vltava (Ma Vlast)* by Smetana, which became a life-long favourite. Also in the programme was Tchaikovsky's *Tatiana's Letter Song*, sung by Joan Hammond. Our first meeting was not long before my planned departure for two weeks in France and beyond, on 29 July 1956. Fortunately, in the meantime, there was time for me to introduce Margaret to my mum and dad. They made her feel very welcome; they developed a fondness for her, a special regard and respect for her which they held for the rest of their lives. When I found myself 'stranded' in a hotel in Dunkerque with a broken leg, with no ready means of contacting my parents, I turned to Margaret; I sent her a telegram and I am sure the wording was "Leg broken. Home on Saturday. Please come out" – I know the telegram is amongst the archives here! When she arrived at my home, she found that my parents were out and so she introduced herself to our next door neighbour, Winnie Maggs; that was the beginning of another long friendship. When it came to the time for Margaret to leave for her home in Bath, Dad insisted on escorting her to her bus. I was confined to the house for some six weeks and spent much of the time in my bedroom. Margaret came to visit me regularly every weekend; with so much time to talk and listen we got to know one another well and it was a period which securely cemented our relationship. It was not until November of 1956 that I had returned to driving and to work and we wished to celebrate. We would have a holiday; where else should we go but Ilfracombe and, of course, to Glendower. Unfortunately, it was the time of the Suez Crisis and there was a great shortage of petrol which was rationed. The kindness and some coupons from a farming friend enabled us to travel confidently, although there was the problem that many filling stations were closed. Nevertheless, it was a wonderful journey on a lovely day. The various countryside colours of late autumn were spectacular and there was an unbelievable absence of traffic.

We used the toll road at Porlock and when we reached the toll-booth we found poultry occupying the road and the warden was astonished to meet a customer. We had a wonderful week in Ilfracombe; for us, a unique winter holiday.

Margaret Elizabeth Moore was born on 25 July 1933, her home was at 51 Faulkland Road, in Oldfield Park. She was educated at South Twerton Junior School and the City of Bath Girls School, remaining in contact with some of her school friends for the rest of her life. She had worked at Toveys the opticians and then, until we married, in the appointments office of the Royal United Hospital in Bath.

Margaret's mother Violet (Harding) was born on 12 September 1902 at Marshfield in Gloucestershire. Her father was Edwin Harding, a verger and gardener. She died on 12 September 1979 at her home, 12 Smallcombe Close, Clandown, with her husband and Margaret by her side.

Margaret's mother had two sisters; May born on 7 July 1900 at Marshfield, married John Silvester on 25 October 1922 at Marshfield and died on 22 September 1970 at Billericay; Ivy born on 5 October 1904 at Marshfield and died on 19 March 1994 at Bath.

Margaret's father was Alec Joseph Moore, who was born on 6 June 1906 at 30 Church Road, Weston, Bath. His father was Joseph Webb Moore. Alec died on 21 March 1988 at St Martin's Hospital, Bath in the presence of Margaret.

Margaret's father had two brothers; Harold born in 1899 at Weston, Bath and died in 1973; Edmund born on 16 April 1904, married Ethel in 1925 and died on 16 March 1992.

Margaret's parents were married in the Parish Church of Marshfield on 24 September 1930. Her father spent his entire working life in the Post Office, retiring as a Postal Inspector, apart from serving throughout the Second World War in the Royal Engineers. He spent much of this time in the Middle East and, during which, he became a close friend of Norman Hill. They shared common Christian beliefs and took the opportunity of spending their leave periods exploring the historic sites of the Holy Land and beyond. Norman Hill remained a life-long friend, and a friendship developed between Norman's daughter Jean and son Ivan and ourselves, which continues to this day. Norman died in 2017 at the age of 98.

Our love of music expressed itself again on Saturday, 8 June 1957 when we drove to Bristol's Colston Hall again for a concert by the London Philharmonic Orchestra, conducted by Constantin Silvestri. The first half consisted of the *Symphony No 9* (From the New World) by Dvorak. Playing his double bass in the orchestra was Margaret's uncle, Jack Silvester. We talked to him during the interval and we spoke of the acclaimed Romanian conductor, Constantin Silvestri. In his matter of fact manner, Uncle Jack commented, "He is supposed to be very good, but we can't understand what he says".

After our holiday in Ilfracombe our relationship continued to flourish, without doubt anticipating that it would become permanent. On 25 July 1957, Margaret's birthday, we became engaged and we began to consider when we might get married and where we might then live. Margaret had come to like Camerton and our situation and, when Mum and Dad offered us two of their rooms, we gave it serious consideration. I know Margaret's Dad had reservations about us living with in-laws, but we wished to have entirely separate accommodation. We had plans drawn up for an extension – a kitchen/dining room and a separate access downstairs and a flight of stairs leading to a bedroom and a bathroom upstairs. In addition, we would have an access provided to each of the two existing rooms. We were delighted with the proposal and the work was carried out by a respected local builder, Mr Tom Cook of Peasedown-St-John for a cost of about £1,600. We then decided on a wedding date; it would be on my birthday, 7 June 1958. As the months passed it became evident that the work would be completed before June. In fact, it was completed well before our wedding and furnished with the gift from my parents of a dining room suite, which was manufactured at the factory of my Uncle Albert Vere in High Wycombe, and a bedroom suite which we had purchased from Silcox, Son and Wicks in Kingsmead Square, Bath.

In view of its significance in our lives we would have been pleased to be married in Bath Abbey. However, Margaret had been a Sunday School teacher at the Church of St Mark's, Lyncombe, Bath and as, at that time, I was Organist at Peasedown St John parish church, we decided that we would be married at St Mark's with the service taken by the Vicar of

Peasedown, the Rev C. Wyndham Hollinshead, that the choir of Peasedown-St-John should be our choir and that our organist would be, my organ master, Stanley Pearce. (The teacher of Stanley Pearce, Algernon Salter, had been organist at St Mark's and I am proud to have some of his books). Our bridesmaids were Margaret's friend Brenda and my cousin Cherry; my best man was Don Dando. We gave much thought to the composition of the service, the music, the hymns, the psalm, etc. It was to be OUR wedding. Margaret insisted that the organ voluntaries should include pieces which I often played – *Air and Gavotte* by Samuel Wesley, *Toccata from the Gothic Suite* by Boellmann, *Minuet from Berenice* by Handel and the *Bridal March from the Birds of Aristophanes* by Parry. The Rev Hollinshead gave an address and during the signing of the registers the Choir sang *Crimond*. It was followed by the *Wedding March* by F. Mendelssohn Bartholdy. After the ceremony, we welcomed guests, choir, etc., to our reception which had been arranged by Margaret's Mum and Dad, in the Red House Restaurant, Bond Street, Bath. With family, friends and choir, it was all a joyful occasion which I remember clearly. We were collected from the Red House by our friend, Mr Jack (Sonny) Coombs of Timsbury. He took us to our completed new home, where we changed, transferred to our car (DOR 695) and set off on our honeymoon. Where? Ilfracombe, of course. We had two weeks of lovely weather, relaxing and walking some of the near coastal walks, including Lee Bay and experiencing a visit to Lundy Island. We returned to a completely furnished and equipped new home to begin our married life.

At this point I think I should introduce Inge to this story. In 1952 an exchange visit was arranged between students in Hadsund, Denmark and students in Bath, particularly, I think, those associated with Bath Abbey. Although Margaret would be unable to visit Denmark, as she was by then working, her parents agreed to accommodate two Danish girls – Inge and Karen. Well, it was the beginning of a most remarkable and wonderful friendship which has continued to this day. In the following years, Inge with her husband Preben, and then with their son Henrik, made many visits to this country. Margaret's parents made two visits to them in Copenhagen and, with Paul and Ian, we visited them by car in 1975. Apart from 'meetings' the relationship has endured and blossomed for approaching 67 years by correspondence, e-mails and, particularly by the telephone conversations between Inge and Margaret which would last for hours and sometimes late into the night and which contained much laughter and hilarity and which they both so much enjoyed.

Following our marriage Margaret was not working, although she was employed for short periods in the next year or so. She adapted to her new life so readily, even joining Mum on her regular Friday morning shopping bus journeys to Radstock and getting to know other passengers.

Margaret had been fond of cats – a photograph of her Timothy is still on display – and we soon acquired Frisky who was followed by Thomas. I had liked Tiger at High Wycombe and we decided to have a dog, a fox terrier, and we named him Prince. Unfortunately, he became difficult to handle and we had to part company. What a different personality we found in Remus, a black Labrador who was to be our friend for many years.

Margaret was also very fond of her two tortoises, George and George, which she had had since childhood. They came with her to Camerton and, in 1997, with us to Trowbridge. Sadly, they did not survive for many years in their new environment; they must have been perhaps about 60 years old.

In 1959 we spent an enjoyable holiday exploring the coasts of Cornwall and Devon and staying in bed and breakfast accommodation. Although Margaret had visited the area before, it was a new experience for me.

On Friday 29 April 1960 our first son, Paul, was born. It had been arranged that Margaret would give birth at the Paulton Maternity Hospital. Remarkably the event coincided with my daily routine. At that time I was working at C.J. Ryland & Co and as I was getting ready for work, Margaret said I think it would be wise if you took me to the hospital before you set off for Bristol; it was only a couple of miles to Paulton. At lunchtime I telephoned the hospital to learn that we had a baby son. I drove to the hospital from the office and then home to tell my parents the joyful news. Visits followed over the weekend, myself and both sets of grandparents. Soon we were all at home – to begin an exciting new phase in our lives.

In 1961 we spent a holiday in a chalet at Dawlish Warren where we were pleased to have a visit from an office colleague, Dennis and his wife Daphne with their young daughter, Julie. I still keep in touch with Daphne and, until her poor sight made it difficult for her, Julie.

In the early 1960s I was the organist at Southstoke Church and as soon as he was old enough, certainly no more than three, Paul would sit with me on the organ stool. It was during this period that we made another visit to Ilfracombe. At that time, we had the Hillman Minx car – FGL 987 – and we took Margaret's Mum and Dad with us. This car had a front bench seat and Paul sat in an attached child's seat between us. He still had a limited vocabulary, but every time he saw an approaching vehicle, he exclaimed "a car".

In 1962 we bought a small tent and planned our first camping holiday. As she did for more than 50 years, Margaret kept a diary of that holiday; the details are so remarkable, I must record them here.

We set off on <u>Wednesday 4 July 1962</u> with, it seems, £18 and £1 for petrol.

Left home at	12.10pm Mileage 52,558
Radstock	12.40pm
Glastonbury	1.15pm
Exeter +	3.15pm – Stop for 30 mins
Newton Abbot	4.00pm
Kingsbridge	5.00pm
Arrived Camping Site (Salcombe)	5.30pm Mileage 52,676

Thursday, 5.7.62

Petrol £1
Toured Salcombe, Slapton Sands and Blackpool Sands.
Lunch 12/-   Mileage 52,728

Friday, 6.7.62

Spent afternoon on North Sands Beach. Paul and Mum went paddling.
Lunch 11/2   Mileage 52,737

Saturday, 7.7.62

Went to Hope Cove.
No lunch   Mileage 52,750

Sunday, 8.7.62

Went to Plymouth to see Mum and Dad. Visited Tamar Bridge.
Lunch at Kingsbridge 15/6!
Petrol 10/- (2 gallons)   Mileage 52,814

Monday, 9.7.62

Went to Thurlestone 'Sands'.
Lunch 12/8   Mileage 52,831

Tuesday, 10.7.62

Went to Slapton and Blackpool.
Lunch 12/7. Petrol 10/-   Mileage 52,876

Wednesday, 11.7.62

Went to North and South Sands.
Lunch 13/1   Mileage 52,890

Thursday, 12.7.62

Went to E. Portlemouth.
Petrol & Oil 14/1 and 1/2d.
Lunch 14/2.   Mileage 52,927

Friday, 13.7.62

Left Salcombe   3.10pm   Mileage 52,930
Lunch 13/2. Petrol 10/-
Stop Taunton + 30 mins
Arrived home   8.10pm   Mileage 53,049
                                  (4½ hrs. 119 miles)

Good Weather – Lovely Holiday!!

This was Paul's first holiday – he was then a little
more than two years old and he does not remember it. I
recall the site; the owner was a Mr Sheppard and near
us was a family from the Midlands with a young son
called Geoffrey.

Wednesday, 9 October 1963 was another memorable
date for us. It was the day on which I was to take my
first choir practice with the boys at Holy Trinity Church
in Frome. It was also at the time when Margaret was
expecting our second child. I left Margaret in the capable
hands of the district nurse, Nurse Pethick from Timsbury,
who did her rounds on her bicycle. With Margaret's
blessing – she had already prepared the choir service

sheets – I left for Frome. I was pleased with the results of that first practice. When I returned, perhaps some three hours later, our son, Ian, had been safely delivered; Nurse Pethick had left and all was under control. Margaret told me, "Paul has been very helpful in getting me drinks, etc". It was another joyful event in our lives.

We believe that it was in 1967 that Margaret's parents sold their home in Faulkland Road, Bath and moved to Smallcombe Close in Clandown, to be just a mile or two from us.

Ever present in life is joy and sadness. Dad would have retired from his work with the National Coal Board in 1963 and shortly afterwards, together with Mum, they undertook the roll of caretakers at Camerton School. They enjoyed this work and also being able to spend more time in the garden. Unfortunately, his 'retirement' was short-lived. His health gradually deteriorated, he was unable to leave the house and, ultimately, his bed, requiring attention day and night. Margaret's dad very kindly shared the responsibility of the nightly vigil. On the morning of Saturday, 2 December 1967 I had an appointment at Holy Trinity Church, Frome to play the organ for a wedding. I returned to find that Dad had passed away, that Doctor Crook had been to certify the death and that Mum had the company of Mrs Kembury of Abbey Farm. Obviously, much of the burden had fallen on Margaret, but she had received the support and help of our near neighbours, Norman and Valerie. With her family near her, Mum recovered to live a fairly active life, tending her garden, etc., for approaching another 30 years.

Paul had begun his education at Camerton School in 1965, to be followed three years later by Ian; here they were very happy and received a fulfilling education under the guidance of the head, Jack Handscombe. When he was due to transfer to a senior school, Paul was offered a place at King Edward's School, Bath, a direct grant school at that time. Anxious that both boys should attend the same senior school, we then arranged for Ian to spend his last two junior years, from 1973 to 1975, at King Edward's Junior School. At the end of that period, we were all very fortunate in that he was granted one of the free places at the senior school, which had been taken up by the newly formed Avon County Council. The ensuing years, from 1971 to 1982 were years of intense activity and involvement, indeed for all of us. Paul and Ian were both very fully occupied with routine school work and membership of the choir and with much work at home. Paul also learned to play the trumpet and was a member of the school orchestra. We were kept regularly informed of all school news, of events, meetings, etc., and we made every effort to attend. Shortly after commencing, Paul discovered that there was only one other boy, Richard, in the form who did not have a television set at home. It was not long before we met Richard's parents at one of the frequent parents' meetings. Remarkably, Margaret had known his mother at the City of Bath Girls School. Also, Yvonne, was the sister of a close friend of mine during my early years in the Inland Revenue. The coincidence did not end there, for when Ian commenced at King Edward's Senior School, in his form he met Richard's younger brother, Peter. Consequently, we all met quite often at parents' meetings and we have remained close friends ever since.

When Paul left King Edward's School he proceeded to study Business Studies at Plymouth Polytechnic where he gained a BA Hons degree. After training at Pearson, May and Co., Chartered Accountants in Bath, he became self-employed in 1993, setting up his own company – Paul Clark Accountants Limited – in 2009 with his wife, Judith, as a fellow director.

After King Edward's School, Ian's route took him to Trent Polytechnic, in Nottingham, to study Accountancy, where he gained a BA (Hons) degree. He too trained at Pearson May and Co, achieving ACA and CTA qualifications. After 33 years Ian remains with that practice.

Ian's first holiday was when he was only about seven months old. It was to Perranporth, Cornwall, where we had booked a chalet at Burrell's Holiday Camp for two weeks. It was situated at sea level, adjoining the beach and the cost was nine guineas per week. Ideal, we thought, for a holiday with two young children – and it was! We travelled in our black Hillman Minx – FGL 987. Again, Margaret kept a diary and it emphasises the remarkable prices of fifty years ago!

<u>Saturday, 30.5.64</u>

Left home 11.30am	Mileage 64,711
Stopped at Tiverton	2.0pm – 3.0pm
Arrived at Perranporth	6.00pm
Hot sunny day.	
Petrol £1.4.2. (5 gals) (162 miles)	Mileage 64,873

Sunday, 31.5.64

Cooked new potatoes and cabbage with a tin of steak. Fruit salad and tin milk for pudding.
After dinner walked to town and beach. Hot, sunny day.

Monday, 1.6.64

Raining.
Went shopping.
Salmon, tomatoes and cheese. Tarts. (at Chalet.)
After dinner went for ride in car to Newquay, RAF St Mawgan.
Bright and sunny.
(32 miles)   Mileage 64,905

Tuesday, 2.6.64

Went to Portreath and Hayle for dinner (Sausage, egg and chips) and on to St Ives when
sun came out!
Back at 6.45pm
Petrol £1. 0. 10 (4 gals) (61 miles)   Mileage 64,966

Wednesday, 3.6.64

Stayed at chalet until after dinner (Steak and Onions, Carrots and Potatoes. Tarts)
Went to Botallack (Mine) and Land's End where it poured with rain.
Bought fish and chips from mobile shop. (Paper plates and plastic forks!)
Back about 9.30pm (86 miles)   Mileage 65,052

Thursday, 4.6.64

Went shopping and then had dinner at chalet. (Steak, peas, potatoes and Jiffi Jellies)
Went to beach in afternoon then back to chalet for tea.
(1 mile)   Mileage 65,053

Friday, 5.6.64

Went for fish and chips for dinner, then set off for Mevagissy.
Had better weather and stayed at Mevagissy until 9.00pm looking round harbour and shops.
Ian still awake when we got home! (about 10.00pm)
Petrol 12/3 (2 gals) (52 miles)   Mileage 65,105

Saturday, 6.6.64

Went shopping for dinner. Cornish potatoes, Steak and Kidney Pie (frozen) and carrots and peaches and cream.
After dinner went to town in car – finished shopping.
Raining most of the day!
(1 mile)   Mileage 65,106

Sunday, 7.6.64

Michael and Paul went to Matins at Perran Church.
Back for dinner and we had chicken, tinned peas and new potatoes. Tinned peaches and Cornish cream.

After dinner we went to Truro and Michael and Paul went to Evensong in the Cathedral.
(26 miles)   Mileage 65,132

Monday, 8.6.64

Spent morning at Chalet.
For dinner tinned salmon, and salad and fruit pies.
In the afternoon went to town in the car and on to St Agnes for tea. Weather not too good, but dry. Had nice tea, sausage, egg, chips and peas. Cydrax.
Petrol 19/8 (4 gals) (13 miles)   Mileage 65,145

Tuesday, 9.6.64

Left chalet about noon and set off for Land's End. Weather glorious!
Had 'dinner' at Sennen Cove (Pasties – with no plates! Egg on Toast) then on to Land's End where we did some shopping and then walked out to the First and Last House in England. Left about 5.00pm via the south coast road to Mousehole and stopped for tea (Cheese and tomato sandwiches, etc.) From Mousehole we went to the Lizard, via Newlyn, Penzance, Marazion and Helston. At the Lizard we had a look at the lighthouse, walked to the most southerly point in England and saw the Lifeboat Station! Left the Lizard at nearly 10.00pm and managed to find the Goonhilly Radio Station and see the Telstar Antenna!! Returned to Perranporth through Helston and Redruth arriving at 11.30pm!!
Petrol 9/10d. Lovely Day. (125 miles).
                              Mileage 65,270

Wednesday, 10.6.64

Paul bought his bucket and spade in the morning and after dinner (Ham and salad and pies) we went up on the sand for the afternoon and got sunburnt!
Back to chalet for tea.

Thursday, 11.6.64

Did washing and shopping and had dinner at chalet (Tinned steak, carrots, new potatoes and fruit flans).
After dinner Mrs 'Scotland' came in for half hour to 'see Paul's bedroom'. We eventually left to look for St Piran's Church in the Sand. We left the car and after walking about one mile over the sand-dunes we found it but it was flooded.
(7 miles)   Mileage 65,277

Friday, 12.6.64

Went shopping in morning and bought fish and chips for dinner and fruit pies.
Weather not very good, so after dinner went in the car to do 'end-of-holiday' shopping. Bought cushions, cups and saucers, etc!
Went back to chalet and took photos of children with Douglas and Fiona. After tea the Fentons left for Aveley and then we took the first steps to packing-up!
(1 mile).   Mileage 65,278

Saturday, 13.6.64

We left the chalet at 11.00 a.m. Stopped at Holsworthy and bought sandwiches and then went on past Torrington and then stopped for dinner from 2.15 – 3.00pm

Arrived at Camerton   6.10pm

Weather mainly fine and dry.

Petrol 19/8d (4 gals). (174 miles).

Mileage	65,452
Total mileage	741
Less	336
Cornish miles	405
Cost of petrol	£5.6.5d
Add	10/-
	£5.16.5d

During all the years from when Paul started school in 1965 to when Ian completed his degree course in 1987 our lives were not devoid of relaxation and pleasurable activities. I recall some of the varied holidays we enjoyed.

One recorded camping holiday was to Daccombe, near Torquay in July/August 1967. I remember the site as being very busy with motorbikes arriving late at night. However, we enjoyed it, visiting places such as Watcombe Beach, Torquay and Goodrington Sands, we went to Ashburton, Buckfastleigh and Buckfast Abbey returning through Poundsgate and Newton Abbot, by train to Kingswear. We visited the Model Village, we returned to Newton Abbot, at Babbacombe we caught an open-top bus to Brixham, we took a coach trip to

Haytor, Widecombe-in-the-Moor and Becky Falls. Yes, an interesting and enjoyable holiday.

In July 1970 we went to Kent, to Westwell, near Ashford to camp in a large field where there were no more than two or three other families – a very peaceful and rural setting. We travelled in our black Hillman Super Minx – FHW 11D – which we had purchased on 1 August 1969. We had also purchased a large frame tent and a trailer in which to transport our equipment. We were able to appreciate the features of the Kentish countryside – this 'Garden of England' and we visited Margate, Ramsgate and, particularly, Canterbury; we also 'found' Betteshanger Colliery, near Deal. My uncle, Arthur Stevens, (Mum's brother) worked at the nearby Tilmanstone Colliery in the 1930s. We had a memorable journey on the Romney, Hythe and Dymchurch Railway. We also had the opportunity of a first visit to France for Margaret, Paul and Ian. On 11 July we drove to Dover and crossed to Boulogne by hovercraft – the *Princess Anne*. It was a very calm crossing and we had many hours to explore the ancient city – its interesting shops in cobbled streets, etc. Our total fare for the journey was £9.0.0. Altogether we had a wonderful holiday in Kent.

Probably, it was in 1972 that we planned a holiday at Wootton Courtenay on Exmoor and near Minehead. The access to the campsite was down a track, past farm premises to a lower level, adjacent to a stream – in good weather, perhaps an idyllic spot. However, one evening we were having a meal in a restaurant in Minehead when a thunderstorm developed. As we sat and watched the thunder and lightning over Exmoor we did not relish returning 'home'. Eventually, after several hours, we felt we had to return. Driving down the track we found it was very muddy, but fortunately, when we reached the bottom, we were pleased to find that our tent was not marooned by floodwater. We were able to spend another night there! However, in the morning we decided that we could not risk being flooded and prematurely and disappointingly we began to pack the tent and all our equipment into the trailer and drove up the track to the road with a measure of relief and continued our journey home. We had not completed our holiday and we were disappointed. We decided that it was the end of our camping holidays; we had to dispose of all the wonderful equipment which we had accumulated, having assumed that it would be the means of future holidays.

On the following day we felt we had to seek some compensation. We decided to drive to Coventry and to visit the famous Cathedral. It was a very rewarding journey. St Michael's Cathedral was mainly constructed between the late 14th century and early 15th century. On 14 November 1940, during the Coventry Blitz, it was almost totally destroyed, leaving the tower, the spire and the outer wall standing. The new cathedral stands alongside the ruins, which is now hallowed ground; it is a modernist design by Sir Basil Spence and was consecrated on 25 May 1962. One of its remarkable features is the tapestry of Christ in Glory by Graham Sutherland. The tapestry was woven in France at the workshop of Pinton Frères of Felletin near Aubusson – some years later Margaret and I had the opportunity to visit the tapestry workshops and to see the weavers exercising their craft. Coventry represented a good day!

During these early years we also had short holidays to Billericay and High Wycombe. Margaret had fond memories of childhood holidays with her Auntie May and Uncle Jack in Billericay and we were pleased to spend a few days with them. Uncle Jack was a great character. He was a musician and had been the principal bass in, I think, all the major national orchestras. We enjoyed listening to his stories. A particular one I recall is of when they were playing in Berlin before the Second World War and in the audience was none other than Adolf Hitler. On that same occasion the principal oboist committed suicide. He told us of a typical rehearsal comment by Sir Adrian Boult, "I think this piece plays itself, gentlemen". Also, at a Sir Thomas Beacham rehearsal, "The fourth trombone is playing too loudly"; to the response, "The fourth trombone hasn't arrived yet, Sir", came, "When he does arrive, tell him not to play too loudly". Uncle Jack's grandson is now the principal bass of the London Philharmonic Orchestra.

High Wycombe had been the destination of my first holidays and it always held a great attraction for me. Uncle Albert was the son of William Vere the founder of the furniture manufacturing company of William Vere Ltd, in 1912. Today, his grandson, Derek, is still managing director and his great grandson, Richard, is also involved in the business now known as Verco Office Furniture Limited.

In 1975 we felt that our holidays should be a little more adventurous; perhaps we should consider going abroad. Naturally we thought of Denmark and Copenhagen. We contacted Inge who was delighted to hear that we might visit them. Immediately, plans began to be laid. Inge found that friends of theirs would be away for two weeks in the near future and that they could sleep in their flat and, therefore, we could live in Inge's flat. We obtained Visitor's Passports and we booked ferry crossings with DFDS – from Harwich to Esbjerg on 23 July sailing at 17.30 and returning on 7 August from Esbjerg to Harwich also leaving at 17.30. However, there was no accommodation available! We didn't hesitate to accept those terms – we were going to Copenhagen! The total cost of the journey was £143.50. Inge sent us copious instructions to help us to find their home and how to use the telephone if necessary. In our Hillman Super Minx – FHW 11D – we drove to Harwich for the overnight crossing on the MS *Winston Churchill* and the drive across Denmark took most of the following day. When we eventually arrived at Ibstrupvaenget 8 we had the most wonderful warm welcome. We had a memorable two weeks, being taken to so many unforgettable sites in and around the capital. Of course, the Tivoli Gardens, Frederiksborg Castle, museums and we even crossed into Sweden for a picnic. On returning to England we took the daring decision to drive through the centre of London. It had been an experience which none of us have forgotten. Sadly, Preben died early in 2012.

It was in July 1979 that we had our first family holiday in France. Travelling in our Hillman Super Minx – FHW 11D – we visited Arromanches, Bayeux, Paris and into Brittany, where our car broke down. I am including a full account of this journey in this 'Miscellany'.

In July 1980 we planned a journey very similar to that which I had to abandon so abruptly in 1956. In our Volvo 144 – NHR 391M – we drove through France, Italy, Switzerland, Germany before returning to France, a total distance of 3,017 miles. It was a wonderful experience. It will be included in *'France – A Journey'*.

In August 1981 we focussed on the Eure-et-Loir, Jura and Herault Departments. Again in the Volvo 144, we travelled 2,568 miles.

In July 1982 we concentrated on the Herault Department; travelling 2,909 miles in the Volvo 144.

August and September 1983 saw us in the Herault Department and beyond. Paul was now 23 and was unable to spend more than one week with us; it was the last holiday for the four of us. Both he and Ian were able to share the driving with me, in our Volvo 244 BAE 980V. We travelled 3,025 miles.

In 1984 we had our last family holiday, with Ian. It was our 'Rhine Valley Holiday'. We booked ferry crossings from Dover to Calais on 27 July 1984, sailing at 13.30 and from Calais to Dover on 6 August 1984, sailing at 16.45. The total cost was £182.00. Again with our Volvo 244 – BAE 980V – we drove to Dover. Our crossing was in the Townsend Thoresen *Herald of Free Enterprise*, which held the blue riband for the fastest Dover-Calais crossing in 53 minutes. However, its glory did not last very long for on the night of 6 March 1987, as it left the Belgian port of Zeebrugge, it capsized killing 193 passengers and crew. The ship had left the harbour with her bow-door open. The assistant boatswain, who was responsible for closing the bow-door, was asleep in his cabin!

In France, we drove to Bruay-en-Artois and the Hotel-Restaurant de L'Univers. We left immediately to visit Notre Dame de Lorette and Vimy Ridge before returning to the hotel at 11.00pm. On the following morning we drove on towards Arras and on to Cambrai. We crossed into Luxembourg for 36 miles and then over the German border to Trier. After crossing the Rhine, we arrived at St Goarshausen at about 10.45pm, where we spent eight nights at the Hotel Erholung; the total cost was £246.60. We had a most interesting time in Germany, visiting Bonn – particularly The Beethoven House, his birthplace in December 1770, Heidelberg and a cruise on the Rhine to Rudesheim. On returning to France we spent one night at Hôtel de la Poste at Ste Menehoud. We visited Verdun, via Bar-le-Duc and la Voie Sacrée, and then the nearby Douaumont Ossuaire. This contains the skeletal remains of at least 130,000 unidentified combatants, both French and German; in the soft gentle light and silence it was a moving experience. The Battle of Verdun, in 1916, lasted 300 days and about 230,000 men died; it was known as the Hell of Verdun. On our journey to Calais we spent an hour at Reims, visiting la Cathédrale. Our ferry crossing was again in the *Herald of Free Enterprise*.

In the succeeding years, with the exception of 2012, we visited France every year, once, twice or occasionally three times, until a final memorable journey by car to Normandy in 2015. We have often driven extensively in the country and we loved France and its people. It has been a privilege to introduce others to France. In 2004, 2005 and 2006 we took our two young grandsons to spend a week in the farm at Vienne-en-Bessin, just five miles from Arromanches, where we have been welcomed many times by Fabienne. On one occasion we took George and Samuel to visit our friends in Bayeux, Paulette and Herve, when George recited a poem in French from memory; it was much admired. A record of the 2004 journey is among this 'Miscellany'.

Margaret always had a fond attachment to Marshfield. It had been her mother's home and in 1942, at the time of the Bath Blitz, they sought shelter and accommodation there, probably with Auntie Bessie. When, in about the year 1990, during a conversation amongst a group of friends the name of Marshfield was heard she was particularly interested. Soon we realised that it had also been the home of Thelma. This led not only to a friendship with Thelma, Bob and their young son, Christopher, but to Thelma's parents in Marshfield, Iris and Desmond, with whom we spent many interesting and enjoyable hours. Holidays with Thelma, Bob and Christopher followed – to Bournemouth and twice to France. We took Christopher on a day trip to Lille from Camerton; it was the first exciting experience of Eurostar for all of us. In August 1998, when he was fourteen years old, we took Christopher for a four-day holiday in Paris. I think the highlights of that visit were the cruise on the Seine and a Paris by Night tour. Now, on 16 June 2019, Christopher and his wife, Alison, have welcomed their first child, Jasper.

I am now unable to visit France, but I still have contact with friends there and I have an abundance of memories which, together with the daily records which Margaret maintained, enable me to recall and reflect on those, days, months, years, perhaps in all two years we so happily spent in 'our second home'. I will continue to create a narrative record in my *'France – A Journey'*.

The past 25 years, a quarter of a century, have witnessed a number of significant events in our family. Firstly, was the happy celebration of the marriage of Paul to Judith Frances Mary Smedley at St Columba The Virgin, St Columb Major, Cornwall on 9 April 1994. Their reception was held at the Tredragon Hotel in Mawgan Porth where, like ourselves, most of the guests assembled on the previous evening, which avoided any possible tensions on the day itself. We all remained until the Sunday morning. It was a very happy occasion. At that time Judith was pursuing a nursing career. We had already developed a very friendly and valued relationship with Judith's parents, John and Joan Smedley, which continued for the rest of their lives.

Unfortunately, Mum had not been well enough to travel to Cornwall. However, at that time we had neighbours living at No 11, Helen and Matthew, who kindly offered to have a key and to periodically visit her. It gave us much peace of mind. Mum continued to spend time in her garden until she caused some injury to her back. Her health deteriorated and she needed the support of carers and, particularly, Margaret. On the afternoon of Saturday, 4 February 1995, with Margaret and I by her side, she slowly passed away very peacefully.

It was just a couple of weeks before her 94th birthday. I went outside and the birds were singing.

If Mum had lived another year or so, she would have welcomed a great grandson, as George Alexander, Paul and Judith's first son, was born on 2 August 1996. It was another joyful occasion for us all.

Following Mum's death in February 1995, we felt we should review our new circumstances. Paul had, by then, purchased his own home in Radstock and the extended property had become too large for the three of us. The big garden was likely to become more than I would be able to manage. Ian bought a house in Keynsham and we decided to move. Rather than seek a new home in the vicinity we felt a complete break would be best and we decided to seek a property in West Wiltshire. After about eighteen months of advertising and searching we suddenly had a prospective purchaser. As a matter of urgency, we had to find a new home. We had never anticipated living in Trowbridge, but Trowbridge it was going to be! We were in a situation of considerable urgency, but all the transactions were completed satisfactorily, and we moved on Friday, 15 August 1997, The Feast of The Assumption. Leaving 10 Camerton Hill after, for me, more than 60 years and, for Margaret, 39 years, was not a joyful occasion, but neither was it a tearful one.

Our move was not exactly smooth – some items of furniture had to be left on the lawn overnight – but with help, particularly from Ian, we gradually settled in. This was a larger property than we had anticipated – 11 rooms – most importantly, it had ample facility for parking and for turning around. It would do!! We proceeded to adapt the property to our needs. We allocated two upstairs rooms as offices. Outside we had a large level garden with grass and a number of mature trees. We erected a summerhouse, a large workshop, Margaret's potting shed, and we created a small vegetable garden. We soon learned that the large house next door to us was a care home and on the other side lived a Mr and Mrs Mills. Although Mrs Mills died soon afterwards, we became close friends of Fred, a lovely and charming man, until his death. On the opposite side of the road was another elderly couple who Margaret befriended until the husband died and his wife left. They were followed for very many years by Geoff and Anne who became good friends. The property is within easy walking distance of the town and of other facilities and it is about half a mile to Tesco. Margaret did not drive and so she appreciated her independence, being able to walk to all the basic facilities. At the end of the West Ashton Road leaving Trowbridge is a signpost to Poole '52 miles'; it would be our gateway to France! We have been very happy here.

Although we had not chosen to live in Trowbridge, we soon discovered benefits. There was a very good rail service to such places as Bath, but also to Waterloo and its link with the Eurostar services. I have already referred to the many concerts we have attended at the Wiltshire Music Centre in Bradford-on-Avon where the Trowbridge Symphony Orchestra performs regularly. We also joined an excellent French Group of the U3A. We met weekly, alternately in Westbury and Trowbridge and it was led by two ladies, Phyllis and Joyce. Phyllis had been the children's book editor of Faber & Faber for 26 years and was an excellent teacher; Joyce had been a French teacher in a local school. During the years in which we attended the group, until sadly both ladies passed away, our ability to read write and to speak French greatly improved.

To increase our familiarity and experience of France and the French language we acquired the means to receive all the French state television channels and we have regularly watched particular programmes, including the nightly *Journal* at 20.00 hours.

We have particularly appreciated *Le Jour du Seigneur* every Sunday morning on the main state television channel – France 2. On 24 December 1948 la messe was transmitted live on television in France, and indeed worldwide, for the first time. The broadcast was from la Cathédrale Notre-Dame de Paris and was a great success. In October 1949 a ninety minute weekly religious magazine programme, incorporating a live messe and a documentary was instituted; the programme, *le Jour du Seigneur,* was born. It has been broadcast regularly ever since and lengthened. It was all due to the inspiration of a Dominican priest, Père Raymond Pichard. We have watched the 'service' regularly and we have found these Sunday morning experiences very uplifting. It is a wonderful experience; one is made to feel present and welcome. La messe is broadcast from a variety of locations, mainly in France, from city cathedrals to delightful little village churches, even in the open air, occasionally from Belgium and sometimes from other countries such as Switzerland and Ireland and from French overseas territories; on one occasion from the

Phillipines. However, it is never from England – how nice it would be to see the appearance of Downside Abbey, for instance! On 12 May 2019 the broadcast came from Berlin, from a lovely church with an excellent organ and choir. In 1966 I took part in such a broadcast in Frome, in England, but those regular broadcasts ceased many years ago – I wonder why? Perhaps it is not surprising that we have known it said to us in France, "We are a Christian country".

On 21 January 1998, in the Royal United Hospital, Bath, Paul and Judith welcomed Samuel Edward, bringing more joy to the family.

In September 2005, we were enjoying our lunch under the Pine trees overlooking the River Loir at La Fleche when we received the exiting news that George and Samuel had been admitted to the Choir of Bath Abbey.

Another happy family occasion occurred on Saturday, 8 September 2007, when we all gathered at Christ Church, Hanham to celebrate the marriage of Fiona and Ian. Prominent in the ceremony were Fiona's daughter Emma and Fiona's parents, the Rev Ken and Grace Wright, her Dad taking part in the ceremony. Ian and Fiona's wedding reception was held on a boat as we cruised along the River Avon. Although Ken and Grace live in Cumbria we have been pleased to meet them from time to time and we have kept in contact, Ken giving me considerable encouragement with my writing.

I am pleased that I still have four first cousins with whom I continue to have contact – Cherry, the daughter of Mum's sister Ivy; Derek the son of Mum's sister Nora; Diana, the daughter of Dad's sister Amy and Una the daughter of Mum's brother Arthur.

Cousins who have passed away include Louisa Williams, Diana's sister, who died in 1943, aged 14; Roger, Derek's brother; Rex, Una's brother and Malcolm, Cherry's brother.

Dad's brother George had nine children of which only four remain.

Margaret had one surviving cousin, John, the son of her Dad's brother, Edmund. Sadly, John died on 14 June 2019; he would have been 90 on Christmas Day next.

Peter, the son of her Dad's brother, Harold; Geoff and Mary, brother and sister of John and Anne, the daughter of her Mum's sister, May all predeceased her.

I don't know whether it is because neither Margaret nor I had brothers or sisters that we have both found great satisfaction in our association with children and young people. I know Margaret enjoyed her work as a Sunday School Teacher, regularly collecting young children on her way to St Mark's Church. I have found teaching children the piano and training young choristers very rewarding and especially in establishing good relationships and mutual respect and being remembered years afterwards. Our 'France – A Journey' has brought us rewards too. On our annual visits to Castelnau Montratier, in the Lot Department, we looked forward to seeing again the young son of Beatrice and Marc, Tristan, who used to refer to me as his grandfather. At Saint-Savin-sur-Gartempe, in the Vienne Department, we always had such a warm welcome from the affectionate young daughters of Bruno and Cécile – Bérénice and Honorine. Also, at Vienne-en-Bessin in the Department of Calvados it has been a pleasure to see the daughter of Fabienne, Amandine, progress to and through her school years. A particular pleasure and privilege was teaching George and Samuel piano and French over a two or three year period.

It has, of course, been a great pleasure to witness the development of George and Samuel.

After attending Somervale School and Midsomer Norton Sixth Form, George studied at Derby University gaining a BA Hons. Degree in History. Following his years as a chorister in the Choir of Bath Abbey he had a love of the Abbey and for about five years he worked as a Tower Guide. That is until he was appointed a Virger (as spelt at Wells) of Wells Cathedral in the summer of 2018. It was a moment of pride for me to see George, wearing his university hood and carrying his staff, leading the full choir and clergy through the nave of the Cathedral at the Christmas Carol Service in December 2018. George lives with his girlfriend, Rebecca, in Vicars' Close, the oldest occupied street in Europe.

Samuel also attended Somervale School and Midsomer Norton Sixth Form. He is now in his third year at Lincoln College, Oxford, studying chemistry. Samuel is a member of the Lincoln College Chapel Choir, which has recently completed a US Tour. Very recently I had the pleasure of a visit from Samuel and his girlfriend, Alice, also of Oxford.

Fiona's daughter Emma has a number of very challenging long-term health issues which she has had to deal with on a daily basis for many years and continues to do so. However, she gave birth to Oakley Jack on 26 June 2018. Oakley is now attempting to walk and talk as he starts to assert himself in the world and, whilst inevitably being very time consuming, brings great joy to those around him. Meanwhile, their family dog, Stitch, continues to provide much affection and entertainment for everyone.

Throughout our marriage we have not initiated any particular celebration of our special anniversaries. However, in 1983, Margaret's Dad took us all to The Vineyard restaurant at Colerne for a meal to celebrate our Silver Wedding Anniversary. The restaurant was owned by Ben Warriss the comedian and we were pleased to be served by him. Our Ruby Wedding occurred in the year following our move to Trowbridge and our family organised a barbeque here; it was an occasion when we saw one or two relatives and friends, sadly, for the last time. We spent our Golden Wedding Anniversary in France and for an hour or two of the day, on a Mediterranean beach.

Early in January 2012 a darkening cloud began to descend over the lives of Margaret and myself. Margaret had been suffering from an ulcer on her right ankle for many years, which had required regular dressing. Then, early on a Saturday afternoon at the beginning of a new year, I suddenly noticed a worrying feature – she became disorientated at home in our dining room. It was a feature which repeated itself in the following weeks and months. After some while we made an appointment to see her doctor. He applied a very elementary test; he did not seem too concerned but said he would arrange an appointment with a psychiatrist. Eventually, on 24 July 2013, we had an appointment at the Memory Clinic when Psychiatrist, Dr Christopher Inegbedion, diagnosed Mixed Alzheimer's and Vascular Dementia. He also referred to Margaret's 'unsteady gait and risk of falls'. He prescribed treatment with Donepezil and we received a copy of a very comprehensive report which Dr Inegbedion sent to our doctor. On being discharged from the Memory Clinic, we were told that monitoring would continue by a Memory Nurse, who would be available in every surgery. In fact, we never received any such further attention regarding her dementia or any advice or guidance as to how best to handle our new situation.

Margaret was now unable to use her phone and computer satisfactorily and often needed guidance in performing routine tasks. I now had to, for me, perform unfamiliar roles such as shopping, preparing meals, etc. Margaret would sometimes fall asleep during a meal and, if left with a cup of tea or coffee, I often found it and the contents on her lap or on the floor. Margaret had, for a number of years, suffered from arthritis, considerable pain in her feet, and her physical disability increased. It was compounded by the emergence of a severe ulcer on her left leg. Apart from her physical difficulty to move from one position to another she became unable to interpret advice regarding moving her feet or body one way or another. Simply transferring from the dining room to the bathroom, the bedroom, etc., became a long and frustrating exercise. I had never been inclined to a nursing or caring role and I often found it difficult to cope. I know that, without thought, I didn't always react to difficult and unwelcome situations in the best way. I know Margaret was aware of the burden she placed on me as sometimes her last words at night were, "You have had a difficult day today". On the few occasions when we planned to go somewhere by car and, particularly, to arrive at a certain time I found it very stressful. The nurse at the Ulcer Clinic recognised this when she arranged for District Nurses to dress Margaret's ulcer at home.

During her last six years, we did, in spite of all the difficulties, have some remarkable experiences and senses of accomplishment. In fact, we travelled to France by train in 2013 and 2014 and, finally, in 2015 once more by car. On each journey we received unbelievable help and support from officials and strangers alike. Recollections and reflections on these last two journeys are included in this Miscellany.

Also, much appreciated and enjoyed, were the days on which Paul, Judith and sometimes George, and with the use of the wheelchair, took us to:- The Courts Garden on Margaret's birthday in 2015, the National Memorial Arboretum on 29 May 2016 and again on 28 May 2017, to visit Samuel, newly installed in Lincoln College, Oxford, to visit George, shortly before the end of his career at Derby University and also Kedleston

Hall, to the Donkey Sanctuary on 28 August 2016 and, finally, with the convenience of a hired car which would accommodate Margaret's wheelchair, to the village of Imber on Sunday 27 August 2017. On this last occasion we continued to Frome for a meal at the Beefeater, where we were joined by Samuel for the last meal we had together. For me, these days also provided welcome relief from the responsibility of assisting and caring for Margaret.

There is one memory which I particularly treasure. In 2016 we planned to go to the Palmer Gardens in Trowbridge on 7 June for some lunch to celebrate our anniversary and my birthday. Unfortunately, when the day came and the hours passed, Margaret showed no willingness to get ready and, disappointingly, we had to abandon the idea. However, come 7 June in 2017, we had similar hopes. On that morning we had a carer, Chelsey, for an hour and she talked to Margaret about the prospect; they even decided what clothes Margaret would wear. It was a great help. We eventually got into the car and drove to the Garden Centre car park where Margaret decided she could walk to the restaurant with the help of her frame. As it was taking so long to cover just a few yards, I found a wheelchair which was available for the use of customers. Established at a table, we had a celebration meal of egg and bacon on toast – it was lovely. After returning home Margaret began to reminisce; she said, with some incredulity, "We have been married for 59 years," and "You are 87 years old"; she added, "In all those years we haven't made many mistakes". Perhaps she thought she might not see another anniversary – and she didn't!

Until the Bank holiday weekend of 2017 we had been receiving the services of a single carer three times per week, but at that time I realised that Margaret had become physically weaker and I had no alternative but to engage two carers four times per day. This effectively was the beginning of the last stage of Margaret's life. The introduction of a range of necessary equipment – a hospital bed, hoists, various chairs, etc., etc., I know she did not welcome. When, one day, she said to me "I don't know whether to live or die," I found it difficult to respond. As the weeks passed, she was reluctant to eat and drink, but she continued to wish to be dressed and brought into our dining room in her electrically controlled chair, where she could view passers-by on the pavement outside. Sometimes she would receive a wave and she would say, "I wish they would come in," but, with the exception of one friend, no one did.

On the morning of Saturday, 18 November 2017 the carers came as usual and washed and dressed Margaret but, for some reason, I suggested that they leave her in her bed. When the carers came back at about 2.00 p.m., Margaret was obviously very weak. Leaving the carers with her, I went upstairs to phone for a doctor, as I thought. Of course, I was confronted with the 111 service. Becoming frustrated by the endless routine questions and to introduce some urgency, I exclaimed, "She's dying!". At the bottom of our stairs I could not believe it, but I was met by two paramedics who calmly said, "It's alright, she has died quite peacefully." It was a shock and a moment of deep regret; I had not been with her. Margaret had been present at the closing moments of the lives of her Mum and Dad and of my

Mum and Dad, but when she herself passed away, she had no members of her family around her. That is a matter of great sadness to me.

At that time, I knew that Ian and Fiona would be on their way to visit Margaret and it was a shock to them to be greeted with the sad news. I telephoned Paul who, with Judith and George arrived soon afterwards. From that moment onwards, Paul and Ian undertook responsibility for all the necessary formalities.

Margaret's Funeral Service was held on Friday 8 December 2017 at Haycombe Crematorium, Bath. Our undertaker and organist was an old friend and we were very pleased for the service to be led by a chaplain of Bath Abbey, the Reverend Canon David Driscoll. The entry music was Mozart's *Ave Verum Corpus;* the first hymn was *Lead us, heavenly Father, lead us*; Paul read verses 1 – 15 from Chapter 3 of Ecclesiastes; George read the poem '*All is Well*' by Henry Scott Holland; Ian contributed a moving Tribute; Samuel read the poem "*I Sit Beside the Fire and Think*", by J.R.R. Tolkien; the second hymn was, *The day Thou gavest, Lord, is ended*; after the Committal and Blessing, we left the chapel to the music of J.S. Bach – his *Toccata and Fugue in D Minor*. It was a very fitting and appropriate ceremony and, I am sure, one for which Margaret would have wished.

Since that time, Paul and Judith, and Ian have visited me almost every weekend, assisting me in any way they can. With the onset of prostate cancer and glaucoma and involving cataract surgery on both eyes, they have transported me to many appointments at the Royal United Hospital in Bath. For all the help I have received, I am extremely grateful. It has enabled me to continue to live a relatively independent life, albeit within the bounds of my home.

Throughout her life Margaret cherished and guarded her family and personal relationships; at the end she was still in contact with three school friends, Grace, Jean and Mary. I have had the pleasure of contact with these same friends since Margaret died.

During the course of our *'France – A Journey'*, the kindness and warmth extended to us has been unforgettable and we have been privileged to form lasting friendships in different parts of the country. In the Lot Department, Ginette (not forgetting the late dear Maurice); also, in the Lot, Alain and Bernadette; in the Department of Corrèze – Anne and Jim; in Calvados – Fabienne and in Bayeux – Paulette and Herve. It is now a great pleasure for me to have news from these friends and, when I feel that my French is adequate, I endeavour to respond.

I have spoken of my thoughts of more than sixty years ago, of my hopes of the kind of person I would like to spend the greater part of my life with. I can now say with gratitude that all my hopes were fulfilled in gracious measure. That 'meeting', that eye contact, that 'message' in Bath Abbey was the key which opened up a wonderful life. Our lives have not been based on romanticism, but on realism, on compatibility, tolerance and harmony, on purposefulness and accomplishment, we have exercised caution in making decisions. Margaret gave her verdict on our 59 years, with which I can only concur. Our lives have not been particularly adventurous; we have never flown, we have never been on a cruise, but we have travelled where our car has taken us, and we have appreciated and enjoyed the fruits of those journeys. It has been a happy and rewarding life and I am blessed with a caring and willing family.

Margaret left me on 18 November 2017, but she left me with the precious gift of time – time to fulfil her wish that I continue to convert her work into a book of 'France – A Journey'.

When, in March 2018, the Consultant advised me of his diagnosis of prostate cancer, he added, "but we can keep you going for a few years", to which I instinctively replied, "I hope so, I have a lot to do". I endeavour to make good use of every single day, constructively and creatively.

I have changed nothing in our home; I have disposed of nothing; her presence is still here and I am guided by her thoughts. I am not heartbroken; I am not morbid; I am grateful for a wonderful life. However, I do wish we had had just a few years in which we could have reflected on the fruits of our life – but that is Life!

Now, another Spring has burst forth, a time which Margaret so much enjoyed. The crocuses, the daffodils and the tulips are presenting their colours; new life is emerging on the silver birch tree and the cherry tree is showing its distinctive colour. Most importantly, a new season is beginning for Margaret's favourite rose, her Papa Meilland. Life continues!

8 April 2019.

OUR FIRST FAMILY
HOLIDAY IN FRANCE

17–26 JULY 1979

We had in mind visiting some of the sites of the early stages of the Battle of Normandy – the D-Day landing beaches, perhaps reaching Paris and, hopefully, discover some of the characteristics of Brittany. We made reservations for our return sea crossing with AA Travel; travelling with Sealink from Weymouth on 17 July 1979 at 10.00 and returning from Cherbourg on 26 July at 16.00; the total cost for the car and four adults was £140.80. We also arranged, very wisely as it proved to be, AA Five-Star Service for a total cost of £34.70. On 17 July we – Margaret, Paul (19), Ian (15) and myself – set off in our car – a black Hillman Super Minx – FHW 11D – which was first registered on 1 February 1966 and which we had acquired on 1 August 1969 (according to the Registration Book!). Margaret recorded the whole of our journey, while Ian maintained a record of distances travelled. It is appropriate that I should quote the first two days of this journal:-

Tuesday, 17 July 79

"Left home 07.05. Good journey to Weymouth where we arrived at 09.05. *The Maid of Kent* sailed for Cherbourg at 10.00 and arrived at 15.00 French time!

Weather perfect! Good road from Cherbourg and out into the Normandy countryside. We drove to Grandcamp-les-Bains, Vierville-sur-Mer and Trevieres, but no accommodation for us all – only one room – then on to Le MOLAY LITTRY and we booked in at the Hôtel du Commerce. In the evening we visited Bayeux and Arromanches where we saw the War Museum and many reminders of the D-Day landings on 6.6.44. Saw the statue of Notre Dame des Flots which overlooks the beach from a hill-top." (167 miles)

I well remember that evening; our first view of the spires of the magnificent Cathédrale, a national monument, and of reaching ARROMANCHES for the first time. I recall parking in the car park near the post office and the small supermarket at the top of the road leading down to the seafront – we have parked there so very many times since! On that occasion Paul and I spent a little while applying the headlamp deflectors, before walking down for a view of those historic remains of the Mulberry Harbour for the first time – how many times have we stood there in awe and wonder since that evening? It is the scene of such momentous events 35 years earlier (now another 35 years have passed and the evidence is still there). Back at the Hôtel du Commerce our rooms were in the top of the building and the nights were very hot; nights which were also punctuated by the regular striking of the nearby clock.

Wednesday, 18 July 79

"Travelled into Bayeux and after going to the Cathedral we went to see the world-famous Tapestry. We were given elongated ear-pieces from which a very English voice gave us commentary on all the many scenes depicted on the Tapestry; these are very detailed. It is hard to realise the age of this fascinating 'work of art'. We spent a short time in the Baron Gerard Museum. Leaving Bayeux, we returned to Arromanches and then made a tour of the coastal towns and villages of Calvados to Honfleur. It was a long journey back to Le Molay-Littry and we had difficulty in finding the correct route in Caen." (145 miles)

Our visit to BAYEUX was the first of many, too. Its magnificent Norman-Romanesque and Gothic Cathédrale de Notre-Dame was consecrated in 1077 in the presence of William the Conqueror. The seventy metres of the Bayeux Tapestry was hung for the first time around the nave of the Cathédrale. Mercifully, the city was virtually undamaged during the Battle of Normandy, having been liberated on 7 June 1944. The poignant Bayeux War Cemetery contains the graves of 3,935 British soldiers. Le MOLAY-LITTRY, about 13km west of Bayeux, had been a centre of coal mining since 1741 and possesses an excellent Musée de la Mine. The Hotel is situated at the side of the large square and on our second morning we were greeted by a weekly market which occupied the whole area. Many years later we sat on the pavement outside a small café opposite the Hotel enjoying a cup of tea with George and Samuel. We have fond memories of Le Molay-Littry.

Thursday, 19 July 79

Before leaving Le Molay-Littry, Paul and Ian visited Le Musée. From the Department of Calvados we headed east towards Paris. We journeyed via Bayeux, Caen, Falaise, Trun, Chambois, Gacé and L'Aigle to VERNOUILLET, which is about 2km from Dreux; here we spent two nights (19 and 20 July) at the Auberge de la Vallée Verte, This auberge was noted as being "Super"! (In 2015 it is described as "Fabulous".) (176 miles)

FALAISE was the birthplace of William the Conqueror; it suffered very considerable damage during the Battle of Normandy. Our route from Falaise to Chambois had been an escape route for the fleeing German Army Group B as it attempted to escape the encircling Allied Armies forming the Falaise Pocket. Along this road, often with high banks on each side, the escaping enemy – men, horses, vehicles and equipment – was mercilessly bombarded by artillery and swooping fighter bombers – Typhoons and Spitfires. This corridor, known as the 'death road', was the scene of unbelievable death and destruction. It was on 19 August that the Polish Army, from the north, and the American Army, from the south, linked up at Chambois. However, many Germans continued to escape and the Falaise Gap was not finally sealed until 21 August. There is considerable uncertainty about the numbers of German casualties and survivors, but it is said that up to 100,000 troops may have been surrounded, up to 15,000 killed, up to 50,000 taken prisoner and up to 50,000 may have escaped. Apparently, General Eisenhower commented, "Forty-eight hours after the closing of the gap I was conducted through it on foot. It was literally possible to walk for hundreds of yards at a time, stepping on nothing but dead and decaying flesh." However, the end of the Battle of Normandy was nearing and, indeed, Paris was liberated on 25 August.

Friday, 20 July 79

Today - a visit to PARIS! Whereas so many towns and villages suffered much damage and destruction in the course of the Battle of Normandy, Paris was liberated virtually undamaged. Although Hitler had ordered that the city should be reduced to 'a pile of rubble', the German commander, General Dietrich von Choltitz, did not carry out his Fuhrer's instructions – Paris was preserved for future generations. We travelled by car from Vernouillet to St-Remy-Les-Chevreux and by Metro to Paris, arriving at 12.30. During the course of a long day, after exchanging travellers' cheques at Châtelet, we explored many of the historic monuments and sites of the city; we visited Le Louvre, la Cathédrale de Notre-Dame. La Seine, Les Invalides, Tour Eiffel, Arc de Triomphe, Avenue des Champs Elysées, Place de la Concorde and le Jardin des Tuileries. We did not leave the Metro station at Châtelet des Halles until 22.15; we reached Chevreux and our car at 23.05 and at 00.45 we arrived at the Auberge at Vernouillet! It had certainly been a long, but rewarding and memorable day. (90 miles)

At the MUSEE de LOUVRE we saw, among many other exhibits, the Mona Lisa by Leonardo de Vinci and the Venus de Milo.

The Palais du Louvre is one of the largest and most magnificent palaces in the world; its construction extended over three centuries and it holds great architectural and historical interest. It first appears in history in about 1204 as one of Philip Augustus's fortresses. The idea of creating a museum in the Louvre first arose in the middle of the XVIII century, but it came to nothing. Eventually, it came to fruition at the time of the Convention, after the fall of the Monarchy; the Museum Central des Arts was set up by a decree of 27 July 1793. Progress was slow, but in 1803 it was named the Musée Napoléon when it must have contained a unique collection of masterpieces. However, in 1815, the treasures were dispersed as a result of the reparation claims made by the Allies following the defeat of Napoléon. Nevertheless, the Louvre's collections rapidly increased under the Restoration and July Monarchy, especially after the transfer into the palace of part of the sculpture in the Musée des Monuments Français and the steady expansion of the antiquities sections. Gradually, the Museum invaded the four wings of the Cour Carrée, leading to what it is today.

Saturday, 21 July 79

We left (reluctantly) Vernouillet at 11.00 and drove the short distance to MAINTENON, where, at 12.00, we booked in at the Hôtel de l'Aqueduc. After establishing ourselves we left for Versailles to visit the Palace and Gardens. (103 miles)

The CHATEAU de VERSAILLES is situated in what was once a country village, but is now a wealthy suburb of Paris. It is a UNESCO World Heritage Site and a foremost tourist attraction. Versailles emerged from obscurity in 1624, when Louis XIII built a hunting lodge here, which he subsequently developed into a small château. However, the real creator of Versailles was Louis XIV. In 1682 it became the centre of power, when Louis XIV moved from Paris and it remained so until the royal family were forced to return to the capital in 1789. The Palace still serves political functions – the Sénat and the Assemblée Nationale meet here in congress to revise or amend the Constitution. We were particularly interested to visit the Hall of Mirrors; constructed between 1679 and 1682 – it is a masterpiece. This celebrated room was, of course, the setting for the signing of the Treaty of Versailles on 28 June 1919 and continues to be the scene of state occasions and receptions for visiting heads of state. Another jewel of the Palace is the Chapel of Louis XIV; with its baroque architecture and wall and ceiling paintings it is an outstanding piece of artistry and workmanship; begun in 1689, it was consecrated in 1710. Of special interest to us was the organ; remarkably, it is situated above the altar, where it faced the King and the royal family seated in the tribune. It is not the original Cliquot organ, but it is a replica housed in the original 1710 case; it was most recently rebuilt in 1995. We learned that this organ had been played by Edward Heath, perhaps when he was on an official visit to Paris in his capacity of Prime Minister from 1970 to 1974! It is not only the interior of this grand and imposing building that attracts vast numbers of visitors; the exterior presents a splendid panoramic spectacle. The GARDENS attract some six million visitors a year. Designed by André Le Nôtre and created between 1661 and 1668, they extend over 250 acres. Although essentially based on the style of a formal French garden of strict geometric principals, the gardens are not monotonous; they remain as they were designed.

DREUX, in the Eure-et-Loir Department, has a long history. Once the capital of the small gallic tribe of the Durocasses, then the crossroads of important Roman ways, a fortified town and the seat of a county in the Middle Ages. Saint Peter's church dates from the 13th century and the Beffroi was built between 1512 and 1537.

MAINTENON, also in the Eure-et-Loir, about 16 miles beyond Dreux and some 40 miles south-west of the centre of Paris, is known for its Chàteau dating from the Middle Ages. In 1574 it was bought by Françoise d'Aubigné who became the secret wife of Louis XIV in 1684. In 1698 she gave Maintenon to her niece on the occasion of her marriage to the son of the Duc de Noailles, Marshall of France. From that time the Château of Maintenon has remained the property of the Noailles family. The design of the gardens is the work of the landscape artist Le Nôtre, who designed the park of the Palace of Versailles. The Aqueduct was built by Vauban and La Hire at the request of Louis XIV to carry the waters of the river Eure to Versailles; it was to have had three levels, but was never completed. The countryside around these towns is attractive, with beautiful forests and picturesque valleys; also, its churches and other buildings provide historical interests.

We enjoyed our visit to the Eure-et-Loire Department; in particular, we found both the Auberge de la Vallée Verte and the Hôtel de l'Aqueduc excellent and Maintenon itself, most interesting; we would be happy to return.

Sunday, 22 July 79

After a little shopping in Maintenon we visited Chartres Cathedral before setting off on a long journey in a south-westward's direction; our route was via Brou, Chapelle-Royale, Vibraye, Le Grand-Lucé, Ecommoy (south of Le Mans) and Sablé-sur-Sarthe. When we reached CHATEAU GONTIER, in the Department of Mayenne and about 19 miles south of Laval, it was an appropriate time to seek accommodation for the night. It so happened that, appropriately, the Hotel Anglais, in Place de la Gare, could offer suitable rooms; suitable it was, but not inspiring, nor particularly inviting, but it was acceptable. In the evening we drove about seven miles south towards Anger for a short tour of the village of Daon, which also sits on the River Mayenne. (175 miles)

Monday, 23 July 79

After leaving Château Gontier, we called at a bank in Châteaubriant to exchange £50 worth of travellers' cheques for 469.85F. This town is situated in the historical and cultural region of Brittany; it is attractive and has a long, varied and important history extending over many centuries – the fair which is held here was founded in 1050!

Continuing the journey, we skirted to the south of Nantes, continuing south of the River Loire and over the magnificent PONT de St-NAZAIRE, which spans the mouth of the river; the toll for this bridge was 28.00F. After driving through the town, we took the coastal road towards La Baule before heading north towards HERBINAC. Here, sadly, just a few kilometres before entering the Department of Morbihan and the Region of Brittany, our tour effectively ended in the late afternoon or early evening. As we reached a junction, and when just considering which direction we should then take, I was in the process of changing gear when I found that the clutch pedal simply went down to the floor without any resistance. Suddenly, we were stranded in the centre of the road, at a junction – in an unenviable, even dangerous situation. What were we to do – of course, mobile phones were unheard of; then, along the road to the right there appeared to be a service station or garage?

Leaving Paul in charge of the car, the three of us walked along the road to the Total Garage to enquire if there was any possibility of assistance. To our relief the gentleman we met willingly came with us to the car having equipped himself with a supply of clutch fluid. Unfortunately, he soon discovered that there was a leak. He was clearly anxious to move us from this embarrassing position and to get the car to his premises and, with some help, he pushed the car along the road to his garage. He seemed confident he could effect a repair straightaway, However, after some while searching through a considerable volume of spare parts on his shelves, he was unable to find what he was looking for – a clutch master pump coupler (?) that was compatible with our Hillman. Clearly there was nothing more he could do until the following day and he was concerned as to where we could spend the night. We were very grateful for his offer to make enquiries and we were relieved when we realised that he had contacted a hotel which could provide rooms for us. Straightaway, he said he would take us there; in fact, to Hôtel Le Bretagne, at PONT d'ARMES, Assérac. How relieved we were and so very grateful to our 'good Samaritan', who was Monsieur JEAN CLOAREC of Cloarec Garage, Herbignac. The accommodation was very acceptable and we were to spend the nights of 23 and 24 July there. (169 miles)

Tuesday, 24 July 79

After successive days of activity, of travel and discovery, today was in complete contrast. We spent the day taking short walks, playing boules and, all the time, waiting and hoping for news of the car. In the evening M. Cloarec came to see us at the Hotel to say that we needed a new clutch master cylinder and that he had been trying very hard to obtain one but, so far, he had been unsuccessful. He was very anxious that we fully understood the position and he took Ian and myself to someone he knew who spoke good English, so that he could explain and be certain that we fully understood the situation. However, there was one more possible source that he would contact in the morning and he would let us know the outcome.

Wednesday, 25 July 79

In the morning M. Cloarec informed us that he had had no luck! Unfortunately, there was not, and there had not been, sufficient time to obtain the part from England before our reserved return journey. We then had no alternative but to invoke the provisions of the AA 5-Star Service. We telephoned the AA and advised them of our circumstances and we contacted Avis Rent-a-Car. The response was very prompt and shortly after 11.30 a red Super Renault 18 (1820 RF 30) was delivered to us. Straightaway, we packed the car, paid our bill for the accommodation, breakfasts and telephone calls, amounting to 236.50F., and said au revoir, with our thanks to Jeanette in particular. Then it was about five miles, via Asserac, to M Cloarec's Garage and our car at Herbignac; we collected our remaining requirements, bearing in mind that we would have to carry our luggage, after abandoning the hired car at Cherbourg.

Although we were restricted to the premises and the surrounding area, our time at Pont d'Armes was pleasant and, having been introduced by M Cloarec, we received the particular concern and attention of Jeanette. An unforgettable memory has been of M Cloarec, of his immediate and willing assistance and how he assumed personal responsibility for our care and needs; it was a remarkable experience – perhaps because we were English? There is a remarkable historical fact relating to this area. Assérac and neighbouring localities, together with the whole area of the Saint-Nazaire Pocket, experienced a prolonged German occupation at the end of the Second World War; in fact, after most of France had been liberated, it continued here for a further nine months from August 1944 to 11 May 1945, three days after the capitulation of Germany.

We set off on the first stage of our journey to Cherbourg, now in an unfamiliar car. I have never had any difficulties in driving on the right-hand side of the road; however, driving a left-hand-drive car (for the first and only time) was a very different matter; I did not find it easy and I was not comfortable. Nevertheless, we safely and successfully proceeded into Brittany and then Normandy. First through Redon and passing to the west and north of Rennes; at Romazy, Tremblay and Louvigné-du-Désert (north of Fougeres) we tried, without success, to reserve accommodation for the night. However, at the little historic village of Le TEILLEUL, in the Manche Department of Lower Normandy, we were able to book rooms at La Clé des Champs, on the Route de Domfront. Appropriately, it was a very attractive and pleasant setting in which to spend our final evening in France and, also, the end of Margaret's birthday. It was already 20.00 hours, but elsewhere in the village we were able to obtain a 'meal' of sandwiches de jambon, frites et jus d'orange! After a short tour of the village we returned to the Hotel. (167 miles)

Thursday, 26 July 79

At 10.00 we left Le Teilleul for Cherbourg; we would, most certainly, have continued into Mortain and then to Vire; from Vire to Cherbourg is a route we have travelled very many times since that day. We made one stop – at Ste-Mère-Eglise – where we saw the effigy of John Steele attached to the tower of the church. He was the American paratrooper who landed on the church tower on 6 June 1944, his parachute being caught on one of the pinnacles of the tower left him hanging on the side of the church; wounded, he hung there, pretending to be dead, until being taken prisoner by the Germans. We have visited Ste-Mère-Eglise, particularly its church, several times since that occasion and many times, as we have driven down the N13, have we glanced to our left for a glimpse of the historic landmark. On reaching Cherbourg we had to replenish the fuel we had used and return the car to the Avis Rent-a-Car Agency. We were then reduced to foot passengers in boarding the ferry. The ship sailed at 16.00 and would have reached Weymouth at about 19.00 (English time). Fortunately, there was still an available train to Frome, where we obtained a taxi to take us home to Camerton. (104 miles)

We were now home safely and satisfactorily, but our car was still far away in France. I had given instructions for the car to be repatriated and delivered to the Meadgate Garage, Camerton and the delivery note is dated 8 August. It was not long before the ever-obliging Mr Reg Coles informed me that the car had been repaired and was ready for collection. The necessary repairs could not have involved major work, for I never received a bill! However, the claims for the additional costs incurred following the breakdown took much longer to settle and it was not until April of the following year that all was finally satisfactorily completed.

Recalling the details of this journey, it is interesting to reflect on a few figures, which I will quote here.

We travelled a distance of 1,296 miles by car.

We purchased 180.75 litres of petrol for a total cost of 533.40F; equivalent to about £56.75.

The average price of petrol was 2.95F per litre; equivalent to about 31 pence per litre. The total cost of our accommodation for nine nights with breakfasts and sundry telephone calls amounted to 1,033.50F; equivalent to about £110.00.

Our rail fares from Weymouth to Frome amounted to £3.30 each.

It was a somewhat inglorious end to our first family expedition to France; we did not quite reach the Brittany we had anticipated, but we had visited many historic sites in Normandy, we had made a long and extensive tour of Paris and we traversed the attractive countryside of Northern France with its numerous interesting towns and villages. Also, the emotions aroused following the sudden failure of the car, the feelings of helplessness, of disappointment, of near despair, were dissipated when quickly followed by displays of concern, understanding, help and support; the incident then became an integral part of the memories of the journey. Subsequently, we have had none but long and happy memories of this first adventure in France. Above all, our experience illustrated the willingness of others to assist when one is in need of help. Yes, as we have experienced so many times since – people are very kind!

A VISIT TO WORCESTER

It is now nearly four months since we returned from our rail journey across France and we have felt that we would like to have a day out before the onset of winter, particularly in the form of much shorter days. There is a wide choice of places one can visit by train from Trowbridge during the course of a day and without having to make changes. The choice includes Weymouth, Southampton and Portsmouth in a southerly direction; otherwise one can go to Cardiff, Gloucester, Cheltenham, Worcester and Great Malvern, for instance. Although the forecast was for fine sunny weather, it also included a warning of very cold northerly winds; we decided that the coast would not be the ideal place to spend a few hours and we chose to go to Worcester, a city we have never visited.

WORCESTER, on the banks of the Severn, is an interesting city with a long history. A village was founded here in about 400 BC and it was the site of an industrial town in Roman times. The Battle of Worcester, in which Oliver Cromwell defeated Charles II, was the last battle of the Civil War. The town was the home of Royal Worcester Porcelain and the composer, Sir Edward Elgar, lived here. The British Medical Association was founded in Worcester. Apparently, during the Second World War,

Worcester was chosen to be the seat of government had the anticipated German invasion materialised in 1940. Lea & Perrins Worcestershire Sauce is made here. Also, like Trowbridge, it is a county town! There is, of course, the Cathedral and in view of our very restricted physical mobility these days, this is where we would spend most of our time.

We had decided that the 09.44 train from Trowbridge, reaching Worcester Foregate Street at 12.16 after two hours 32 minutes and the 17.02 from Foregate Street arriving at Trowbridge at 19.29, a journey of two hours 27 minutes, would be the only suitable trains; both journeys involving no changes.

After an interrupted night we did not begin the day with any great enthusiasm, or anticipate a day out with much determination. However, as the morning took its normal course we began to feel that, providing we had a trouble free journey to the station and that we found a parking space without difficulty, we could still reach the station by 09.44. Eventually, we left more with hope than certainty and, fortunately, all the various traffic signals were green and we were able to park near the entrance to the platform at which we would arrive on the return journey. While I purchased a ticket (for £3.20), Margaret went ahead with the help of her stick and crossed the bridge safely; having joined her we were fortunate to find no queue at the ticket office and we had made it; we were relieved!

The train arrived, more or less on time; it had come from Weymouth, but there were only two coaches.

We boarded without assistance, but there were no double seats available; that is until a very kind lady, recognising our disappointment, offered that which she was occupying. We were, however, travelling backwards and as soon as we had the opportunity, at Bradford-on-Avon I think, we moved to a seat facing in the right direction. This was clearly going to be a 'stopping' train. After Bradford it was Avoncliff, Freshford, Bath Spa, Oldfield Park, and Keynsham to Bristol Temple Meads. Here there was a delay until we eventually reversed out of the station; we were going backwards again! Shortly afterwards we stopped at Filton Abbey Wood, then at Bristol Parkway, Yate, Cam and Dursley and Gloucester. Here we change direction again and once more we are going forward. At Cheltenham Spa the Times Literary Festival was well advertised and we had heard a lady passenger tell a 'friend' on the telephone that she was visiting the Festival. Next stop was Ashchurch for Tewkesbury, then Worcester Shrub Hill and, finally, Worcester Foregate Street. It had been a long tedious journey, not a very comfortable one and, in particular, a noisy one; at times alarmingly so. Otherwise, there was not a great deal to comment on, passing through Bath, Bristol, Gloucester, etc., but as we approached Worcester, we could distinguish the Malvern Hills in the distance. As we were about to alight we could not believe what we were confronted with; it was a 'gap', well, more like a gulf between the train and the platform. I did not know how Margaret, in particular, was going to negotiate this challenge, until the conductor, who had been assisting another passenger, recognised our predicament and came to our rescue. Once on the platform we realised that this station is situated above street level. First we found the toilets; they were very satisfactory, but a notice on the door stated that they would close at, I think, 7.00 p.m., because of 'misuse' – a sad commentary on the times we live in! Next, we were pleased to find that there was a lift to take us down to street level. Because of its situation this station does not have a frontage at street level and, consequently, no forecourt where I had hoped we would find some waiting taxis. However, further along the street and on the other side there appeared to be a couple of taxis, but it was quite a long way and we had to cross the busy road; there was a crossing for pedestrians with lights, but in two stages. I approached a car, not being sure that it was a taxi, but the driver did not appear to respond. I opened the door and asked if he could take us to the Cathedral; I got little more than a nod. Although he could see that it was difficult for us, he did not attempt to assist us to get into the vehicle. I had read that it was a short walking distance from the station to the Cathedral, but because of the route we had to take and the volume of traffic it took quite a while. I do not know what the nationality of the gentleman was, but his English was extremely difficult to understand. I mentioned that we had travelled from Trowbridge by train and he commented that Great Britain was truly "great", but he kept repeating that the rail system was terrible. Eventually, we could see that we were near the Cathedral, but as we left the car at a taxi rank we had to walk back in the direction in which we had come. However, we stopped to view and photograph the excellent bronze statue of Edward Elgar and to read the interesting inscription on the paved area. Then we had to cross another very busy road by means of more pedestrian lights. As we approached, we could not see an entrance to the Cathedral, but then noticed some people who seemed to be going in. We noticed some cars parked quite near and I wonder if we could not have been driven somewhat nearer our destination!

EDWARD ELGAR was born in the nearby village of Lower Broadheath in 1857; he died in 1934. Although himself a self-taught composer he had a musical background in that his father was a piano tuner, violinist and organist and owned a music shop in the town.

The CATHEDRAL of Christ and the Blessed Virgin Mary was founded in 680. Saint Oswald built another cathedral in 983 and established a monastery attached to it. In 1084 Saint Wulfstan began the present building. The monastery continued until 1540 when it was dissolved by Henry VIII. Before going inside, through the north porch, which was built in the 1380s, we would like to have spent a few moments studying the statues above the arch, which date from the 1860s replacing those destroyed in the 16th century; however, it was bitterly cold and we were anxious to reach the warmth of the inside of the building. Warm it was, as we were instantly welcomed by a lady guide in a very friendly informal manner. She gave us a leaflet containing a plan of the layout of the church and she drew our attention to several features, such as the tomb of King John and Prince Arthur's Chantry; she also pointed out the location of the café and toilets. While talking to the guide I asked her if I was right in thinking that there is a window recording the victory of Edward III over Philip

VI of France in the Battle of Crecy, but she was not aware of one. Almost immediately, we noticed the Beauchamp tomb of 1388; a name we have been familiar with in Somerset and in France. Before venturing very far I made a quick tour to ascertain the precise situation of the café, etc. As I returned from the direction of the Cloisters I was greeted again, by a gentleman guide and I took the opportunity of asking him if he was aware of a 'Crecy window'. He was not aware of one either and pointed out that all the stained glass windows in the cathedral are Victorian. However, he looked up some handwritten records and took me to the Cloister windows where we found some referring to the 14th century, but nothing specifically relating to Crecy. (I have since ascertained that the window I had heard about is in Gloucester Cathedral) We began to explore the building from near the entrance to the Tower and made our way to the Tomb of King John who died in 1216. This was a particularly interesting discovery as we have visited Fontevraud Abbey near Chinon where his father, mother, brother and wife were buried (Henry II, Eleanor of Aquitaine, Richard I and Isabella of Angoulême). Although the recumbent effigies on the tombs are impressive, there are now no corporal remains. It seems that John's heart was also buried at Fontevraud! Close by King John is Prince Arthur's Chantry; Arthur, born in 1486, was the eldest son of Henry VII, but he died in 1502, soon after his marriage to Catherine of Aragon. One wonders how the history of England and the Church, particularly here in Worcester, would have been written had he reigned instead of his brother, Henry VIII. It was time for some refreshment, as well as medication, and we already knew the location of the Prior's Parlour. In its very friendly atmosphere we enjoyed a delicious toasted cheese and pineapple sandwich with side-salad and a sausage roll with a slice of Victoria sponge. We were sitting on conventional chairs, but seating on the opposite side of the tables was provided by the stone seats, suitably cushioned, where the monks sat to receive their visitors. After welcome rest and refreshment we continued our tour. Nearby is the magnificent Chapter House, construction of which began in the early 12th century. We then walked into the medieval Cloisters and we were particularly interested in the display of five medieval bells displayed in the east cloister, where, until the 14th century, was housed the bookcases of the monk's library. As we returned from the cloisters there was a public invitation for a brief period of quiet and prayer culminating in a reading of the following words of Saint Francis of Assisi:-

> *"Lord, make me an instrument of thy peace.*
> *Where there is hatred, let me sow love,*
> *Where there is injury, pardon;*
> *Where there is doubt, faith;*
> *Where there is despair, hope;*
> *Where there is darkness, light;*
> *And where there is sadness, joy."*

It was a surprising, but short and moving episode. We wished, then, to spend a little more time in the Quire to see the splendid new Quire organ and to take some photographs of King John's Tomb and have a second look at Arthurs's Chantry. As we descended the steps from the Quire, obviously extremely cautiously, a lady member of the staff offered Margaret a hand of support and made some reassuring comment; this was indicative of the atmosphere which permeates this place. However, although it must be very interesting, we decided not to venture down further steps and visit the Crypt, which was begun by Wulfstan in the 11th century. We were anxious to allow time to visit the gift shop as we must not leave without a guide book and some cards. Nearby, at the west end, is the Baldwin Memorial where is buried Stanley Baldwin, who was three times Prime Minster. Close by is the Gerontius Window, a tribute to the life and work of Sir Edward Elgar who performed many times in this building. Another interesting window, which we did not see, is in St George's Chapel; it depicts a Worcester priest who served as a chaplain in the Great War. He was the Rev'd Geoffrey Studdert Kennedy, who was known as 'Woodbine Willie' for his offering of comfort to soldiers, sometimes injured or dying, holding a New Testament in one hand and offering a Woodbine cigarette with the other. Studdert Kennedy was awarded the Military Cross for bravery; he wrote a number of War Poems and he is buried in Worcester.

There is so much to see in this Cathedral and more than one can appreciate in a single visit, but we knew we had to return to Foregate Street Station by 17.02 and at about 16.00 I felt we should begin to proceed in that direction. As we were about to leave by the north porch another lady guide came to speak to us and say farewell and, again, made us feel that we had been very welcome; she said that we should be able to find a taxi without difficulty. Yes, it had been a warm place in every way; however, as soon as we emerged the contrast was great; it was no less cold than when we had entered. As we made our way back towards the taxi rank it was obvious that we were approaching a 'rush hour' period. Crossing the road again was not easy and there were many people about. We thought we could see a taxi at the rank, but, unfortunately, when we reached it there was none. We waited and waited, but no taxi arrived and then suddenly a car left the stream of traffic – it was a taxi. However, a lady appeared – perhaps she had been waiting for a taxi – she was much more mobile than we were and she reached it first. We had to carry on waiting, but traffic was at a standstill for seemingly long periods and there seemed little hope of a taxi arriving. We had been given a card by the morning taxi driver; I telephoned the number – sorry, no taxis available! We were afraid to have regard to the time, the prospect of not catching our train loomed ever nearer and the thought of a later journey, with perhaps one or two changes, frightening. I don't know what the time was, but suddenly there was movement in the constant queue of traffic and I noticed a white vehicle approaching which could be a taxi; we hoped that it was empty and I stepped out and made a determined attempt to stop it. It pulled into the rank and we hurriedly clambered aboard. We explained the urgency and the driver decided to take a route which he hoped would be less busy, but there did not appear to be any uncongested roads in the centre of Worcester at that time. Incidentally, this driver was not of English extraction either, but his English was much easier to understand and he was very friendly. Eventually, we reached the taxi rank in Foregate Street; we must now cross the busy road and get to the station entrance with much urgency and effort. When we arrived, in the morning, I noted that it was at number one platform; therefore, I decided that we must go directly to the lift for platform number two. On reaching this platform I could see no reference to a train for Bristol, etc. On enquiring, I was told that we should be on platform number one; another desperate rush to the lift and down to street level again and across to number one lift. Finally, we were on the correct platform and the train had not arrived. I cannot now say what the actual time was, but we had a couple of minutes to spare and the train was then about two minutes late. What an experience, what a panic! There were many passengers waiting for this train and, again, there were only two coaches. It was a very competitive situation and we had to move as quickly as we could to board, crossing the 'gap' again; fortunately, we found a seat for three, with much relief! We began to reflect on the day so far and, particularly, on the past hour.

Our attention was soon drawn to our new environment. This train is obviously much used by many passengers travelling regularly from their various places of work to their homes and it was very full, with many people standing, for much of the time, but there were only two coaches. At the frequent stops, many would leave the train, often to be replaced by other travellers. It was soon evident that the door near us, on the side normally adjacent to the platforms, was not working; at station after station anxious passengers would be pleased to be first to the door; how their facial expressions changed when they realised they then had to join a queue at another entrance! Although this is, no doubt, a regular daily routine for many people it was noticeable that no one appeared to recognise or speak to anyone. As soon as they were established, on a seat or even standing, the first priority for most was to make a desperate search for their electronic gadgets, phones, laptops, etc., etc., as if it is essential to escape from this human world.

A smart young man opposite had his 'mobile' for company. A gentleman sitting next to us carried on a lengthy business-like conversation on his telephone in a way that we could all hear his side of the conversation, but it was of no interest to any of us. A lady came to sit opposite and immediately produced her laptop to seemingly continue, in a very determined way, the work that had been interrupted on leaving her office; it seemed that she completed her task before reaching her station as her facial expression changed from one of anxiety to one of satisfaction accompanied with a brief smile. Of course, this is simply supposition! Oh yes, one lady, standing, was actually reading a book and another, who had found a seat, was reading *The Times*. Daylight was beginning to fade and during a brief stop at Bristol Parkway we noticed the illuminated screen advising of trains to such distant places as London, Manchester and Penzance. Not surprisingly, there was quite an influx of passengers at Filton Abbey Wood. We stopped at all the stations we had visited on the outward journey with two bonuses, being Stapleton Road and Lawrence Hill. At Bristol Temple Meads, Keynsham, Oldfield Park and Bath Spa more people left the train than joined. In fact, after Bath there were fewer and fewer new passengers as the train's journey would terminate at Westbury. On reaching Trowbridge, there was no sign of any likely assistance and, indeed, we realised that we had not seen a conductor during the whole course of the journey and, still, there were only two coaches; our tickets had not been checked! However, we were now very glad that we had been able to leave our car so close to the platform and it was then only a few minutes journey to Green Lane.

We had completed our 'Visit to Worcester', but it was an experience of great contrasts. The Cathedral is a wonderful building, a treasure, full of interest and very welcoming. However, the train journey is not one which we would be keen to repeat, but I must say that the trains were virtually on time and the fares of £28.70 return each seemed very reasonable for a five hour journey.

It is evident that many people use the rail system already and, no doubt, many more would do so if it were more attractive. Surely, substantial investment in the tracks and rolling stock is justified and the opposition to the proposed innovative HS2 will not serve future generations well.

TOUR OF SOMME AND YPRES SALIENT BATTLEFIELDS, AGINCOURT AND LA COUPOLE – 2001

A journey from 1415 – (Agincourt) – to the present – (Space travel)

<u>27 April to 7 May 2001</u>

<u>Friday, 27 April</u>

We left Green Lane at 8.55. It was a very slow journey via West Ashton, Edington, West Lavington and the A360, until reaching the A303; thence the M3 to Junction 5 and then the A287, A3016, (Farnham) A31, (Hog's Back) A3, (Guildford) stopping for 20 minutes at a Services and continuing to the M25 (Junction 10); M26 and M20. We arrived at the Tunnel Terminal at 12.20. The weather was good. (168 miles)

After driving through a 'bath' of disinfectant we boarded the Shuttle (Upper deck) and left at 13.19. We ate salmon and cucumber sandwiches (No meat or dairy products allowed because of foot and mouth restrictions) and arrived at the terminal at 14.55 (French time) and drove through a further 'bath' of disinfectant.

We drove to Cite Europe and purchased a bottle of brandy, etc., at the Tesco Store. After verifying that our One to One phone operates in France we left Cite Europe at 16.45. We travelled on the A16 and A26 to Junction 9, stopping briefly for a snack at the Autogrill Rely on the A26. Before leaving the motorway it began to rain very heavily and continued for the rest of the journey, however, there was very little traffic. After leaving the A26 and joining the D917 we encountered a 'Route Barre' and we had to take a somewhat improvised route to RANCOURT. However, we arrived at Le Prieure at 19.30. (The same time as last year). Our room, No 27, was very satisfactory and we ate some crisps and made three phone calls. (287 miles)

Saturday, 28 April

A dark and damp morning. Stopped raining and we left the hotel at 11.20. Drove to Bapaume for petrol (40 litres). Returned to Rancourt and retraced route of Remembrance Tour – Combles, Guillemont and Montauban. Near Montauban we noticed a house with a sign 'Gite – English spoken' and decided to call. We were welcomed by Christine who told us that the house was the rebuilt stationmaster's house on the pre-Great War Albert to Peronne railway and a few yards along the track was the rebuilt station (1922) which has been converted into a gite. It is hoped to retrieve the original station nameplate from a loft in England. Nearby is the site of a dressing station. We learned that Christine's husband's grandfather bought the property in the 1960s. We noticed an old 1970s photograph of a very old gentleman riding in a pony and cart and we were told that that was grandfather who was a great character and always used that form of travel. Although grandfather has been dead for some years, we were amazed to hear that the horse is still alive on a farm in Montauban; if he survives until next year, he will go into the record books!

We continued past Bernafay Wood to stop at Bernafay Wood British Cemetery. We then drove on to Longueval and to the Delville Wood car park where we had a snack and a drink. We visited the shop and purchased the 'Montauban' book which contains photographs of the station before and during the Great War. Our next village was Martinpuich where we located the remains of a German 'Concrete Tree' on the Bazentin road. We then joined the busy Bapaume to Albert road near Courcelette towards Pozieres; we stopped at the Windmill and Tank Memorial and then continued to the Australian Memorial and Fort Gibralter. From Pozieres we took road D73 and stopped at the Mouquet Farm Memorial, the Thiepval Memorial and the Ulster Tower.

Mouquet Farm, or Mucky Farm to the soldiers, was part of the German second line of defence; it was hoped to take this on 1 July, but it was not finally captured until 26 September. We then drove down into the valley of the Ancre river, where, in the Hamel area, we hoped to locate a memorial we photographed last year but had been unable to identify. We found a situation which resembled the site of the memorial, but there was no memorial. We took a number of photographs to compare with last year's and explored the immediate area and reluctantly decided to continue the tour. We proceeded towards Auchonvillers and, after a short while, we found the memorial we had been looking for – more photographs; we then stopped briefly at the Newfoundland Memorial Park. Next, via Puisieux and towards Gommecourt past Owl Trench Cemetery and Rossignol Wood Cemetery to Rossignol Wood to which we will return. We returned to Rancourt via Puisieux, Achiet-le-Petit, Achiet-le-Grand, Bihucourt and Bapaume reaching Le Prieure at 19.25.

Weather much improved during the day. (361 miles)

We found that there was a wedding reception in the main restaurant of Le Prieure, but we were able to have a meal in the bar area.

M and M E - Pâté, etc. (Not ordered)
M and M E - Petit rôti de gigot d'agneau – gâteau de pomme de terre au lait de sa mère.
M – Glace fraise avec crème légère a la pistache.
M E – Sorbet poire avec langues du chat au gingembre.
Château Turcaud rouge; café au lait.

Sunday, 29 April

Phoned Paul – his birthday!

Left hotel at 11.20. We first returned to Montauban Station as we realized that we did not take any photographs there yesterday. Stopping in the road near the station-master's house we saw someone looking out of a bedroom window – it was Christine's daughter who happily agreed to be photographed. We then drove in to be welcomed again by Christine who was very pleased for photos to be taken. We then continued via Longueval (where a ceremony was taking place at the memorial – uniforms and bagpipes), Martinpuich, Courcelette, Adanac (Canada backwards) Military Cemetery (3,172 graves – many Canadian), Miraumont, Puisieux and to Rossignol Wood. We left the car in a nearby storage area for road making materials and some shells! It was near Rossignol Wood that the Reverend Theodore Hardy won his Victoria Cross for fetching wounded men from close to a German pillbox. On 5 April 1918 Padre Hardy, helped by a sergeant, rescued a wounded man from a position very close to a German pillbox. We walked 120 paces along the edge of the wood from the road to Bucquoy and just inside the wood we found the remains of a German pillbox, almost certainly the one where Padre Hardy rescued his wounded man. On 11 October 1918 Padre Hardy was fatally wounded crossing a plank bridge over the River Selle at Briastres; he was heard to say, 'I've been hit. I'm sorry to be a nuisance" and he died in Rouen a week later, two days before his 55th birthday.

We returned to the car and, after a snack and a drink, we set off for Le p'tit Train de la Haute Somme at Froissy. We arrived just in time for the 14.30 train to Cappy and Dompierre-Becquincourt and return – it was the first operating day of the season. This five miles of two-foot gauge track is the last remaining section of the network laid by allied armies in 1916 for the Somme battle; it was used to transport men and materials to the front near the sugar beet factory at Dompierre. On the return journey we were joined by a reporter from France Bleu radio station who asked if we would like to be interviewed; however, he agreed that our French was not up to that standard, but he spent the rest of the journey talking with us. We returned to the Museum, had a snack in the car and then walked between the railway and the Canal de la Somme to Cappy; it was very beautiful and peaceful with many birds (including a cuckoo) singing – in sharp contrast to the conditions in 1916. We left Froissy at 19.10 for Albert to obtain details of train times and fares to Amiens (a visit to the Cathedral was recommended by the reporter). From Albert we returned to Rancourt via La Boisselle, Contalmaison; we stopped at the Longueval Memorial and then continued through Guillemont and Combles, reaching Le Prieure at 20.40.

Lovely day and plenty of sunshine. Crisps, etc! (420 miles)

Monday, 30 April

A wet morning. Left Hotel at 11.00 for Albert and parked near the station (free). Walked to the Museum which by then was closed. Visited Albert Basilica which has a golden Virgin and Child statue on the top of the tower. On 15 January 1915 a German shell caused the original statue to start leaning over; engineers managed to secure it the following day and it remained in a horizontal position for the next three years; during the German occupation of Albert British guns finally destroyed the tower of the church on 16 April 1918; the statue fell and was never found. We returned to the car for some food and drink.

We then caught the 13.24 train to Amiens. On the journey we noticed some of the flooding which this part of France had suffered from so much recently. We arrived in Amiens at 13.48 – still raining and very cold. In view of the weather we made our way straight to the Cathédrale Notre-Dame. This is the largest in France and was built to house the head of St John the Baptist, brought back from the Crusades in 1206 and which we saw still displayed in the Treasury; the nave is 42 metres high; there are many carvings and statues in stone and wood both inside and out – a very impressive and beautiful building which miraculously survived two world wars, although the surrounding centre of the city was destroyed during the 1939–45 war. While we were in the Cathedral a funeral took place. Before leaving the Cathedral, we visited the shop where we were directed to les Toilettes – single capsule type which operated automatically after depositing the appropriate coins – very clean and efficient. Still wet and very cold, we eventually found a Salon de Thé where we had pastries and coffee – all very nice and enjoyable. When we left the café we found that it had stopped raining and we were able to walk to and take photos of the Hôtel de Ville, the exterior of the Cathedral, trained street trees, flower beds, a year 2000 decorative clock and a war memorial. We returned to the station and caught the 18.45 train, arriving at Albert at 19.21. The trains were on time, swift, smooth and clean and the conductors wore uniforms with peaked caps and were in charge – the return fare was 52 FRF each (about £5)! We returned to the car and looked for the mobile food van near the Hôtel de Ville without success; we then drove on to buy frites at McDonalds drive-in on the Bapaume road.

We returned to Rancourt via la Boisselle, Contalmaison, Longueval, Guillemont and Combles, arriving at 20.40. Crisps, etc., and brandy! (449 miles)

Tuesday, 1 May

Labour Day and a public holiday in France. Although not raining a very thick mist! Left the Hotel at 10.25 and returned to Albert. We visited Le Musée des Abris Somme 1916 – in a tunnel 206 metres long and 10 metres underground – it takes you into the very midst of the Great War trenches, etc. – full of displays, re-creations and memorabilia of every kind. It was raining when we emerged from the tunnel, but we walked around the gardens before returning to the car for an extended 'lunch'.

At 15.15, as it had brightened a little, we left by car towards Peronne. We visited Dartmoor Cemetery at Becordel-Becourt and we found the grave of Lt Henry Webber who, aged 68, is believed to be the oldest soldier killed in action during the war; we also located the graves of father and son Sgt George and Cpl Robert Lee, both killed on 5 September 1916. The civilian cemetery opposite was flooded. We then continued to Fricourt visiting Fricourt British Cemetery and viewing Fricourt Church; we drove along rue du Major Raper whose family gave funds for the rebuilding of the church. We visited Fricourt German Cemetery which contains 5,056 marked burials and 11,970 in mass graves at the rear – the black metal crosses mark up to four burials. We then drove along a very long track and located the extremely impressive 38th (Welsh) Division Dragon memorial, overlooking Death Valley and

Mametz Wood – the exuberant, winged red dragon spits fire and grasps the enemy's barbed wire in its powerful claws. This memorial was unveiled on 11 July 1987. Our next stop was at the Dantzig Alley Cemetery where on a clear day there are extensive views of Death Valley, etc. Next, we visited Carnoy Military Cemetery and the grave of Capt W.P. Nevill, who, before 1 July, bought footballs for each of his four platoons. He offered a prize for the first ball to be kicked into a German trench during the assault on Montauban on 1 July. Nevill kicked off but did not survive to award his prize. Two of the footballs were retrieved and are preserved. Via Contalmaison we paid a second visit to McDonalds near Albert for supper.

On our way back to Rancourt we made a short stop at le Grande Mine at la Boisselle, where a Remembrance ceremony takes place at 7.30 on 1 July every year, and then we visited the impressive Caterpillar Valley Cemetery, the second largest on the Somme, with 5,539 graves and the New Zealand Missing Memorial. We reached Le Prieure at 21.15. (500 miles)

<u>Wednesday, 2 May</u>

We left Rancourt at 10.50 for Albert where we purchased petrol (30 litres) and a video in a newsagent/ bookshop where some alterations were being carried out and I was surprised to see some large packaging materials from Viking Direct! We have purchased many items of stationery and office equipment from Viking Direct! We then drove via Doullens, Frevent, Hesdin to Agincourt. (566 miles) We parked in the square and visited the small but interesting museum; we drove round the battlefield route frequently marked with appropriate displays, stopping to photograph a memorial and then back to the square. There is a memorial near the Château de Tramecourt and the family of Chaboy-Tramecourt still own part of the ground on which the 1415 battle was fought; they had a father and two sons killed in that battle and a second group of father and two sons died in German hands for being associated with the Resistance in the Second World War. We had some lunch in the car and visited the church. It seems remarkable that the French, having been decisively beaten in the battle by Henry V's weary and bedraggled army and losing 6,000 men compared with the English losses of some 300+, should make such an interesting, attractive and inviting setting of the battlefield site. Unfortunately, it rained during most of our visit.

We continued at 16.00 via Fruges, Fauquembergues, St-Omer and Hazebrouck to the Belle Hotel at BAILLEUL, arriving at 17.15. A good journey. (621 miles)

We received a warm reception and room 152 was very nice.

We had an enjoyable meal in La Pomme d'Or.
M and M E – Entrecôte Grillée beurre Maitre.
M – Mousse au chocolat.
M E – Coupe Panachée 3 Parfums.
Château Beausoleil rouge.
Café.

We phoned Ian.

Thursday, 3 May

Left the Belle Hotel at 09.20 for Ypres via Dikkebus; we parked near the Menin Gate (free) and joined the Salient Tours minibus at 10.00 with three other visitors for a four-hour tour of the Ypres Salient. Our driver and guide, Tony, was very knowledgeable; we visited Cement House Cemetery at Langemarck, in which burials are still being made (the remains of about 100 men were found last year); Essex Farm Cemetery (to which we will return); Langemarck German Cemetery (which contains 44,292 burials, including one mass grave of 25,000 soldiers, the sculpture of four mourning figures and the remains of some massive German blockhouses); St-Juliaan (the Brooding Soldier memorial marking the area of the first gas attack on 22 April 1915 in which 2,000 Canadians died); Tyne Cot Cemetery (this resembles a great church and is the largest British War Cemetery in the world containing 11,871 graves and on the wall at the back of the cemetery the names of almost 35,000 soldiers who have no known grave – it contains two German block-houses; at the suggestion of King George V, the Cross of Sacrifice was built over a large German pill box which, after its capture, was used as an Advance Dressing Station); Passchendaele (unable to enter centre area of village because of extensive road works); the Canadian Memorial at Hill 62; Sanctuary Wood Museum (preserved trenches and dugouts and the stumps of trees outside (it was raining) and many, many exhibits and 3-D pictures inside – this area has been in the ownership of the Schier family since the Great War); Hell-fire Corner and back to Ypres. A memorable tour!!

We returned to the car to eat and it rained and rained and eventually we drove into the centre of the town to park at the rear of the Cathedral. We then visited the In Flanders Fields Museum – a very realistic presentation with films, audio-visual presentations, etc. We then visited the Cathedral.

We decided to have a meal in Ypres and we found a Tea-Room – 't Ganzeke (The Goose) nearby. It was very nice, friendly and the waitress spoke English.

M and M E – Ham and salad followed by ice-cream.

After leaving the restaurant we walked to the Menin Gate to witness, with many others from across the world, the Last Post at 20.00 hours. This ceremony has been performed here every night since 1929, except during the period of occupation in the Second World War.

We left a very cold Ypres at 20.15 and reached the Belle Hotel at 20.55. (648 miles)
Phoned Thelma.

Friday, 4 May

A damp morning. We walked into the town, bought some films and viewed the remains of the church and the 'flying angel'.

At 11.40 we set off for La Coupole near St-Omer arriving at 12.35. Raining!

The Germans began building La Coupole in 1943 to be the launch base for the new V2 stratospheric rocket which, it was hoped, would destroy London. First, a railway tunnel was constructed, designed to receive trains loaded with rockets from Germany and then nearly seven kilometres of galleries were bored into the chalk plateau for the storage of rockets. To protect the site an enormous reinforced concrete dome, 71 metres in diameter and five metres thick, was laid on the surface of the plateau to increase resistance to bombing, the chalk then being excavated from underneath to form a vast empty room. However, the French Resistance informed London of the existence of the abnormal work site. Sometime afterwards it was attacked many times from the air and some 3,000 tonnes of bombs were dropped, however, the dome remained intact. Hitler ordered the site to be abandoned on 28 July 1944 and no rocket was ever fired from La Coupole.

After the war the German designers of the V2 rocket, Wernher von Braun and his team, moved to America and then became the engineers of the Saturn V rocket which took man to the moon. La Coupole was adapted as an historical centre and opened in 1997. The entrance is through the tunnel and galleries to a lift which rises 42 metres to the area beneath the dome, which now houses cinemas, displays, models of rockets, etc., and, in particular, a record of life in occupied France. A very interesting and impressive experience.

When we emerged into daylight it had stopped raining and there was some weak sunshine.

We left La Coupole at 18.50 and returned to Bailleul via Cassel, where we parked the car in the centre and walked or 'climbed' the short distance to the top of Mt. Cassel (176 metres high) – magnificent views all around, but bitterly cold.

We continued to Bailleul to enjoy frites in the car, in the centre.

We returned to the Belle at 21.15. (704 miles)

Saturday, 5 May

Blue sky and sunshine, but very cold wind.

We left the hotel at 10.30 for Poperinghe, a cloth town in the Middle Ages and the material produced here became known as 'poplin'. We parked the car (free) and walked to the square and into the street – Gasthuisstraat. Our first stop was at No. 43 – Talbot House, this was the rest house for soldiers, established by Padre Philip (Tubby) Clayton and opened on 11 December 1915. This extraordinary club was named after Gilbert Talbot who was killed in the Salient; the name was shortened in Army signallers' language to 'Toc H'. It has been described as the last stop before Hell. Although it now provides self-catering accommodation, we were able to enter several rooms and, particularly, the Chapel on the top floor, which looks much the same as in the time of the Great War.

Other properties in Gasthuisstraat associated with the War which we traced were; No. 12 'Skindles' (a wartime café now a pharmacy), No. 26 'Hotel Cyrille' (no longer a hotel), No. 57 'Skindles' No 2 (no longer a hotel). In Boeschepestraat we found No. 11 'The Savoy Restaurant' (an officer's hotel). We continued into the Grote Markt and visited the Cathedral and the local War Memorial.

We returned to the car for some 'lunch'. We then continued on the road towards Ypres to visit Brandhoek New Military Cemetery and the grave of one of the truly brave heroes of the war – Capt Noel Chavasse, a Medical Officer and the only Double VC winner during World War One (last year we found the area near Guillemont in the Somme where he won his first VC). Next, we visited Hop Store Cemetery – the nearby hop store building was used as an Advanced Dressing Station and here worked the Reverend Charles Doudney, Vicar of St Marks, Bath (where we were married); 'Charlie' Doudney is buried in Lijssenthoek Cemetery. We then continued to Wlamertinghe Military Cemetery, but we were unable to find the grave of P Fuller. We then went to the nearby Hospital Farm Cemetery – this was closed because of foot and mouth. We then crossed the railway and main road to Vlamertinghe New Military Cemetery. Here we found the grave of Gunner P Fuller MM (the uncle of Iris Hope), we also recorded the Register entry. We also found the grave of Major Adrian Drewe, the son of the founder of the Home and Colonial Stores of Castle Drago. Also buried in this cemetery is CSM John Skinner, VC, a colourful character who had been wounded eight times before being shot and killed trying to rescue a wounded man.

We then made a second visit to Essex Farm Cemetery. Outside the cemetery is an Albertina Memorial to

Canadian Medical Officer, Colonel John McCrae, who wrote the poem 'In Flanders fields the poppies grow', which bears the date 3 May 1995, the eightieth anniversary of the writing of the poem; nearby, are some concrete dugouts which were used as a dressing station and it was either while sitting on the roof of these dugouts or sitting on the bumper of a nearby ambulance that McCrae wrote the poem. Thence the poppy became the symbol of remembrance. In the cemetery is the grave of Pte Thomas Barratt who won the VC as a sniper – an unusual achievement; another grave is that of 15-year-old Pte V.J. Strudwick (not the youngest to die); we also noticed a number of headstones touching one another which indicates that the soldiers died touching one another.

Leaving the cemetery, we drove into Ypres for a meal at 't Ganzeke.

M and M E – Lamb chops (4 each), chips and very assorted salad with dressings.

Left Ypres at 21.00 and reached the Belle Hotel at 21.30. (746 miles)

Made phone call.

Sunday, 6 May

Took photographs of the Hotel and left at 11.30, then bought petrol (36.25 litres) nearby. We drove towards Pomeringhe to the Lijssenthoek Military Cemetery, but we were very disappointed to find that it was very securely closed because of foot and mouth – a very beautiful and interesting cemetery and deserving of another visit. We had some lunch, sitting in the car outside the cemetery walls, which have wisteria growing over them. We then decided to visit the German Cemetery at Vladslo and drove via Ypres and Diksmuide, but we found that all roads into the village were closed because of foot and mouth. Reluctantly we abandoned the visit and returned towards Diksmuide. On seeing the official signs to the Cemetery, we decided to make a further attempt and eventually reached the Cemetery which is, in fact, outside the village. It contains 25,664 burials in virtually one mass grave with standard flat markers listing about 20 names each. In the Cemetery is the famous pair of statues, 'The Grieving Parents' created by the sculptress Kathe Kollwitz in memory of her 18-year-old son, Peter who is buried in front of the statues; he was killed in battle nearby in what Germans described as 'The Massacre of the Innocents'. As the statues are now deteriorating the Germans wish to remove them to their country; the Belgians have not agreed, and it is likely that they will be put in the nearby Kathe Kollwitz Tower in Koekelare and replaced with replicas. As we were about to leave a group of perhaps 30 motorcyclists, etc., arrived and we made a swift departure.

We returned to Ypres by 17.30 and decided to visit St. George's Memorial Church. However, a service was about to begin, but we were welcomed and we stayed for the Annual Pilgrimage Service, which included the dedication of kneelers and wall plaques and ended with the 'Last Post'. A very interesting church.

After the service we went to 't Ganzeke for a meal.
M E – Ham, bread and salad (shared).
M – Jam pancake.
We returned to Bailleul at 20.55. (823 miles)
A dry, brighter and less cold day.
Made phone calls.

Monday, 7 May

Left Belle Hotel at 10.00. Purchased petrol in Bailleul
(12.13 litres – 7.09 FFR per litre). Travelled via
Hazebrouck, Aire-sur-la-Lys, St-Omer, A26 to Calais
(motorway, but very little traffic) arriving at Cite Europe
at 11.40. Visited Tesco and left car park at 13.15 for
terminal. Shuttle left at 14.21 arriving at English terminal
at 13.55 (English time). Continued via M20, M26, and
M25 to Junction 10, A3, A31, A3016, A287, M3 and
A303, stopping at Popham Services at 15.55 for coffee
and biscuits at the Little Chef. We could not help noticing
the appalling volumes of litter in and around the car
parking area here – it was repugnant, particularly as we
had seen so little litter in France and Belgium. At 16.40
we continued via A303, A360, B3098 to Edington, West
Ashton, arriving at Green Lane at 17.50. (1056 miles)

A dry and warmer day.

The day after we left France was another public
holiday – the anniversary of VE Day, 8 May 1945, the
end of the Second World War (in Europe)! France also
has a public holiday on 11 November, the anniversary
of Armistice Day at the end of the Great War.

A moving and memorable experience.

THE WINTER OF 1962–63

SOME PERSONAL RECOLLECTIONS

Much has been said about the severity of the weather in this current winter (2009–10) in relation to that of previous years. It has been suggested that it may be the most severe for 100 years and also that it is the worst for 30 years. Personally, I would think that the latter is the most likely. Certainly the winter that we recall very vividly and that which we shall never forget as being by far the most severe in our lifetimes was that of 1962–63. As it is now approaching 50 years ago I thought it would be sensible to record our recollections of that very difficult time while they are still very clear in my memory.

It was on Boxing Day 1962 that Gran and Grampa Moore (Margaret's parents) came to us at 10 Camerton Hill, Camerton from their home in Bath. They would have travelled by bus, with the last mile or so on foot. They intended to return by the same means. There was no snow during the afternoon, and we paid no attention to the conditions outside after it became dark; all enjoying the warm festive atmosphere with Paul, then aged two, and my parents. That is, until at about 10.00pm when it was time for me to take Margaret's parents about a mile up the hill – Skinners Hill – to meet the bus on the main A367 road between Radstock and

Peasedown. On looking outside we were amazed to find that several inches of snow had fallen on the already frozen ground. However, we were even more surprised to find that, as it was fresh snow and there had been very little traffic, I succeeded in driving up the hill to the bus stop and we parked in the lay-by opposite. Shortly afterwards we were a little surprised to see a double-decker bus for Bath appear, more or less on time, above the brow of the hill from Radstock. Obviously the driver was also surprised to find passengers waiting at that isolated spot at that time on such a night. He clearly delayed braking and when he did so the bus turned round completely in the road, coming to a stop facing back towards Radstock. However, getting it to face in the correct direction did not present any difficulties; the passengers boarded and they all set off towards Peasedown and, we hoped, Bath. I returned home with no more difficulty than I had encountered on the outward journey. That was that – or so we thought! We did happen to hear on the radio later that night that the town of Weymouth had been completely cut off and so we realized that the snowfall had been very widespread. We had no telephones in those days and it must have been quite some days later that we would have received a letter explaining that, in fact, the bus got no further than the bottom of the hill in Dunkerton and Gran and Grampa had to walk the remainder of the journey to Bath, some three or four miles, in very unpleasant conditions.

In the following days we realized that Camerton too was cut off; the roads between the crossroads south of Camerton Farm and the junction with the A367 road and also the road between the top of Red Hill and

Meadgate were filled in with snow to the tops of the hedges. One of our first concerns was to obtain some milk. This was no great problem because nearby Abbey Farm had milk which they were unable to dispose of as the tankers were unable to reach the farm. Secondly, after a few days we needed, of course, to do some shopping. The only option available was to walk to Radstock which I remember doing on several occasions; because the road from the crossroads to the A367 was completely blocked I had to find a way across the field. It was a task which took some hours!

Snow fell on and off for it seemed weeks and one of the features of that time was that the frost was intense and deep; any slight thawing of snow during the days quickly became ice as darkness fell. Consequently, it was not just a case of moving the snow, but of breaking up the ice.

Our most unpleasant experience and most difficult time was after we discovered that our water supply had ceased. Obviously the water in the pipes had frozen somewhere in the course of 120 yards or so from the road in Camerton Hill. I suspected that it had occurred at the side of the road in Camerton Hill where motorists had clearly been attempting to dig out soil, etc., to throw on the icy road surface so that vehicles could obtain some grip. Late one evening I actually tried burning some rags soaked in paraffin where I thought the problem might lay, in the hope that it would raise the temperature sufficiently to thaw the pipe beneath. Of course, it was to no avail. We felt helpless! For three weeks we had to carry all the water we needed from a well in Abbey Farm opposite Camerton School and because of the very low temperatures we found that we were having to walk on the surface of the frozen snow. It was not easy! In addition to that difficulty, at that time we had a back boiler in the fireplace of our living room and, as there was no water supply, we could not have a fire. Consequently we had to heat with kettles, etc., all the hot water we required – for washing, etc. We had to resort to an electric heater. Tolerating and coping with the difficult conditions outside was one thing, but not being able to wholly escape from them indoors was another.

It was 'the last straw', with no sign of the weather coming to our assistance we asked a company in Radstock for their help. They suggested running an electric current along the metal pipe. Two men came and connected an extension cable to the water pipe at a stop tap at the far end (in the garden of Hill Cottage) and at our end and then to our electricity supply. We sat and waited and waited. After a couple of hours or so they were beginning to come to the conclusion that their mission had failed and were talking of packing up and leaving. I don't know who suggested it but, at the last moment they decided to leave the electricity connected and go to the Jolly Collier for some lunch. We were left to continue our 'vigil'. Not long before the men returned we were absolutely delighted and relieved when we suddenly saw a drip from the tap. Success! After three weeks it was the beginning of the end. We have never been more pleased to be able to draw water from a tap – not even when we first had a mains supply about 20 years earlier.

At that time I was working in Bristol – at Berkeley Square – and travelling by bus and I am not sure how long it was after Christmas before I first went to work. There were no buses through Camerton for six weeks and the first service (occasional) that I became aware of was from Radstock to Bristol via Pensford as there was no route through Burnett between Marksbury and Keynsham. I used this service a number of times, but it was a very long journey taking about three hours from the office in Berkeley Square, including the long, difficult and lonely walk from Radstock, to home. Subsequently a service from Bristol to Timsbury was restored which I then used as this was a shorter walking journey. For several weeks I only went in to work two or three times each week. When travelling into Bristol one morning I clearly remember seeing workman using pneumatic drills to break up the ice on the surface of the road at the top of the hill from Pensford towards Whitchurch. I have very clear memories of walking home from both Radstock and Timsbury perhaps between 7.00 and 8.00pm. Particularly, one evening I was passing the home, at the top of Redhill, Camerton, of the late James Sellars, who was in his 90s, when he was listening, presumably, to the Stock Market Report; indeed I could hear it in the road. Generally everywhere was deserted; there were virtually no cars on the roads and I was unlikely to meet another pedestrian. For most of the way there were no street lights, but everywhere and everything was covered with a clean white sheet and there was a remarkable silence and an atmosphere of peace and calm. I don't think I have ever experienced anything like it. Yes, it was quite wonderful.

Eventually the end of our six weeks of isolation from the bus services came. It was, I believe, one Sunday afternoon when we heard and then saw a double-decker bus climbing up Camerton Hill and we were delighted to see that it successfully passed between the School and Abbey Farm - that was the real test! Shortly afterwards we were able to drive the car on to the road – again. After six weeks it was a great relief to feel that we were once again connected to the outside world. However, it was not the end of the winter and of the snow. In fact, the last remaining snow that I witnessed was near the road between Farmborough and Marksbury and it was in early March!

At that time I was also the Organist at Southstoke Parish Church, near Bath and, obviously, I was unable to carry out my duties for a period of about six weeks.

There have been other winters in my lifetime when we have had some severe weather, notably in 1967 and in the early 1980s (the date of the latter has not made a sufficient impression!), but none of them stand out in the memory to the extent of that of 1962–63.

There are, of course, many 'official' records of circumstances and events of that winter and I would be surprised if I do not have relevant newspaper extracts and cuttings among the 'archives' here. Very many people have personal memories and only today I have spoken to two people who have been keen to tell me where they were and the particular circumstances on the evening of Boxing Day 1962. For many it was a memorable evening! For everybody it was a memorable winter!

A FIRST VISIT TO FRANCE FOR GEORGE (7) AND SAMUEL (6)

NORMANDIE 2004

Saturday, 17 April

George and Samuel arrived at Green Lane on Friday evening and we completed as much packing of the car as was possible. After a rather short night we were all up and ready in good time and we left in the early light at 06.10 and travelled via West Ashton, Edington, West Lavington, Shrewton and the A360 to Salisbury encountering virtually no traffic. We continued on the A36, M27 and M275 to Portsmouth Ferry Port, arriving at 7.50; the motorway section of the journey was quite busy.

After reporting to Southfield that we had arrived, we quickly passed the ticket and passport checks only to be directed to the security checks where the over efficient officer, appearing to lack any degree of discretion, asked us if we were carrying any guns, knives or other weapons and, despite the obvious answer, still decided to inspect the very full boot of the car; he chose one of the larger bags to pass through the screening process and, that not being enough, the driver had also to be screened! Apparently being satisfied that our mission was entirely peaceful he allowed us to continue and we then boarded Brittany Ferries *MV Normandie* and sailed at 08.45.

George and Samuel found it interesting exploring some of the nine decks – there were very few people on board. We passed close by the *Victory*, the *Warrior* and Portsmouth Harbour Station and we could see the new two-legged observation tower which stands on the harbour front and which is still under construction. The boys phoned home, we visited the shop and we had a meal of fish and chips. It was a very pleasant and enjoyable crossing and we were able to stay viewing the French coast as we approached and entered the harbour at Ouistreham until just before docking, when we had to return to the car deck. We docked at 15.30 (French time) and we were soon off the ferry and in the town of Ouistreham and then out into the French countryside in warm sunshine. We passed through Colleville-Montgomery and Cresserons to the town of Douvres-la-Delivrande with its twin spires, where we decided to do some shopping. We soon found a boulangerie-patisserie and the '8 a huit' which clearly had all that we required and where the butcher showed a great interest in the boys, asking them if they were on holiday and they soon felt very comfortable and welcome in France. We returned to the car with numerous bags of shopping and, in view of the fact that the car was full when we left Trowbridge, it was somewhat difficult to accommodate them all! However, George and Samuel were very helpful and with some improvisation we succeeded. As we continued on the journey it transpired that Granny had forgotten to buy any butter or margarine at the supermarche, but it was not long before we were passing through the small village of Reviers where we noticed a typical small village shop which was able to supply our further needs.

After passing through Tierceville we soon found Vienne-en-Bessin and La ferme des Chataigniers which we had visited in October last year. It was about 18.00 and we very anxious to inspect the gite and Samuel was the first to do so, exclaiming, "George come and see this – this is great". It was indeed very satisfactory and in a very rural environment. We went to visit Fabienne Fortin, the owner, to let her know that we had arrived but, although her door was open, she was clearly not in!!! After a while she arrived at the gite apologizing for being out and talking too much! She was accompanied by Amandine (two and a half years) who soon found the boys who had already discovered a box which contained 20 games! When the 'visitors' left we all proceeded to unload the car and to get established in the gite. We phoned Southfield and, eventually, had a meal of ham, tomatoes, etc. Finally, and rather late after the beds had been prepared, it was bedtime. A very successful day – we had arrived!

Sunday, 18 April

After rising rather late (about 09.00) but following a good night it was breakfast of croissants, etc., though a little later we discovered that we were the lucky recipients of a dozen eggs and some vouchers for entry reductions to places of interest. As the weather was very unsettled and stormy it was difficult to decide what to do, but at about 13.35 we set off towards the coast at

Arromanches. At the entrance to the village of Ryes we noticed le garage and in the centre we stopped to observe certain features:– le aux morts, la mairie, l'ecole, la justice de la paix, la poste, la boulangerie/patisserie – a complete village perhaps? On leaving the village we paused again near the entrance to l'eglise where stands an inscription recording a nearby meeting in the year 1070 (?) between William the Conqueror and a local lord.

We then continued to Arromanches and George was very excited when he spotted a Berkeley coach (T4 POW) in the coach park at the entrance to the village. Berkeley Coaches are based at Paulton, the adjacent village to Camerton. We drove to the sea front where the boys had a glimpse of the remains of the Mulberry Harbour but because of the weather we did not stop. We continued up the hill to the east and parked (for two euros) in the car park of St Come de Fresne Table d' Orientation. Again, the rain did not allow us to leave the car. We then continued eastwards along the coast to Asnelles, Courseulles and Bernieres, where, in addition to many reminders of 1944, there is much post-war development and, as we travelled, the weather became drier and brighter.

We then passed through Douvres and Colleville again to the village of Benouville to visit Pegasus Bridge. We spent some time in the Café looking at the mass of memorabilia and photographs and making a number of purchases; Madame Arlette Gondree-Pritchett, la Propietaire, was there and, as a child, she had been in the building during the momentous night of 5/6 June 1944. However, we were not able to speak to her, but we talked to another lady who was very interested in George and Samuel and clearly impressed by their willingness and determination to speak as much French as they could. While in the Café we all enjoyed a cup of tea. As it was still dry we then walked across the present bridge to the area of the memorials which mark the spots where the three gliders landed. We photographed the bust of Major John Howard who was in command of the successful operation to capture the vital bridge. We did not have time to visit the new museum on the opposite side of the road, but we could see the original bridge which is erected near it. We returned to the car, but barely in time to avoid another heavy storm which included hailstones.

We returned to Vienne via Douvres and Creully. We then all enjoyed a late evening meal of vegetables and the pork which was purchased in Douvres the previous day. Eventually, after telephone calls to report the day's activities, it was another rather late bedtime!! A good day.

Monday, 19 April

After another good night and a late breakfast, we set off late in the morning to Ryes and Arromanches then heading westwards along the coast to Longues-sur-Mer. Here we spent some time viewing the four German gun positions, the Longues Battery. These guns had a range of nearly 13 miles, but they were put out of action on D-Day and the garrison surrendered on the following day. However, three of the guns remained almost intact while the fourth had received a direct hit from the

French warship Georges Leygues. George and Samuel were very interested in tracing the various remains of this gun imbedded in the surrounding area. We then continued along the coast, past Port-en-Bessin, to Colleville-sur-Mer. We parked in the car park of the American Cemetery at St. Laurent, but because of heavy rain we had to remain in the car for some time. However, we were able to make a phone call and we occupied ourselves by having a snack and a drink. Eventually, the rain eased and we walked into the cemetery to view the 9,286 graves and the impressive Memorial. We walked to the viewing area to look down to the landing beaches below and saw the new walkway leading to them, which is being constructed. We returned to the car and continued via a diversion along the D517 which, at Vierville, took us past a number of the Mulberry Harbour pier sections which are being restored in preparation for display to coincide with the 60th anniversary of D-Day. We intended to visit Pointe du Hoc, but the construction of a new access road and car park made it unfamiliar and because of the uncertain weather, we decided to continue our journey. We stopped at Grandcamp-Maisy in dry weather and walked along the front and around the harbour and passed the hotel Duguesclin, where we have spent a few nights in previous years. After leaving Grandcamp-Maisy we passed close by the famous Isigny-sur-Mer dairy products factory before joining the N13 for Ste-Mere-Eglise. We parked in the square outside the church and the boys were very pleased to see the effigy of John Steele hanging from the church tower. As mentioned earlier in this book, John Steele was an American paratrooper whose parachute got caught on a flying buttress and he hung there, pretending to be dead, for some two hours. He was eventually released and survived. We spent some time inside the church and afterwards called at a patisserie. We returned to Vienne by the quickest route – the N13.

We had an evening meal of tinned beans and sausages with scrambled eggs, etc., and bedtime was again quite late, but it was a good day and we had all enjoyed it.

Tuesday, 20 April

Another good night and a late breakfast of croissants or cereals. Later in the morning, when we were all ready, we drove into Bayeux. However, we had some difficulty in finding the car park off the ring road and also the rather spread-out park nearer the centre where we have parked in the past. After driving down the main street for the third time the boys thought that by then they knew the way. Eventually, we parked (free) and set off for the attractive café named le Triskell, with its interior walls decorated with paintings of Dinard. Again, the proprietor acknowledged and took an interest in George and Samuel which pleased them. We all had a crepe and a drink. Refreshed, we then proceeded to the Centre Guillaume le Conquerant to see the Tapisserie de Bayeux. With the assistance of the personal commentary in English we all found it, and the short film we saw afterwards, very interesting and remarkable even if it was not for the first visit for two of us! We then spent time in the shop making purchases, etc. Afterwards we visited the magnificent Cathedral which was consecrated on 14 July 1077 in the presence of William then Duke of Normandy! Parts of that Cathedral which remain today include the crypt and the piers on the west front. Before leaving, George and Samuel lit and placed a candle in memory of the late Mr Mills, our friend and neighbour at Trowbridge. This decision, entirely their own, was very moving.

It was now time for a cup of tea and so we chose the salon de thé we were near. After sitting down and about to make an order a gentleman at an adjacent table commented that we were obviously English. We had quite a long conversation with him and he was a most interesting man. His name is Charles Hargrove; he lives in Paris and has a property, a former 'rectory' near Omaha Beach. He was born in Leeds (?) – his mother was French and his father British; at the beginning of the last war he was a student at Peterhouse College in Cambridge; he landed in France on D-Day; sometime after the war he was the Paris correspondent of the Times for 16 years; he was involved in advising French Television regarding a recent programme relating to L'Entente-Cordial and mentioned some links with the British Ambassador to Paris. His wife is French and her father, a musician, knew Saint-Saens and Faure; his two sons, now in their mid-forties, went to Downside School and he knew Stratton-on-the-Fosse and Bath well; he was interested in our visits to Downside and in the fact that George and Samuel will be going to Wells Cathedral School in September. Finally he mentioned that he has written a book, in French, *"A Gentleman of the Times"* and said that we might be able to obtain a copy from the book shop next door; he said that if he had our address he would send us a copy, but no doubt a copy could be obtained from *The Times* Paris office. A most interesting encounter. We eventually finished our tea and almost left forgetting to pay the bill.

We called at Marche Plus to do some necessary shopping before returning to the car. When we did so, we thought it wise to buy petrol before returning to the gite; however, we found that the route to the garage we know on the ring road was barred and we had to reach it by going the reverse way round the ring road! Eventually we returned to Vienne.

Another late tea accompanied by discussions and questions, followed by phone calls and another late night. However, an interesting and good day.

<u>Wednesday, 21 April</u>

A good night and a late breakfast. We decided to make the trip to Falaise and we took the road to Tilly-s-Seulles via Vaux-s-Seulles, Carcagny and Chouaint. We continued to Villers-Bocage and Aunay-s-Odon, then along the D6 through very attractive countryside to Thury-Harcourt and Falaise. There was no charge for parking outside the chateau. First, we viewed and photographed the majestic statue of William on horseback. We spent a considerable time inside the chateau following the audio-visual tours around the keeps and climbed to the top of the tower. It is extremely interesting – a great deal of restoration work has been completed and much is still in progress. We spent time in the shop making purchases. Leaving the chateau shortly before it was due to close, we then enjoyed a cup of tea in a salon du thé – Serais Gourmand – nearby and called at a boulangerie next-door. We returned to Vienne via the N158, Caen and the N13. The N158 was very quiet, but there was much traffic around Caen.

After a meal it was another late night, but following a very good day.

Thursday, 22 April

Again a good night followed by a late breakfast. Late morning, we went via Bayeux and the D5 to le Molay-Littry. It was market day and so we proceeded to the Musée de la Mine – it was closed for lunch, but we remained in the almost empty adjoining car park in pleasant warm sunshine to have a snack. When the museum was due to open there was a party of school children waiting to enter. The museum was created in 1902 and is the oldest mine museum in France. Coal was first extracted in the area in 1747 and the last mine was 'flooded' in 1880, however, two pits were reopened in 1941 and heavily exploited after the end of the German occupation in 1944. The mines closed permanently in 1950. The museum has many exhibits and photographs and also large scale working models. The reconstructed gallery is very realistic with the use of lighting and sound effects. This is an excellent museum and the visit is totally automatically controlled by modern technology. After leaving the museum there was time to visit the Moulin de Marcy, a restored 19th century flour mill and farm, a short distance away. At the entrance to the property we were able to watch a donkey being shod. This mill was transferred to the local authority following the death of the last miller. It is in a beautiful setting and is excellently preserved with working equipment.

Before setting off for Vienne we returned to le Molay-Littry; the market having closed, we were able to park in the large square outside the Hotel du Commerce, where we spent our first night in Normandy in 1979, and to visit a boulangerie. We then returned past the mine museum and the route to the mill before passing through Cerisy-la-Foret and then along the D13 through the very attractive Foret de Cerisy to l'Embranchement. We then continued along the D572 passing through Noron-la-Poterie where salt glaze pottery has been produced since the 13th century – there are a number of displays alongside the road. We returned to Vienne via Bayeux.

Another late tea and not an early night, but a most interesting and excellent day in good weather.

Friday, 23 April

Another good night and the usual late and casual breakfast. We felt we could not leave Vienne without exploring the village and, as it was a pleasant morning, we walked past the entrance to La Ferme des Chataigniers and a number of attractive properties; past the village school (we could hear the children at the rear), past the Marie, to the Church. Unfortunately, we could not go into the church, but George and Samuel were very interested in the layout of the cemetery and certain inscriptions on gravestones particularly the one of a local doctor. Returning to the gite we noticed Fabienne and we had an interesting chat.

We then decided to make a specific visit to Arromanches and we passed through Ryes for the third time and, as we passed the church, we saw again a shrine in a field nearby and, not for the first time, Samuel said, "I would like to walk out to that shrine". Unfortunately, to have done so would not have allowed time in Arromanches to make a worthwhile visit to the museum. We parked in the usual car park in Arromanches and walked down to the 'front'. Before going to the museum, the boys could not resist the temptation of an ice-cream. On entering the D-Day Museum we were welcomed by a lady who spoke good English and she first gave us a very detailed and vivid description of the construction and operation of the Mulberry Harbour; she clearly spoke with pride when she said that it was named Port Winston. She told us to look around the Museum, but she advised us when each of the two films were due to commence – these were extremely interesting. After we had visited the 'shop' she spoke to us again; she was very interested in George and Samuel and impressed by their use of French. She was pleased to tell us that her two daughters are learning English. We told her we were very grateful for the welcome and help she had given us and, as we left she gave both boys a kiss. We had been treated like very special guests.

After leaving the Museum George and Samuel were pleased to have a ride on a merry-go-round, followed by a run on the beach. We then enjoyed a cup of tea at the Café Six Juin. It was then time (or past the time) to return to the gite.

We had a meal and then did a certain amount of tidying-up, but we could not do any serious packing until the morning. In addition, there was a lot to talk about and it was not an early night, but it had been another excellent day.

Saturday, 24 April

A good if short night. We had to be at Ouistreham by 08.15 and we decided that we must leave Vienne by 07.30 at the latest. We were up at 05.20 and the boys by 06.00., assuming that that would allow us enough time – it was not enough! Breakfast, packing bedding, towels, food, etc., etc., and all the items we had acquired during the week, etc., and into a car which might not accommodate it all took a long time. Fortunately, when we were nearly ready to leave, Fabienne called and, therefore, we did not have to spend time returning the keys to her. It was by then a lovely morning and, eventually, we left at about 07.45. However, we had not travelled very far when we found ourselves in thick fog. This was so all the way to Ouistreham making it difficult to see directions to the ferry port, etc. After having to change direction a couple of times we reached the port at about 08.30; we quickly passed the ticket and passport check points and we were very relieved to join the end of the boarding queue for the *Mont St Michel*. The ship seemed immense and the car deck cavernous. Emerging on to the upper deck we found the sun breaking through the fog and we had excellent views of the port and coast as we sailed at 09.00. It was an excellent crossing in a large modern ship with many and varied facilities and not very full. We passed some of the time having a snack and later a meal before arriving a Portsmouth at 13.45 (British time). On our way into the harbour we were able to see the various 'landmarks' and many naval vessels.

We disembarked without delay and were soon on the M275 and then the M27. We took the A36 for Salisbury and Warminster and returned to Trowbridge via Westbury, reaching home at about 15.50. (499 miles)

Throughout the week the boys had been very helpful and extremely interested in all that we had done and seen. They had been very busy, reading, drawing, (they each did an excellent map of Normandy entirely on their own initiative) discussing history and asking questions, listening to and participating in French language cassettes, completing their diaries and, obviously, very anxious to tell Mum and Dad about their experiences.

It was remarkable how many French and also English people spoke to us because of George and Samuel; the French, in particular, much appreciated the fact that they used their knowledge of French whenever they were able to do so.

This had been a very successful, happy, enjoyable and rewarding week for all; George and Samuel having contributed much to its success.

Pour nous quatre c'était une expérience inoubliable!

THE GREAT WAR

THE FINAL YEAR – 1918

At this time of remembrance, I recall that my father, Reginald Samuel Clark, served during the latter part of The Great War. He was born on 11 June 1898 but, as a miner, he had been exempt from military service. However, in March 1918 it was decided that a certain number of men from each colliery would have to serve and selection was by placing all names into a hat; those drawn out were the unfortunate ones, and Dad was one of those. He served in the Machine Gun Corps of the 51st Highland Division from 19 April 1918 until 27 January 1919. His Regimental No. was 172454 and he was awarded the British War Medal and the Victory Medal. I have wondered why he was called up at that particular time, but I now believe that this further mobilisation followed the German Spring Offensive of March 1918. The initial German successes had alarmed Whitehall. I know that Dad was in the Arras area and we have seen orientation tables near Arras indicating the position of the 51st Division. It is clear to me now that Dad must have been involved in the horrifying and terrifying actions and witnessed the appalling scenes of death and devastation. However, like most participants, he never spoke about his experiences.

It seemed, therefore, an appropriate time, when so much attention is being drawn to the final months and weeks of the War, to learn more about the events of the year during which my father served. My source has been mainly the excellent book by A.J.P. Taylor, *'The First World War'* and I have made a brief summary of the events of the final stages of the 'war to end all wars'.

Revolution in Russia had changed the course of the war and the Russians were no longer capable of fighting a war with Germany. It would be brought to an end by the Treaty of Brest Litovsk. However, the Russian delegation refused to discuss or even read the terms of the Treaty. Trotsky simply advocated a state of 'No war, no peace'. Nevertheless, on 8 March 1918 they signed, in silence, the dictated terms of the Treaty of Brest Litovsk. Under the terms, Russia lost the conquests of 200 years of the Tsars – the Baltic States, Poland and the Ukraine which, in practice, were added to the German Empire.

Following the Treaty, some German Divisions remained on the Eastern Front, but 52 Divisions were transferred to the Western Front. With increasing numbers of American troops arriving in Europe, the respective armies were about equal. General Ludendorff decided that it was an appropriate opportunity to launch a decisive offensive that would win the war for Germany. It was to be against the British Fifth and Third Armies which held the front from the Somme River to the English Channel. Offensive 'Michael', the Spring Offensive, began at 04.40 on 21 March 1918 with an artillery bombardment of targets over an area of 150 square miles; it was the biggest barrage of the entire war and over 1,100,000 shells were fired in five hours. On the morning of the attack there was dense fog allowing the stormtroopers leading the attack to penetrate deep into the British positions undetected. By the end of the first day, the British had lost 7,512 dead and 10,000 wounded; the Germans had broken through at several points of the front. After two days the Fifth Army was in full retreat and had become separated from the Third Army, which also retreated to avoid being outflanked. On 28 March an attack was launched at Arras against the left wing of the Third Army in an attempt to widen the breach in the Allied lines, but it was repulsed.

Marshall Foch had now become Commander-in-Chief of Allied Armies in France; he adopted a policy of holding reserves back and using them to counter-attack. However, the Germans made greater advances and more gains than ever before. In allowing them to do so, Foch restored the war of movement – the only way it could be won. Lloyd George responded to the challenge; on 23 March he went to the War Office and ordered that all available troops be sent to France. General Pershing agreed, temporarily, that American troops be brought in as reinforcements for the British and French armies. Allied commanders rarely consulted each other and thus there was no fully coordinated plan of campaign; three separate armies fought to the end. However, the Germans were unable to move supplies and reinforcements fast enough to maintain their advances and the German offensives petered out. On 28 March General Ludendorff expanded his offensive northwards towards Arras, where there were strong British forces; he only acquired a salient, not a breakthrough.

On 5 April the offensive was halted. The Germans had inflicted great losses and had suffered great losses; they had not achieved a breakthrough. Ludendorff's forces were running down, but he was still eager for his second blow in the north – the diversionary offensive of St George or Georgette! On 9 April the German's attacked in Flanders towards Hazebrouck; they were lucky, the line was held by a single Portuguese division. They broke on the first onslaught. The British abandoned Passchendale, which they had won in the previous year. Haig feared for the Channel ports. On 12 April he issued his famous order, "With our backs to the wall and believing in the justice of our cause, each one of us must fight to the end". This had much effect in England. By 29 April the German attack had been stayed. The danger of a German breakthrough had passed and they had suffered heavy losses; the tide had turned. During May German forces moved south – Ludendorff planned to attack on the Aisne. On 27 May, 14 German divisions broke through the British line and advanced 10 miles in a single day. The War Cabinet were alarmed. By 3 June the Germans had reached the Marne – the 'Marne' brought terrifying memories of 1914 - and were only 56 miles from Paris. But the Germans marched into a sack and had not broken the French front.

The decision rested with Ludendorff for the last time. Victory had eluded him despite repeated success. The German's assembled divisions east and west of Rheims and mounted a new, and last, offensive on 15 July.

The Allies were not taken by surprise. The Germans advanced towards Paris, but the French mounted a counter-attack on 18 July and the German forces were halted. However, the German line remained intact until the end of the war. Ludendorff planned to launch offensive 'Hagen' on 20 July. However, the Germans were forced back across the Marne and 'Hagen' was called off. It was the turn of the tide.

On 24 July Haig, Pétain and Pershing went to Foch's headquarters – he told them the time had come for a general offensive, using better tactics and greater resources. The British were to attack in the north, around Ypres; the Americans at the southern end, near Verdun; the French would maintain pressure in the centre. Events led to victory, but not as Foch had planned. His immediate concern was to free the railways east of Amiens. Canadian forces were moved secretly and were aided by the Australians who possessed, in Sir John Monash, the only general of creative originality produced by the First World War.

On 8 August – it was the beginning of the Hundred Days Offensive – the British forces attacked. They had learnt at last the lesson of Cumbrai, 456 tanks were used; morning mist played its part and the British advanced six miles. The tanks went faster than the cavalry, the infantry lagged behind both. Foch and Haig wanted to press the attack in the old way, but there was resistance by the subordinate commanders. Their policy was to stop when the enemy proved obstinate and attack the weak points not the strong ones, but Foch and Haig took the credit. For four weeks there was a succession of Allied attacks – short and sharp – French on 10 August and 17 August, British on 21 August and 26 August and American on 12 September. Ludendorff called 8 August 'The black day of the German Army'. However, the fighting from 8 August to 12 September nowhere broke the German line. They had abandoned the salient they had conquered since 21 March and withdrawn to stronger positions and the Allies had suffered the heavier losses. The real effect of 8 August was psychological; it had shattered the German faith in victory. The German soldiers no longer wanted to win; they wanted to end the war. Ludendorff admitted that the war would have to be ended by negotiation, not by victory. Foch agreed with him.

By mid-September it seemed too late to launch the final campaign. Still, the great attack started on 26 September. The vital stroke was to be delivered by the Americans in the Argonne. However, they had not yet learnt from experience; Pershing used the old method of attacking strong points instead of by-passing them. The troops often waited for the mist to clear instead of welcoming it. They suffered over 100,000 casualties; discipline often broke down and in one week they advanced less than eight miles. The British did better and actually got beyond the Hindenburg line. In Flanders, mud triumphed once more. The Germans had not been encircled as hoped; they were holding on the two flanks and yielding in the centre, thus shortening their line and improving their position. Yet, suddenly, the great moment came. On 29 September Ludendorff insisted that there must be an immediate armistice. Partly because he feared, mistakenly, that the Allies would do so first, but much more because of news from the distant forgotten front at Salonika.

On 29 September Bulgaria asked for an armistice and withdrew from the war. Southern Europe was then wide open and the war effectively ended when 'western' and 'eastern' strategy combined. Ludendorff did not envisage unconditional surrender. He imagined, with childish cunning, that an armistice would permit the German armies to withdraw from conquered territory and then to stand on a more formidable defensive position in their own country. Ludendorff thought an armistice was a means by which he could avoid defeat and emerge from the war undiminished.

On 4 October Germany formally requested an armistice. The German note was addressed to President Wilson, not to the Commander-in-Chief Foch and it accepted Wilson's Fourteen Points proposal as the basis for peace negotiations. The Allies had never accepted the Fourteen Points, nor had the American people. Wilson hoped for a peace without victors or vanquished; he did not consult the Allies. Germany was being offered a harmless, innocent peace merely at the price of withdrawing within her own frontiers. The European Allies were alarmed; the Germans were delighted. On 12 October Prince Max replied to Wilson that Germany accepted the 14 Points.

On 12 October a German submarine sank the *Leinster*, a ship running between England and Ireland – 450 passengers were drowned, some Americans. Wilson was offended. Ludendorff was now for fighting on; the great Allied attack was running down and the German army was neither encircled nor being broken. The German generals and admirals were overruled. Wilson's condition of a military armistice was accepted on 20 October with assurances that Germany had become truly liberal. Few Germans had appreciated anyway, the legend of the 'Imperialist Germany' or the bitterness against the Kaiser. They imagined that they had atoned for the events of the war by becoming democratic on Wilson's instruction. They did not realise that they would have to surrender territory to Poland. On 23 October Wilson announced that he was satisfied with the German answer. He asked the Generals to draft an armistice and invited the Allies to accept the Fourteen Points as a basis for the future peace. A strange way for the war to end!

The United States had borne least of the burden and done least of the fighting, yet dictated terms to the Allies and enemies alike. The Allies had not formulated any aims except victory. The armistice was to be a military agreement which would end the fighting. Ludendorff, by insisting on an armistice instead of negotiations for peace, brought on Germany the defeat which he had intended to avoid. Haig would have accepted a withdrawal from all occupied territory. On the other hand, Pershing wanted no armistice at all and wanted more military success. Foch was determined to get the Rhineland for France. The British Admiralty insisted that the German fleet be handed over or interned. The British got the German navy, Foch got the Rhineland. The Germans were to hand over a large part of their fighting material. The political leaders eventually accepted the 14 Points.

Lloyd George and Clemenceau insisted that the Germans pay for damage caused to civilians and their property in Allied countries. Wilson thought he had won, but at his moment of triumph, the Republicans won the elections to Congress. Wilson's position crumbled. The American people repudiated Wilson's programme; they did not want the United States to be embedded in an idealistic peace, they only wanted to defeat Germany. The German position was crumbling also. On the Western Front they were still holding their own; their defensive line remained unbroken. Devastation, lack of communications and nests of machine gunners held up the Allied advance. However, in their rear the German allies collapsed; the Ottoman Empire was the first to dissolve; a British Army under Allenby reached Damascus on 1 October and another was moving up the Euphrates to the oil wells of Mosul. On 30 October Turkey signed an armistice of surrender with a British admiral. The British Navy steamed through the Dardenelles. Constantinople (now Istanbul) passed under allied control. The Allies were free to advance up the Danube against Germany and also free to intervene against the Bolsheviks in southern Russia. The Sultan was a virtual prisoner of the Allies and the Ottoman Empire was at an end.

The Habsburg Empire vanished at about the same time. Austria-Hungary had been rocking on her feet throughout 1918. The Austro-Hungarian Government asked President Wilson to arrange peace on the basis of the Fourteen Points. He could not do so, as the Fourteen Points had assumed the survival of the Habsburg Monarchy with 'autonomy' for its various nationalities. Since announcing them, Wilson had promised independence to the Czechs and Poles and less formally to the Rumanians and South Slavs. Wilson replied that it was these nations, and not he, who must decide on the peace terms.

This was the signal for revolt. The so-called 'subject' nationalities of Austria-Hungary learnt that they could escape the burden of defeat and become Allies merely by becoming independent nations. The revolutions were harmless. In Prague the Imperial Governor rang the Czech National Committee and they met in the Castle. The Governor handed over his seals and keys and left. The civil servants remained at their desks. In ten minutes, an independent country of Czechoslovakia had been created. Likewise, with the South Slav Committee at Zagreb; the Croats and Slovenes, subjects of the Habsburg Emperor Charles, suddenly became, along with the Serbs, subjects of King Peter Karageorgevich. In Vienna Count Bilinski, last Austro-Hungarian Minister of Finance, locked his office and took the train for Warsaw, where he became first Polish Minister of Finance. In Hungary, Michael Karolyi, an opponent of the war, became Prime Minister on 31 October. Two days later he proclaimed the independence of Hungary and became Hungary's first President. The Germans of Vienna were the last to leave the sinking ship. Emperor Charles was still at Vienna on 12 November, when his German lands proclaimed themselves part of the future German democratic state. The Czechs, the South Slavs, the Poles duly became Allies, as did the Rumanians. The Hungarians and German Austrians were not so lucky; they alone were treated as heirs of the dead Empire and saddled with its guilt. They were compulsorily disarmed and theoretically charged with reparations. Democratic Hungary and republican Austria paid a penalty for retaining their former imperial names. The Austro-Hungarian army continued. but after action against the Italians they deserted; the Italians taking 300,000 prisoners and an armistice was hastily signed on 3 November.

The German rear was now wide open and the Allied armies were preparing to advance into southern Germany. On 26 October William II dismissed Ludendorff and three days later left Berlin for army headquarters still confident of a long successful defensive period. The Government urged him to return, but he defied them. The German admirals were defiant also. They resolved to send the High Seas Fleet into action against the British again, although they had not been in action for more than two years. Orders were issued to raise steam and prepare for battle. On 29 October the crews began to mutiny. Two days later they went ashore and carried the mutiny through the streets of Kiel. By 3 November Kiel was in their hands; it was the beginning of the German revolution. Soon the news reached Berlin. Prince Max and his colleagues were convinced that revolution would soon spread throughout Germany. They were resolved now to bring the war to an end – no longer to avert defeat, but to prevent revolution.

Erzberger, leading figure of the Centre, was put at the head of the Armistice Commission, which did not include any representative of the High Command. It was thought that a military representative might be inclined to prolong the war. On 7 November Erzberger requested a meeting with Foch. He and other delegates were driven across the fighting line during the night. At eight o'clock the next morning they met Foch and Admiral Wemyss in a railway carriage at Rethondes in the forest of Compiegne. Erzberger asked for an armistice and Foch read out the harsh terms on which the Allies had agreed. Events had made the German Government grasp at an armistice on almost any terms. On 9 November the revolution finally took fire. A republic was proclaimed in Berlin. Prince Max handed over his position as Chancellor to Ebert, leader of the Social Democrats. The generals told William II that the army might fight for Germany but not for the Emperor. William retired to his special train and steamed away early the next morning. He then changed over to a car and drove to the Dutch frontier. After some hours delay, he was allowed to cross. Two days later he signed his formal abdication as King of Prussia and German Emperor. He never saw Germany again, but the income from his vast German properties continued to roll in until his death in 1941.

The new government was too busy staving off revolution to spend time discussing the armistice terms and Erzberger, having gained some minor concessions, was instructed to sign at once – at 5am on 11 November. He handed over a declaration which ended 'A nation of seventy millions of people suffers, but it does not die'. Foch replied, "Très bien" and withdrew without shaking hands. At 11am that morning the fighting stopped. The war was over. The German army, still unbroken, stood everywhere on foreign soil, except for a few villages in Alsace, which the French had held throughout the war. Canadian troops entered Mons an hour before the armistice came into force. The British army was back where it started.

The Germans were to hand over vast stocks of war material and most of their fleet. They were to withdraw from all invaded territory in the west and from Alsace Lorraine. The allied armies were to occupy German territory on the left bank of the Rhine and the bridgeheads for fifty miles beyond it. The treaties of Brest Litovsk and Bucharest were annulled. This was the crushing victory to which the Allies had aspired, though by no means the destruction of the German army, still less the dismemberment of the German Reich. The German revolution was not the cause of defeat. On the contrary, the revolution was caused by Ludendorff's confession that the war was lost. More than this, the revolution saved both the German army and German unity. The armistice came when Germany still held together. The Allies themselves had to desire a strong German government if the armistice was to be maintained or a peace treaty signed. Future victory was snatched by the Germans from present defeat.

On 11 November 1918 the Allied peoples burst into rejoicing. All work stopped for the day. Crowds blocked the streets, dancing and cheering. In Trafalgar Square Canadian soldiers lit a bonfire on the plinth of Nelson's Column. As evening fell, the crowds grew more riotous. The celebrations went on for two more days. Things were quieter in Paris after the first day. The death toll of the French was too great to be forgotten even in victory. In Moscow the news of Germany's defeat was received with sombre triumph. The Bolsheviks imagined that revolution would now sweep across Europe; many in the West feared that it might.

What happened on the 11 November 1918? Was it the military defeat of Germany? Or the triumph of idealistic principles enshrined in the Fourteen Points? Or was it the prospect of imminent revolution? Or was it little more than a temporary cessation of fighting, albeit for some twenty years? The peoples and their leaders now had to seek answers and solutions; to determine the future of a damaged and disturbed Europe!

A DAY AT WEYMOUTH

This is the first year for some 35 years that we have not made at least one visit to France; a long period during which it has become a kind of 'second home'! Although, principally, it is for reasons of health, there is also the fact that the Brittany Ferries cruise ferry service between Poole and Cherbourg had been withdrawn. Apparently, the company has suffered losses in recent years because of increases in the cost of fuel and changes in the exchange rate and it is reported in the French press that, in view of its financial difficulties, it has proposed reductions in the salaries of its employees. This decision was followed by strikes and on 21 September the company decided to immobilise all its ships; there were, in fact, no services on any of its routes between France and Spain and England until 2 October. The many thousands of passengers affected have been directed to either Calais or Dover. Also, services from Weymouth to the Channel Islands have been transferred to Poole, but that is because of structural work on the ferry berth.

Fortunately, Trowbridge is well served with rail services, one of which is to Weymouth on the Heart of Wessex Line. First memories of Weymouth are of Sunday school outings by coach and I clearly remember the sight of many young men in naval uniform, obviously from the nearby Portland naval base; this must have been in the years prior to the Second World War and it made a lasting impression. Many years later, but still some 30 years ago, this port on the south coast was our regular gateway to the Hexagon when the crossing to Cherbourg was operated by British Rail! Of course, Weymouth has other links with the shores of Normandy. In the circumstances, what better place than Weymouth in which to spend a few hours of a very pleasant day at this end of a 'summer' which has offered so few such opportunities?

We decided to travel on the 10.29 train from Trowbridge which does not involve a change and which is due at Weymouth at 12.09. We allowed about half an hour to find a parking place close to the appropriate platform and to cross the bridge to purchase our tickets. Unfortunately, I was told at the booking office that, on its journey from Gloucester, the train had been held up at Bristol Parkway by signal problems and was likely to be 20 minutes late. In fact, it was further delayed and when the two coach train eventually arrived it was about 30 minutes late, but we had been able to spend most of the extra waiting time in the car. Our first stop was at Westbury and the next at Frome and we were soon travelling through the delightful rural countryside of Somerset and then Dorset passing through or near many small villages, Whitham Friary, Bruton, where it skirts the Kings School, Castle Cary, where there were many cars in the car park, no doubt, belonging to commuters to far off places, Sparkford, Marston Magna and then to Yeovil (Penn Mill station). Continuing into Dorset the route crosses an Area of Outstanding Natural Beauty before sweeping over the South Dorset Downs to the Jurassic Coast; in the course of which it serves the towns and villages of Thornford, Yetminster, Chetnole, Maiden Newton and Dorchester (the county town of Dorset). It was then just a short distance past Upwey and Broadwey to Weymouth, which we reached without any extension of the initial delay. It had been a very enjoyable journey; being able to observe such rural scenes, not now so familiar to us – in Trowbridge, as large herds of cattle grazing contentedly on the verdant pasture lands and the occasional small village distinguished by the perpendicular tower of its church. The train did not appear to be particularly old, presumably what is known as a Sprinter diesel multiple unit train dating from the late 1980s and 1990s; it was in good condition and clean and tidy except for newspapers left by previous passengers. However, we could not avoid noting that it was a noisy journey, particularly comparing it with similar journeys we have made on regional routes in France. But why did governments of past decades fail to invest in the infrastructure of the system as many travellers use the services and, no doubt, many more would do so if it were modernised and more efficient? The original large station at Weymouth was demolished in 1986 and replaced with a much smaller terminus; it is neat and tidy and with the basic facilities one would expect – booking office, a shop and toilets, etc. Apart from the service we have used there is a frequent service to London Waterloo from here, but services to Cardiff have been reduced. This station also has the advantage (for us) of being a very short distance from the sea front. In fact, until 1987 mainline trains ran through the streets and along the Weymouth Harbour Tramway to the Quay station at the eastern end of the harbour, to connect with ferries to mainland Europe. It was now about 12.30 and after leaving the station our first priority was to look for something to eat. We did not have to go very far; after reaching and crossing the road which leads directly to the landmark clock we noticed an inviting fish and chip shop – the Sea Chef – which had an adjacent small restaurant. We had a most welcome and enjoyable meal – of fish and chips – and in a very friendly atmosphere.

WEYMOUTH has a long and interesting history and has a population of 50,000–55,000; it has been twinned with the town of Louviers, in the department of Eure in Normandy, since 1959. The town developed from the middle of the 12th century and by the middle of the 13th century it was an established seaport. Melcombe Regis developed separately and is known to have been a licensed wool port in 1310; however, French raiders found the port easily accessible and in 1433 the trade was transferred to Poole. It is thought that Melcombe Regis was the port at which the Black Death first came into England in 1348. The towns of Weymouth and Melcombe Regis were united by an Act of Parliament in 1571 and together have become known as Weymouth, although Melcombe Regis represents the main town centre. The architect, Sir Christopher Wren was the Member of Parliament for Weymouth at the beginning of the 18th century and controlled nearby Portland's quarries from 1675 to 1717. When he designed St. Paul's Cathedral he had it built with Portland stone. Sir James Thornhill, who was born in the White Hart Inn in Melcombe Regis, became the town's MP in 1722;

he became an artist and it was he who was responsible for the interior decoration of St Paul's Cathedral! Weymouth became a tourist destination after the Duke of Gloucester, brother of George III, built a residence there, Gloucester Lodge; the King himself spent his summer holidays in Weymouth on fourteen occasions between 1789 and 1805. There is a painted statue of the King on the seafront, which was renovated in 2007/8. The esplanade features terraces constructed in the Georgian and Regency periods between 1770 and 1855; the terraces form a long continuous arc of buildings facing Weymouth Bay; the buildings being commissioned by wealthy businessmen some of whom were involved in the growth of Bath.

It was just a few yards to walk from the Sea Chef to the esplanade and to the Jubilee Clock, which was erected in 1887 to commemorate Queen Victoria's Golden Jubilee. I wonder how many memorials have been constructed to mark the Diamond Jubilee of Queen Elizabeth II, for future generations to admire. Immediately we reached the sea front we were reminded of Weymouth's role in the recent Olympic and Paralympic Games. We last visited Weymouth in June 2002, by train also, and since that time and, particularly, in preparation for the Olympics there has been much redevelopment of the esplanade, providing Victorian-style shelters, a number of seasonal kiosks, a sand art pavilion, seating areas with raised beds of plants, etc., etc. All of which has enhanced the pleasure of a leisurely walk for many people on this comfortably warm and sunny afternoon; always with a panorama of the splendid bay and a view out to sea towards France. An early point of interest was the memorial to the American Rangers who left Weymouth on 6 June 1944, "Showing courage and endurance beyond belief. 3,000 died on D-Day while fighting to secure the beachhead and strategic Pointe du Hoc, spearheading the invasion of Normandy". We recalled the Rangers Museum on the seafront at Grandcamp Maisy and visits to the Pointe du Hoc! On 11th October 2002 the Rangers have added a tribute to the men and equipment of the Landing Craft Assault (LCA) flotillas of the Royal Navy and their contribution to the successes of the assaults at Pointe du Hoc and Omaha Beach. It also records the loss of 749 men during a D-Day training exercise when a convoy of LSTs was attacked by E-boats off Portland on 28 April 1944 and the fact that, on 24 December 1944, 802 died when the troopship *Leopoldville* was sunk by a torpedo off Cherbourg. In fact, Weymouth played a very important role in the invasion of Europe as more than half a million men, together with about 140,000 vehicles, embarked through this place to fight in the Battle of Normandy.

Further along the esplanade I crossed the road to photograph the impressive over life-size statue of Sir Henry Edwards, which is in white Sicilian marble standing on a Cornish granite plinth. Sir Henry was Member of Parliament for Weymouth and Melcombe Regis from 1867 to 1885 when it ceased to be a parliamentary borough; he made generous gifts to the town. We eventually walked to near the Pavilion Theatre which was built in 1960. This area of some 10 acres was planned to be entirely redeveloped to provide many and varied amenities, including a World Heritage Site visitors' centre, a new ferry terminal and a 140 bed four-star hotel, etc., in time for the 2012 Olympics; unfortunately, because of delays to the project, this aim was not achieved. As we slowly made our way back in the direction of the Clock we saw again the little land train which we had been tempted to join, but one of the purposes of this day had been to walk as much as possible while in a very conducive environment. However, we could not resist taking advantage of one of the many kiosks that are available and we bought an ice cream to enjoy while sitting on a 'garden' wall; at the same time observing the gradually changing scene as we approached the end of the afternoon.

Coaches were arriving to collect the many departing visitors; some, certainly, had a quite long journey ahead of them – South Wales, for instance. As the sun was beginning to shine from a westerly direction it presented a changing view of the bay and emphasized, in particular, the white cliffs on the eastern side; we took some photographs. Stall holders on the beach were beginning to pack their wares away for the day. We had to pause to 'meet' and photograph four donkeys which were also coming to the end of their day's work. Eventually and reluctantly we had to leave the esplanade and continue towards the station even passing the Sea Chef as we did not feel that we had sufficient time for a cup of tea. However, we found that we had ample time at the station. When our train arrived we chose a seat on the right-hand side again, where we would not be looking into the setting sun and so that we would have the views opposite to those of the morning. Again it was a similar two coach train and seemingly very full. We left on time at 17.30 and were able to enjoy the different scenery.

It was a pleasant journey, although the space between the seats was somewhat narrow; for economic reasons perhaps! When we reached Frome there was a delay of some minutes – apparently to allow other trains to pass through Westbury. However, it would appear to have been allowed for in the timetable as it seems that we reached Trowbridge more or less on time, shortly before 19.30.

A very successful, enjoyable and interesting day!

NICE AND COTE D'AZUR – 2002

<u>Wednesday, 8 May 2002</u>

We left Green Lane at 11.40 by taxi (A & D) for the 12.07 train to Waterloo which was a few minutes late. Arrived at Waterloo a few minutes after the due time of 14.06. We entered the departure lounge for France as soon as it was possible, and the waiting time quickly passed, eating sandwiches, etc. Boarded Eurostar 9148 in a First Class compartment – very roomy and comfortable with individual seats. Left on time at 16.27 and, after a few minutes, dinner was served – Champagne or orange juice; Chicken, orange and basil pate served with a cucumber and orange salad; Medallion of turkey in an apricot and chive sauce, set on a bed of sautéed Mediterranean vegetables; Blackberry mouse and a set wild berry coulis on a light sponge cake soaked in blackberry syrup and topped with chocolate; Taurus, a washed rind cheese produced in Somerset, with a strong smooth taste; Coffee and chocolates. The meal had been served and eaten by the time we reached the tunnel – it was excellent.

We reached Lille on time at 19.29 (French time) and walked the short distance to Hotel Lille Europe and went to our room 801 on the eighth floor. After making phone calls, we walked to Les 3 Brasseurs for a drink and then back to the Hotel.

Thursday, 9 May

At breakfast we spoke to a couple who told us that the TGV journey to the south coast was a memorable experience and recommended a visit to St Agnes near Menton. We walked to the station in good time for the 10.20 train (5012) for Nice. We found the First Class accommodation very comfortable – only three seats across and a wide corridor, reclining seats with head rests and plenty of leg room; the increased spacing between the seats allowed good views to both sides of the train. The train was not full on leaving Lille, but appeared to be full for a large part of the journey. We left on time and stopped at Haute Picardy (10.50), Aeroport Charles de Gaulle (11.20), Marne La Vallee-Chessy – for Disneyland (11.33). At 13.00 we had a snack and a drink. The next stop was Valence for 15 minutes (13.33) and then at Avignon (14.15) (We had a view of the Pont du Gard) and Marseille, St Charles for 20 minutes (14.50). The train, in reverse, continued to Toulon (15.45), Les Arcs – for Draguinan (16.25), St Raphael/Valescure (16.40), Cannes (17.10), Antibes (17.20), arriving at Nice at 17.40 (It was due at 17.39). It was a remarkable journey with splendid views of beautiful scenery, particularly along the coast from St Raphael to Nice.

The journey of between 700 and 800 miles completed in less than seven and a half hours with a top speed of 186 mph and arriving only one minute late, was certainly memorable. All the stations from Calais and Lille to Marseille are new. We found our way to the station entrance and almost instantly a taxi offered its services; we were driven through a very, very busy city to the Hotel Vendome arriving by 18.00. We were welcomed by Valentin and given the 'key' (a token) to our room 404 on the fourth floor – it was very satisfactory. We made some phone calls and then, armed with a street plan, we made our way in the direction of the sea and, in the Avenue Felix Faure, Place Massena, we found a number of restaurants. While studying the menu at one, Le Pont Neuf, a polite and helpful lady of the staff enquired if we needed any assistance. We decided to go in and we enjoyed a very nice meal, in a very pleasant atmosphere contributed to by both staff and other customers and accompanied by very pleasant live keyboard music provided by one of the staff.

M - Poulet Grille and frites, followed by Glace.
M E – Poulet Basquaise and frites, followed by Glace.
All with water, wine, coffee and chocolates.

While finding our way back to the Hotel, a passing MPV slowed and a passenger enquired for some directions; after explaining that we were English and complete strangers in the city he apologized, and they drove on. To our amazement, when we reached the Hotel Vendome there were the people who had asked for directions, just getting out of their vehicle! They were clearly amused that we had been unable to help. On returning to our room we were concerned to find that we apparently had no electricity; we contacted Valentin, who advised us that we had to insert our door 'key' into a socket just inside the door to restore the supply to our room!

Friday, 10 May

After a satisfactory breakfast, buffet style in the relatively small dining room, we decided that our first task was to explore Nice and with a view to discovering the surrounding area, the Cote d'Azur. We first walked to the railway station (Gare SNCF) and obtained details of services and fares to various places along the coast and, in particular, inland to Sospel. We then set off to find the bus station (Gare Routiere); unfortunately, although we found the centre for local 'Sun Bus' services, there was no evidence of services to places beyond the city. We then walked through the famous Flower Market in the old town and through an arch onto Quai des Etats-Unis and then along to the Promenade des Anglais; here we sat for some while having a snack and watching the very frequent flights coming into and leaving Nice Airport – the second busiest in France. Eventually, we walked back along the Quai des Etats-Unis, past the very impressive and unusual war memorial set into the cliff. and on to the harbour, which contains some very expensive yachts. It then began to rain, and we were able to shelter in an antiques market, but we could see the very threatening storm over the mountains. After less than an hour the rain stopped, and we walked back along the front and decided to search again for the Gare Routiere. This time we were successful, and we obtained useful timetables of services to Cannes, Grasse, Menton and Eze. It was then time for a meal and we decided we could do no better than return to Le Pont Neuf.

M – Cotes agneau (3 lamb chops) and frites, and glace.

M E – Cotes agneau (3 lamb chops) and haricot verts, and crème caramel.
A bottle of Badoit and a glass of wine.

We returned to the Hotel where we were able to have coffee in the foyer.

Apart from the fairly brief storm it was a dry day.

Saturday, 11 May

After breakfast we set off for the Gare Routiere again and for the 11.15 bus to Menton. The 75-minute journey took us through Villefranche, Beaulieu, Eze Gare, Cap d'Ail, Monaco, Monte-Carlo and Roquebrune, with superb views of magnificent scenery, interesting buildings and luxurious yachts; the return fare was €4.90 each (about £3.10). On reaching MENTON we bought some pain-aux-raisins which we ate in the nearby park. We then walked past the Casino to the front – after a while we were surprised to see an elderly lady sitting on the beach wall who had been near us on the train journey from Lille to Nice. We were looking for toilets and all we found were the automatic operation cubicle type and we did not have the appropriate coins and, in any case, there were people waiting to use them, so we enquired in a bar if we could use their toilets. As we walked in, the lights went out and we realized that the business was closing for the afternoon, but yes, of course, we could use their toilets and when we left they all said, "Thank you" to us! We walked along and around the very attractive front, and eastwards to the harbour; we were sure that, in the distance, we could see the

Italian frontier and we were tempted to walk on to it, but decided that it might prove too far and take too long.

We returned to the front via the very attractive Vieux Ville (Old town) and then made our way back to the Gare Routiere. However, we still felt we would like to go into Italy and we found a local bus which was going in that direction, but first it did a 'tour' of Menton picking up and setting down local people who all appeared to know the very friendly lady driver (they also seemed to know the fares in the new currency); eventually, we went a very short distance over the frontier and then returned to France and to Menton. It was a very interesting experience. We left this bus on the front and walked back to the Gare Routiere for the bus to Nice. Unfortunately, on the return journey the bus clearly developed a problem which we thought might be that it had run out of fuel, and we had to get off in Monaco and wait for the next bus, which arrived after about 15 minutes. When we reached Nice it was time to look for a meal and we decided to try the Lafayette Restaurant. We chose jambon et frites and, although the food was good, the portions were far too large; we chose some wine, but despite only wanting a glass we, unfortunately, asked for a bottle! We were, however, willingly provided with a cork and were able to take the remaining wine away with us. This was not the most successful meal!

We returned to the Hotel.

However, it had been a fine day!

Sunday, 12 May

We decided today to go along the coast in the other direction and to Antibes. We walked to the bus station in good time for the 11.00 bus for Antibes and Cannes; we found the bus marked Cannes and the appropriate service number (200) and several people waiting. However, as 11.00 passed with no sign of a driver, one of the other would-be passengers found that the correct bus stop was one with an official timetable fixed to it at the other end of the station. Consequently, we then had to wait for the 11.30 bus which we boarded for the 50-minute journey to Antibes.

We stopped at the Aeroport Nice where we spotted the athlete Daley Thompson waiting for a taxi. We continued via Cagnes and Biot to ANTIBES. The fare each way was €4.10 each. We sat for a while in the pleasant Place du General de Gaulle, where we left the bus, and after making a phone call we found our way to the front/harbour which is very attractive and where we made more phone calls. We noticed, in particular, the railings on the sea wall were chromium plated and they had not been vandalized! We then decided to have a meal in Le Tea Pot.

M – Grilled faux filet (sirloin) and frites.
M E – Peppered grilled filet de boeuf and frites.
Also, wine and coffee.

This was a very nice meal in a most pleasant restaurant.

Afterwards, we walked past a very large open-air Sunday market (perhaps a sort of car boot sale?) and in the direction of the Cap d'Antibes. Margaret was very fond of a Papa Meilland rose, and interested in its history, which we have in our garden and she understood that Meilland Rose Nurseries were established on the Cap years ago and which, from roadside advertisements, still exist there. We hoped to find them, and so we continued. However, although we walked and walked as far as the first tip of the Cap, Pointe Bacon, we found no reference to the nurseries; clearly, it was going to be impossible to walk all the way round the Cap, and back again, in the time available. Disappointed and reluctantly we decided that we must return to the 'front', not knowing how near we had been to achieving our objective. On the way back, we visited the still open market. After lingering, to enjoy the 'front' for the last time, we walked past the Château Grimaldi and into the busy Vielle Ville, along the Rue de la République and back to the Place du General de Gaulle for the return journey to Nice. Back in Nice we walked along, and sat on a seat in, the Quai des Etats-Unis and enjoyed eclairs and a can of drink. We stayed until after sunset and although there were many people about, particularly young people some of whom were on roller skates, we did not feel uncomfortable in any way. We noticed in particular that, as it had been a busy day, most of the fixed waste bins along the front were full to overflowing; however, many had tidy piles of plastic bags full of additional rubbish piled around them. This was clearly not England!

We returned to the Hotel.

Another fine day and warmer.

Monday, 13 May

Breakfast and, once again, to the Gare Routiere, this time for the 10.30 bus to EZE Village. The fare for this 20-minute journey was €2.40 each, each way (about £1.50). This was a spectacular journey to a dramatic 'village perche' and a centre of the perfume industry. First, we enquired about a visit to the Parfumerie Galimard Museum, but there would be no guided tour in English for a while – the Japanese had just arrived! We had a patisserie and coffee in Le Beleze Restaurant nearby and then walked up the steep climb to the ancient village and to the Church and then on to the Jardin Exotique on the summit of the rock. This is 1,400 feet above the sea affording marvellous views of the coast and surrounding mountains and as far as Corsica; we could see what may have been two cruise ships anchored in the bay far below. We returned to a lower level and the main road, did some shopping and then caught the bus back to Nice.

We called at the Hotel to leave unwanted baggage and then walked to the Gare SNCF to do some shopping. When we returned to the Hotel again we asked the receptionist if she would book a taxi for our journey to the station in the morning, but she said it was not necessary; she said, just come down when you are ready, and we will then order a taxi and it will be here in five minutes.

We decided that it would be nice to have our final meal in Nice at Le Pont Neuf.
M – Poulet Grille and frites.

M E – Poulet Basquaise with rice.
Crepes with chocolate sauce (shared)
Water, wine and coffee.
€46 (About £29).

We walked back to the Hotel and did most of the necessary packing.

Again, a fine day.

Tuesday, 14 May

An earlier breakfast (about 8.00), and then finished packing. With plenty of time to spare we paid the bill, the taxi was ordered, and it was there in five minutes! A very polite, courteous and helpful taxi service for €14. We had quite a long wait for the train for Brussels, which originates in Nice; it left on time at 10.31 and stopped at the same stations as on the outward journey, reaching LILLE on time. Unfortunately, we had perhaps the worst possible seats for viewing, alongside the division between two windows – the consequence of the train being nearly full when we booked and having to travel back second class! We walked to the Citadines Apart'Hotel; we were given the key (token) for our apartment 1106 on the 11th floor. This was very large with a lounge and kitchen as well as a bedroom, toilet and bathroom; also, a wonderful view of Lille Flanders railway station. After making phone calls we walked into the city for crepes, wine and coffee at La Taverne Flamande.

Back to the apartment.

A very satisfactory and trouble-free day.

<u>Wednesday, 15 May</u>

A leisurely breakfast and, after the limited packing, we left our cases, etc., with the receptionist and spent an hour or so strolling around Lille. We returned to collect our luggage and walked to Lille Europe Station; we arrived with plenty of time to spare and, after passing through passport, etc., controls, waited in the departure lounge. When we were allowed to descend to the platform for our train, we found we had a very long walk to the appropriate boarding point as we were in the 17th of 18 coaches; we were very pleased to have a case with wheels! The train, from Paris, arrived and left on time and after a very smooth two-hour journey, we arrived at Waterloo ahead of time. There was, however, much congestion on the platform as a large number of Indian tourists had arrived on the same train. We managed to extricate ourselves and then avoided the crowds by spending some time at a snack bar where we had a pastry and a drink. Eventually, we went up to the main line level for the train to Trowbridge (and Manchester). Surprisingly, it left on time, but after two minutes it stopped for 10 minutes. We reached Trowbridge about 20 minutes late. After leaving Warminster I telephoned A & D Taxis only to find that they had no car available in the next half hour.

When we left the train, we could find no information or telephone numbers of taxi firms, obviously there was no directory in the telephone kiosk and a member of the station staff could not help! However, we saw that there were two taxis parked outside the A & D office near the entrance to the station car park and so I thought we should enquire again. I was told by the gentleman in the office that there were three taxis in various places, one of which was stuck in traffic in Bradford-on-Avon and his comment was, "What can I do about it?". I said I felt that this was typical of England and I asked if he could give me the number of any other taxi firm. Seemingly somewhat reluctantly he scribbled the number of Alpha Taxis on a scrap of paper after checking the number in the Dentons Directory. I left the office; rang the number I had been given – it was the wrong number!!! We decided that we would simply have to walk home to Green Lane and we secured all our cases and bags to the one case on wheels and set off via The Shires. As we reached the main road an A & D Taxi drove in; we returned to the office and, although the 'controller' seemed unwilling to agree to him doing so, the driver said that he had time to do a short journey and so, eventually, we had a taxi home, arriving at 18.00.

Our experience on returning to England was in sharp contrast to the welcoming, friendly, helpful, efficient and purposeful attitudes we experienced and witnessed everywhere we went in France; one is invariably greeted with a "Bon jour Monsieur/Dame", when eating with "Bon appétit" and when parting with a "Bon journée".

The public transport system, particularly the railways, is a revelation. The cities are clean and tidy and in Nice, in the mornings, the streets appear to have been washed.

The Euro has been accepted and adopted as if there had been no other currency and yet the French are still French!

We saw little or no litter or evidence of vandalism in either Nice or Lille or anywhere else. Nice is, in fact, France's largest tourist resort and fifth biggest city!

LILLE AND ARRAS

OCTOBER 2014 (Tuesday, 21 October – Thursday, 30 October)

This year, 2014, has been marked by the special anniversaries of two momentous events in European history – the 100th anniversary of the commencement of the Great War and the 70th anniversary of D-Day. Television has provided us with memorable pictures of numerous poignant commemorative events which have taken place in many historic locations but, of course, it is even more deeply moving to visit relevant sites in person. However, the year was now passing so quickly and we were approaching the Autumn Equinox; with the days rapidly becoming shorter it was too late in the year to plan a visit by car to Normandy. In the circumstances, we decided to travel by train and spend a few days in Lille and Arras in the Nord-Pas-de-Calais Region; this would be quite a challenge involving six separate train journeys. I contacted Eurostar and SNCF and I was assured that services for the handicapped were still available. In fact, the Accès Plus service is apparently provided at virtually every station in France.

Following exploratory internet visits to hotels and rail services, we concluded that we could make an outward journey to Lille on 21 October and return on 30 October, also a convenient onward journey to Arras and return, whilst reserving acceptable accommodation at hotels in both cities. As all the pieces of the jigsaw fitted together we made firm reservations straightaway.

As the date of our departure approached it was essential to give careful consideration to the matter of luggage, etc. In particular, should we take with us Margaret's three-wheel-walker and/or walking stick. Both would be useful at times and I had been assured by Eurostar that the former could be accommodated on their trains. However, when not in use I would have responsibility for handling it, particularly the folding and opening, in addition to our general luggage. Although we could rely on assistance at the stations, it was clearly most beneficial and practical for escorts to employ a wheelchair and we could not expect them to take responsibility for another piece of equipment. We decided to make do with a stick! We had to restrict our luggage to three items, a case on wheels, a bag which could be attached to it and a haversack, all of which I could carry or control and still have a free hand. All was prepared by the previous evening – essential documents, clothing, vital medications, etc., etc. However, overnight I recalled that on the previous journey a bag attached to the case had become somewhat uncontrollable and I decided that a second haversack would be more manageable – one on the back and one over the shoulder, which would still leave me with a free hand. Therefore, in the morning there was some urgent repacking to be done. Nevertheless, and quite remarkably, we were more or less ready by the time we planned to leave.

Tuesday, 21 October

Shortly before 09.00 our taxi appeared at the gate and with the driver's help we were quickly aboard and on our way to Trowbridge Station. This station provides very easy access to the trains and we were deposited adjacent to the platform. We had quite a long time to wait as our train, to Waterloo, was due at 09.27 and it was a little late. Although it was not a pleasant morning it was dry. When the train arrived a couple nearby realised that we had our hands full and offered their help. Unfortunately, they were travelling second class and we had booked seats in the first-class compartment. We had to scramble on board as quickly as we could, and we were relieved to find two empty seats at the end of the carriage with ample room for our luggage; although the seats were facing the wall, we were quite content to remain there. We sent a number of text messages to family and friends to let them know that we were on this stage of the journey. It was generally an uneventful journey with the usual stops but, compared with the same journey last year, there was no one to engage in conversation with.

When we reached London Waterloo, no one, staff or passengers, offered assistance, except that, when on the platform, one gentleman did show his concern. However, we had ample time and our plans had been based on the assumption that, at times, we might have to manage without help. We know where the toilets, particularly the disabled facilities, are situated and we decided to make use of those before continuing. Afterwards we slowly made our way to the taxi rank

– again it was very helpful to have made this same journey last year. When our turn came for the next available taxi we were assisted into the vehicle by a very polite and friendly driver. However, we were separated from the front of the vehicle by a screen and it was not possible to carry on a conversation with the driver or to have the route explained to us as we did last year.

When we reached St Pancras we were taken as near to the entrance as possible, for which we were grateful. When inside we found that the handicapped reception centre was no longer where it was last year; in fact, it is now immediately inside the building on the right and consists of no more than a desk and a computer. We were received straightaway, our details taken, a wheelchair provided, taken through border controls and to an area in the departure lounge which was for the specific use for passengers such as us, without any delay whatsoever. Margaret was allowed to remain in the wheelchair and we were assured that, when the time came for boarding, someone would come and assist us to and onto the train. It seemed that, within minutes of arriving at St Pancras, we had, I suppose, legally left the country; it was a remarkable experience!

Of course, we had a long time to wait, but it was a relaxing and interesting situation and the usual facilities, refreshments, etc., were available. We observed the variety of activity and we noticed, in particular, quite a number of men passing in front of us very casually in twos and threes; they were not formally dressed but were all wearing a casual type of 'blazer' and each carrying a small 'haversack'. Obviously they were all part of a large group, a club perhaps, even a football club. Eventually, the time came for us to be taken to the train and as we were passing along the side of the train our escort said, "We have the Arsenal Football Team travelling with us today – they have reserved two complete coaches". We were quite excited and as soon as we had been installed in our seats we sent text messages to say how privileged we were. George, in particular, exclaimed "You're not!" The team was, in fact, on its way to play a Champions League match in Belgium on the following evening. As we sat patiently, or impatiently, we received a text from Ian saying that we would not be delayed and at the precise appointed moment of 15.04 we began to move, silently and very slowly at first, but we quickly gained speed. These moments bring a special sensation, of achievement and of the adventure of setting off on an international journey. No doubt many who make this journey frequently find it simply a very routine experience. In any case, the route to the Channel Tunnel does not have many scenic virtues and then for 20 minutes we are under the sea, but after emerging in France we are welcomed to a very pleasant tranquil rural landscape.

How different it would have seemed to the hundreds of thousands who travelled in this direction in 1914–18! On time, of course, we approached Lille and we had to arouse ourselves and struggle towards the luggage racks and the exit. Fortunately, there often seems to be someone who recognizes that one would welcome a little help and here was no exception. However, as soon as the train drew to a halt, there again was 'our man' waiting at the door with a wheelchair. What a welcoming, comforting, reassuring sight it was; all our concerns and worries evaporated; we are truly in France. As we made our way up from the platform and towards the handicapé centre our escort asked us where we planned to spend the night and on being told that we had a reservation at Hotel Lille Europe, he said, "I will take you there straightaway". Remarkably, about 100 minutes after leaving London we were established in our room (512) at the hotel in Lille. As it was now approaching 18.00 and as we had accomplished our task for today, we decided to remain in our room; it is small, with a view of other uninteresting tall buildings, but it is comfortable and quite acceptable. Time now to relax, to send some messages and, in particular, to enjoy our excellent Tesco sandwiches, together with a drink from the cold cabinet. Unfortunately, we found that we had forgotten to bring our travel clock and so we had to arrange for a wake-up call. Having done so, we could now take advantage of the opportunity of a very early night.

Wednesday, 22 October

A varied and generous petit-déjeuner is available here over a long period, to meet the needs of guests who have early morning appointments in the city and those who may be leaving early by train or car. Also, it suits the arrangements of those, like ourselves, whose timetable is somewhat more leisurely. Towards the latter end of the session there is usually an opportunity to choose a table which provides a grandstand view of the busy activity in the streets below, with a comfortable feeling of detachment. However, we too are continuing our journey today and, therefore, we are required to vacate our room by 11.00. We returned our keys to the reception desk and confirmed that we will return to the same room on Monday next. It is only a short distance to Lille Flanders, but it involves crossing a very busy route; there is a lights-controlled crossing and in such situations we always wait until the lights change to green to allow ourselves the maximum time for crossing; we had allowed ample time for the journey.

At the station there were many staff in evidence, but we found an office where we were advised, quite informally, to wait in the nearby waiting room where someone would meet us with a wheelchair and accompany us to the platform for our train to Arras at 12.02. Indeed, a gentleman did so and he led us to the train and kindly assisted us into suitable seats with adequate room for our luggage; the train left on time! The journey took about 40 minutes with one stop at Douai; it took us across very flat countryside with numerous level crossings and much evidence of mining in earlier years; this was, of course, a battlefield and we noticed a military cemetery close by a level crossing. As we drew into the platform there was a uniformed SNCF man, with a wheelchair, waiting for us. Our exit involved travelling down in a lift, along a subway and up to street level by another lift. He led us out into the station car park and directed us to Hotel Mercure just ahead of us. What a great help this service had been. By 13.00 we were at the hotel, a very modern building; we were received by a very friendly receptionist and given the keys to our room – 304. As we emerged from the lift there was our room, just opposite; as we entered we were very pleased with what we found – it was spacious and welcoming and the bathroom, in particular, was designed and equipped for use by handicapped guests. On opening the curtains, there was the view! In the immediate vicinity there was a fairly busy road leading to Amiens in one direction and to Cambrai in the other, but the streets were lined with buildings which displayed a variety of façades and, notably, and not too distant, two towers – on the left the famous Beffroi and on the right, the tower of l'Eglise St Jean Baptiste. It was all very enticing; we had made a good choice!

The city of ARRAS is the capital of the Pas-de-Calais Department and has a population of about 43,000. Its long history and its architectural inheritance, attracts many visitors. The Romans were here, in 1430 Jeanne d'Arc was imprisoned here and Napoléon visited the city in 1804. The squares – Place des Héros and Grand Place – date from the year 1000 and the surrounding houses from the 12th and 13th centuries. The Beffroi and Hôtel de Ville date from the 15th and 16th centuries and were built over a century from 1463; built in flamboyant Gothic style it is a World Heritage Site. During the Great War Arras suffered terribly; being less than five kilometres from the front line, it was shelled relentlessly by the Germans. Architectural heritages such as the Beffroi and the Hôtel de Ville were virtually destroyed; the Cathédrale and the Abbaye Saint-Vaast greatly damaged and, in fact, some 95% of the buildings of the city were either destroyed or severely damaged. My father was in Arras in 1918; it must have been a scene of great destruction and desolation at that time. However, in 1919 an ambitious programme of reconstruction was commenced, and it took 12 years to identically rebuild the Place des Héros and the Grand Place; this time the new town hall was built on concrete foundations!

The afternoon was dry and still young and we decided to, at least, attempt to walk to the centre of the city. Crossing the Boulevard de Strasbourg by carefully observing the crossing lights was not difficult; passing La Poste on our left to another crossing in Rue Gambetta, continuing along a pedestrianised street towards the church of St Jean Baptiste and a short street took us to the entrance to the Place des Héros. This is an arcaded square formed by splendid buildings with a great variety of baroque façades. On the far side is the magnificent Hôtel de Ville crowned with its wonderful 77 metre high Beffroi; this building houses the Office de Tourisme. When we made a short visit to Arras in April 2000, we spent time in the tourist office; we will make it our first port of call again today as these offices are an important source of information, advice, etc.

We are pleased we did so as our attention was quickly drawn to an interesting exhibit displaying information, pictures, etc., relating to the experiences of Arras in the Second World War. By the end of 1939 Commonwealth armies were deployed in Northern France, the British Army GHQ was established at Saint-Vaast Abbey, troops were arriving at Arras station in large numbers and the Artois countryside became a vast training centre. All this was barely 20 years after the end of the Great War and, as we know, it was all to no avail. At 11.00pm on 14 May 1940 Arras suffered its first bombardment and on Sunday 19 May at 3.17pm the station and surrounding neighbourhoods were bombed by 18 enemy aircraft, killing more than 110 people. The Germans were at the gates of Arras and many civilians left. Overnight on 23/24 May the British evacuated the city which was then occupied by the Germans on 24 May. The Town Hall was requisitioned to accommodate the Kommandantur and four long years of German occupation began. On 1 September 1944 British tanks entered Arras without opposition; it was the Regiment of the Welsh Guards which liberated Arras, the Regiment which had been the last defender of the city in May 1940. This was a very interesting exhibition. Also, one cannot avoid being attracted to three giant figures – 'Les Géants d'Arras – Colas (4.6m), Jacqueline (4.3m) et Dédé (3.8m)', dressed as 18th and 19th century local peasants; they have a most interesting background. In Northern France and Belgium the tradition of giants goes back to the 16th century; it was revived in the 19th century as towns and cities identified themselves through huge figures representing a founding hero, a brave protector, or which embodied a trade symbolic of the town's history. The late 20th century saw a further revival of the tradition; new giants were created and a number of baptisms and weddings held at that time. The Giants of Arras are market gardeners of a nearby village; in fact, the Place des Héros is a market square where, several times a week, growers have come to sell their produce. Colas and Jacqueline existed in song from 1812; in 1891 they appeared in the form of giants. Destroyed during the bombardments of the Great War, they made a comeback in the 1920s only to be obliterated again in the Second World War. They were reborn in 1981 and the family expanded in 1995 with the birth of Dédé. The guardians of the giants are the Jouteurs d'Arras, who provide an entourage for Colas, Jacqueline and Dédé during Arras's festivities. We took photographs of the interior of the 'town hall' and we bought an excellent little book *'Balade au Coeur d'Arras'*, which includes pictures of beautiful facades, gables and sculptures which adorn so many buildings.

It was now time we began to make our way slowly back to the hotel and as we did so we took further photos of the 'square' as well as of l'Eglise St Jean Baptiste and, particularly, of a plaque recording the bravery of two sapeurs pompiers who fought a fire at this church during a violent bombardment on 10 July 1916. We looked forward to spending a pleasant leisurely evening in the hotel restaurant and to an enjoyable meal; we were not disappointed. We wasted no time and made our way to the restaurant, on the ground floor, shortly after it opened at 19.00. We were warmly welcomed, and the young waitress suggested that we might like to sit at a table for three or four situated in a corner a little detached from the main area, but with a view of the whole restaurant, as well as of the activity in the streets beyond the far windows of the building. Although we were quickly joined by quite a number of other guests, including a very large group, we were continually shown much personal concern, attention and friendly interest by, on this occasion, Estelle. Our meal, yes; for our main course we had gigot d'agneau, but I cannot recall our chosen dessert; it was all certainly enjoyable, but the lasting memory was of the convivial atmosphere. Before we left, after some three hours, the hardworking young waitresses, Estelle and her colleague Melody, were preparing the setting for the next day and petit-déjeuner. Time now, for us to wish them goodnight and return to our room. We had had a good day!

Thursday, 23 October

Needless to say, the waitresses supervising petit-déjeuner were not those making the preparations on the previous evening, but they were equally welcoming and helpful. The menu was very comprehensive and the proceedings informal and leisurely. After enjoying a very adequate breakfast, and before making plans for the remainder of the day, we made use of the shower and how convenient is was to use – an open area in the corner of the room with no restricting screen, no tray to negotiate and a seat fixed to the wall, but foldable when not in use. It may be designed specifically for disabled but is very practical for many others. Some years ago we visited the France Exhibition in London where we found an exhibit of the Arras Tourist Office particularly interesting. Talking to one of its representatives we were told that a further aspect of the town's history had recently been revealed to the public; it was the ancient quarries under the town. We were told that we should make a point of visiting them; well, now is our opportunity.

It was at the Chantilly Conference on 16 November 1916 that the plans of General Nivelle for an offensive by the British in the Artois Region, followed, a few days later, by an attack by the French at Chemin des Dames (near Reims), were adopted; amazingly both Petain and Haig were not in favour. Chalk quarries had existed beneath Arras since the 16th century and the decision was taken to develop these quarries as a holding point for the troops; in fact, actually beneath no man's land. The work of linking and adapting the quarries by a series of tunnels was done by about 500 New Zealand tunnellers, who named them the WELLINGTON QUARRY. Facilities incorporated included electricity, running water, railway lines and the exits for the day of the battle. Kitchens were required as the provision of adequate meals, etc., was essential in maintaining morale; the British soldiers were particularly demanding regarding hygiene and sanitation and latrines, showers and water tanks were installed; the arrangements for sleeping provided little comfort in the cold and damp conditions; all the time, walking around was banned. The total underground network stretches for 12 miles and, ultimately, the Quarry accommodated 24,000 British soldiers. It was Easter Sunday on 8 April 1917 and, with an improvised altar, a service was held in the Quarry; it is still possible to see the black traces on the walls, left by the candles.

At 5.00am on 9 April 1917 a better than normal breakfast was provided, even a glass of rum for some; the last letters home, the last goodbyes, were posted. Ordered to leave great coats behind, at 5.30am these brave young men climbed the steps to burst out into the early daylight and the field of battle; the Germans had been taken totally by surprise. The great Artois Offensive stretching from Vimy Ridge to Bullecourt Plain mounted by British and Empire soldiers, preceded by a lengthy bombardment, had begun; initially it was a great success, but German counterattacks from 14 April halted the offensive.

The British had gained some 12km, but at what a cost; during a period of two months 4,000 men died every day. Many of the 24,000 soldiers who climbed out of the Quarry early on that Easter Monday morning would not return to collect their great coats; the goodbyes had, indeed, been the final goodbyes. As Laurence Binyon wrote:-

"They shall grow not old, as we that are left grow old,
Age shall not weary them, nor the years condemn.
At the going down of the sun, and in the morning,
We will remember them".

Although we were told that the quarries were not far away, behind the station, we felt that it was not a likely walking distance for us; the receptionist ordered a taxi and within minutes we were at the doors of the entrance. We did not have to wait very long for the next tour and after being provided with the obligatory tin helmet and an optional personal hair net, we were taken to a lift. We descended about 20 metres into this amazing subterranean world. It has been made accessible to the public by the construction of a wooden walkway with a rail on each side; it is dimly lit, reminiscent of the times of its original use. As we proceeded, our well-informed guide pointed out various areas and features by the use of a torch; we noticed the graffiti on the walls, the drawings, inscriptions, messages, names and prayers engraved by the soldiers as they awaited the battle. I had noticed that the temperature in the Quarry was 11C; one cannot imagine what it would have been like, living, eating and sleeping and unable to move about, in these conditions for any length of time. This is a very moving experience. Towards the end of the tour, our guide was very interested to know that my father had been in Arras in 1918 (not at the time of the Battle) and I wonder if he had been in this Quarry; it is possible. Our visit concluded with a short film realistically simulating the battle into which the young soldiers were instantly thrust. Of all the very many places of evidence of the Great War surely this must be unique and one of the most poignant. We spent a while surveying the items for sale and we bought a souvenir book; it contains two verses

The General

"Good morning, Good morning!" the General said
When we met him last week on our way to the line.
Now the soldiers he smiled at are most of 'em dead.
And we're cursing his staff for incompetent swine.
"He's a cheery old cart," grunted Harry to Jack
As they slogged up to Arras with rifle and pack.
But he did for them both by his plan of attack.

Siegfried Sassoon, wounded at the Battle of Arras.

All of the night was quite barred out except
An owl's cry, a most melancholy cry
Shaken out long and clear upon the hill,
Speaking for all who lay under the stars,
Soldiers and poor, unable to rejoice.

Edward Thomas, killed in action on 9 April 1917.

The Battle of Arras continued from 9 April to 16 May 1917. The British casualties numbered nearly 160,000; what a terrible price to pay for so little gain.

Nearly 100 years afterwards, at 6.30am on 9 April of every year, a tribute is paid to the soldiers of Britain and the Empire at the foot of the Battle of Arras memorial wall.

How shall we spend the remainder of the day? Firstly, we need a taxi. Once again help was willingly offered at the desk; a taxi would meet us in a matter of minutes. As we were driven away, we asked the driver to take us to the centre of the city where, perhaps, we could find somewhere to eat; he took us to the Place des Héros. The cost of our two taxis had been €5.60 and €9.00. Unfortunately, it was still too early for evening meals, but at Café Leffe we were able to have Crepes au Sucre and, at the same time, to savour a typical busy early evening setting with lively friendly background conversation. When we left, we first walked the very short distance into that other, and larger, magnificent square the Grand Place. Darkness had now descended and, back in the Place des Héros, we spent awhile absorbing its captivating scene and atmosphere now that natural light had been replaced by the gentle light of the street lamps and the interior lights of the buildings, all silently guarded by the towering Beffroi; this is the Place of Heroes which, in years gone by, has presented very different scenes – of destruction and desolation.

We had little alternative but to return to our hotel on foot which we did very slowly and with not a little discomfort and complaining. Back in the comfort of our room and after a short rest we felt sufficiently refreshed to spend an hour or so in the 'bar' area adjacent to the restaurant and to enjoy a cup of coffee. We found one sole gentleman there enjoying a glass of beer. We suspected that he was a coach driver and, after a while, he was joined by a number of ladies. We could not avoid overhearing their animated and excited conversation and we were in no doubt that they originated from the South Wales area; they did not appear to be conscious of our presence. Our small cup of coffee kept us occupied for a long time but, eventually, it was time for us to retire and, as we left, we wished the group "Goodnight". They were a little surprised to discover that we were English and a short conversation ensued. They told us that they were members of a choir and were on their way to visit a twin town in the west of Germany beyond Strasbourg; yes, the gentleman was the coach driver! How nice to end a memorable day sharing the anticipation and joys of others.

Friday, 24 October

Today, we will endeavour to visit l'ABBAYE SAINT-VAAST and la CATHEDRALE. What an interesting saint Saint-Vaast is! As a priest, he was called upon by the Bishop of Reims to teach the catechism to Clovis, King of the Franks (509–511) and he moved to Arras to evangelize the Artois Region. According to legend, he miraculously healed two sick beggars and he was also known for his ability for taming bears that had terrorised the region; the museum possesses a fragment of the tapestry depicting St Vaast and his bears. When Saint Vaast became Bishop of Arras; he erected a chapel and he repaired the church in which he was buried, when he died in 540. In about the year 650 St Aubert, Bishop of Cambrai and Arras, founded an abbey on the site of the chapel and decided to transfer to this place, on the banks of the river Crinchon, the relics of St Vaast. Although the abbey was razed by the Normans in the ninth century and successively burnt down and rebuilt, a Benedictine monastic community became established; it was to be one of the most prestigious north of Paris and continued until the Revolution. The original abbey church was built between the 11th and 14th centuries; by the 18th century it had fallen into disrepair and the monks decided to renovate and rebuild all the abbey buildings. When the Revolution broke out in 1789 the work had not been completed; the abbey was taken over by the forces of Revolution, desecrated and partially destroyed; the monks were forced to leave. In 1804, Emperor Napoleon I decided that the remains of the once beautiful Gothic cathedral should be demolished and a new Arras Cathedral constructed, "limiting the work to the requirements of solidity and decency"; it was completed in 1834. The remainder of the abbey was bought by the town and now houses the Musée des Beaux-Arts and a library. During the Great War the Cathedral was almost destroyed; on 26 June 1915, it was ripped open by a massive shell and from 5–10 July both the Cathedral and St. Vaast were in flames. Reconstruction began in 1920 and it was reopened in 1934; it was damaged again by a bomb in 1944. In fact, the Cathedral has never been completed, as the planned bell tower was never constructed. Therefore, the building is only 75 feet tall at its highest point.

Our interpretation of the street plan suggested that it might not be a practical walking distance from our hotel to the ABBAYE SAINT-VAAST. Hence, the receptionist promptly booked a taxi and we were soon set down at the entrance gates. Inside, the spacious courtyard is enclosed on three sides by an impressive three story building. On the far side, in the centre and raised above the level of the courtyard, is the entrance to the Musée des Beaux-Arts. It is not a particularly auspicious entrance and there was little sign of activity. However, we found a door which was open and we were pleased to find that the museum was, in fact, open. Once inside we were instantly enveloped in the atmosphere of a museum richly endowed with its many treasures, testimonies of Arras's history, sculptures, porcelains and tapestries, in addition to paintings by significant artists. Also, at this time and for a period of eighteen months, the museum is displaying 100 masterpieces on loan from the collection of the Château de Versailles; they include the bust of Louis XIV (1665), the Dauphin's writing desk (1745), the sculpture Latone and her children (1670) from the Latone fountain and the remarkable sculptural group, Apollo Served by the Nymphs (1675).

Altogether, this was a wonderful exhibition of many and varied treasures and works of art, appropriately housed in this superb eighteenth century monastic complex. Although spread over a considerable area, we succeeded in viewing all parts; however, we were grateful for being reminded that there was an occasional chair placed at certain intervals! During the course of our tour we were able to see and photograph, through the windows, the splendid cloisters. We left through the 'shop' and, as we did so, we enquired how we could reach the CATHEDRALE most directly; we were told to go left after passing through the gates and then to take the next turning to the left and go straight ahead. With these straightforward instructions we set off; however, as we walked along close to the side of the buildings it became evident that this complex was, indeed, one of the largest religious sites in France. With no 'cathedral' in sight I decided to go ahead to reconnoitre to ensure that we were going in the right direction. It was quite a long walk before I saw what appeared to be a large individual building; it was not impressive, with scaffolding implying that it was undergoing some much needed maintenance. Of course, there was no tower or spire to distinguish it! Indeed, I was still not convinced that it was the building we were seeking and I descended a set of aging stone steps to a door – surely this is not the entrance to a cathedral! I opened the door and then I was in no doubt. I hurriedly retraced my steps to meet Margaret who had continued to make slow progress. Together, we were finally inside this huge and impressive church and yet it is of remarkable simplicity. It was constructed in ancient temple style from plans by the architect who, later, built La Madeleine in Paris. There is much of interest in this cathedral; we looked at the Chapelle de la Vierge in the apse; we noted, particularly, the magnificent organ, the work of Roethinger of Strasbourg, which was inaugurated in 1964; it is said that, in the Choeur are relics of Saint Jacques le Majeur, Saint Vaast and Saint Thomas Becket. In the transept there is a small shop and we talked to a gentleman there; in fact, he produced a chair for Margaret's use. I talked to a lady and asked her if la messe would be celebrated here on Sunday; she replied, "non, fini" and promptly found a street plan and highlighted the churches where there is a service regularly and noted the times. We purchased a small book *'La Guerre 14–18'* and collected one or two information leaflets. Although we had spent some time here, it is a building which deserves more attention. However, we felt that we should begin to make our way back to our hotel. Firstly, we would head for the Office de Tourism but, by now, it was becoming dusk and difficult to read the street plan. We returned along the road back towards the museum and then turned left in what we hoped was the right direction. After some distance we asked a lady if we were going towards the Office; she assured us we were – she was going that way herself and suggested that we follow her. Her speed was somewhat superior to ours and after a while we lost sight of her. At one point we found ourselves alongside a taxi, but we soon realised that he was already responding to a call and our hopes quickly faded.

Eventually, to our relief, we recognized the rear of the Hôtel de Ville. We could not contemplate walking the further distance to the hotel and we asked an assistant at the Office de Tourism to order a taxi for us. However, most taxi drivers appeared to be very busy and it was only after many calls that a taxi was contacted which could collect us in a matter of minutes – we could meet him outside the fish shop, we were told. Unfortunately, the fish shop was closed and I didn't recognise it and, while searching for our taxi on the further side of the Place des Héros, the taxi driver had found Margaret and was looking for me near the Tourist Office. Eventually, we were all united and, somewhat relieved, safely delivered to Hôtel Mercure. The fare for this taxi was €8.50; however, this cost and the physical efforts required to enable us to visit these wonderful buildings and their contents were well justified.

After a period of recuperation in our room we did not find it difficult to make our way to the restaurant, anticipating a relaxing and enjoyable couple of hours. We were welcomed again by Estelle and Melody and we were pleased to find that we could occupy the same table as on the previous occasion. This evening was a fairly busy one, but we were again given generous attention by, in particular, Melody. Both waitresses speak commendable English and Melody clearly enjoyed exchanging brief comments with us as she busily went about her work. When speaking to Estelle, she said that she felt she needed a holiday; in fact, she is going away next week, to Chinon. We were pleased to be able to tell her that we know Chinon well and we wished her, bonnes vacances! Perhaps it is surprising that, although we recall such aspects of the evening, we cannot remember the details of our chosen menu. However, it was certainly enjoyable as, indeed, was the entire evening; an appropriate conclusion to a very interesting day.

Saturday, 25 October

Of the numerous battlefield sites of the Great War perhaps few are more widely known and visually recognisable than VIMY RIDGE. In fact, The Ridge extends over some fourteen kilometres, while the memorial stands on Hill 145, the highest point. As at Arras, the Artois Offensive began here at 05.30 on the morning of 9 April 1917, when thousands of Canadian and British soldiers emerged from tunnels and trenches and, preceded by a heavy artillery bombardment, stormed the Ridge. They achieved all their objectives with the exception of Hill 145, which was captured on the following day. Although out of 10,602 casualties 3,598 Canadians died, it was a significant victory of the War and it brought honour and pride to the young Canadian nation.

We have visited Vimy Ridge on previous occasions, but we felt we would like to do so once again. We obtained a Salient Tours leaflet detailing minibus tours from Arras hotels; unfortunately, neither I nor the hotel could obtain a telephone response. In the circumstances, we decided to make the journey by taxi. Again, the hotel arranged a taxi for us. When driving in this area many years ago we had discovered an orientation table showing the disposition of the various armies during the war; one of these units was the 51st Highland Division of which my father was a member (the Machine Gun Corps, in fact). I cannot remember where exactly it was; I had hoped that we might locate it again, but we did not spot it on this journey. Nevertheless, it was good to travel over this historic landscape again, even though we did not have the independence to stop or take diversions whenever we felt it might be interesting to do so. Our driver took us to the Visitor Centre of Vimy Ridge, a situation we did not readily recognize for we could not see the massive monument.

We spent some time in the Centre, looking at photographs, exhibits, etc., and we talked to the supervisor, a young Canadian gentleman – perhaps he was a student or a member of the military. He told us that a new Visitor Centre was to be constructed nearby during the next two years to commentate the 100th anniversary of the battle in 1917. We realised that we now had some walking to do and there was no doubt as to the direction we should take. There is a clearly defined route for pedestrians at the side of the road and one must not stray from this path. The area is now reverentially forested and the very uneven surface neatly grassed, for, no doubt, it still conceals human remains. The area is pock-marked with shell holes from artillery bombardment and mine craters from the fierce underground war. Here, the earth's surface has been turned over and over again by the tunnelling, the trenches, the shelling and the underground mines; one cannot imagine how human life survived amidst such a hell. As we walked and walked, albeit very slowly, we still could not see the Monument. Quite suddenly and remarkably we found ourselves talking to a couple going in the opposite direction. Perhaps it was the use of the walking stick which attracted their attention and prompted them to make some comment. However it was, we had quite a long and very friendly conversation – they were aged 80 and 81; they live in Vimy and they told us that they walk this way every day. They clearly have much respect for this site. We spent quite a few minutes talking and, I think, we said 'good bye' three times. What an uplifting encounter.

Eventually, we continued on our way and, after a while, we saw the first glimpse of the towering Monument standing on Hill 145. After reaching the open area and the car park it is still quite a long way to the base of the Monument and suddenly a buggy drew alongside us; it was the young Canadian gentleman we had been talking to earlier. He asked if he could take us the remainder of the way; we thanked him, but we felt that the appropriate way to approach this revered site is slowly and on foot. However, he did offer to come and collect us in 30 minutes or so; this we accepted.

The MONUMENT stands on land ceded by France, in perpetuity, to Canada in 1922 – it is the Vimy Ridge National Historic Site of Canada. It was designed by a Canadian sculptor and architect, Walter Seymour Allward, who said that the design came to him in a dream; his aim was to produce 'a structure which would endure, in an exposed position, for a thousand years – indeed, for all time'. The work began in 1925 and it took eleven years to complete; the memorial was unveiled on 26 July 1936 in the presence of King Edward VIII. Some facts relating to the construction of the Monument are, in themselves, awe-inspiring – the foundations are formed of 11,000 tonnes of concrete reinforced with hundreds of tonnes of steel; the pylons and sculptured figures consist of almost 6,000 tonnes of limestone transported from a former Roman quarry in Croatia; the figures were carved where they now stand from huge blocks of this stone, the largest being of a sorrowing mother (representing Canada) mourning her dead; one of the massive twin white pylons bears the maple leaves of Canada while the other bears the fleurs-de-lys of France; carved on the walls are the names of 11,285 Canadian soldiers who were killed in France and who have no known grave. Barely three years after the unveiling, France and Germany were at war again and when the German Army occupied France, there were fears for the preservation of this priceless treasure. However, there was one person who had admired it, as a monument to peace rather than a celebration of war. Incredibly, that man was none other than Adolf Hitler and he assigned special troops from the Waffen-SS to guard Vimy Ridge. About 70 years after its construction major restoration work was carried out on the Monument with particular care and craftsmanship, including repointing the two massive pylons and cleaning the twenty statues; work which took two years to finally complete in 2007.

Although the Monument is not a building, and is in a very exposed situation, its huge presence pervades an atmosphere of sacrosanctity. It was a lovely warm afternoon; there were many visitors – we had noticed a coach of Glovers of Ashbourne – and people were silently appreciating the experience; however, as we have found on earlier visits, some felt they wanted to express their emotions – one man turned to me and said, "this is the most beautiful place". Indeed, a visit here is a deeply moving experience. Nearby, sheep are grazing peacefully now. Looking beyond the Monument and across the Douai plain to the east we can see symbols of a different kind, slag heaps; a reminder that this was a mining area in bygone years. We had spent quite some while at the memorial when our buggy duly arrived to take us back to the nearby car park He enquired how we were continuing our journey and, when we told him that we required a taxi to return us to our hotel in Arras, he was able to telephone a taxi driver. The response was, 'would we be willing to share a taxi with another couple', to which we readily agreed.

It would be some while to wait, but the weather was still good and we spent the time sitting on the wall near the flags of France and Canada and with a more distant view of the Monument. When the taxi arrived for us it still had to collect the other 'couple'; however, we soon discovered that it was, in fact, two young Canadian men. Our journey back to Arras was, therefore, very interesting; they told us that they are backpacking around Europe by train and so our taxi delivered them to the station at Arras before taking us to our hotel. The cost of our return journey to Vimy Ridge was €26.60 and €15.00; this was well justified. We are now grateful that, with the benefit of the nearby lift, it is only a few short steps from our room to conclude the day with a very pleasant evening in the restaurant. However, tonight is l'heure d'hiver, which means that all clocks move back one hour!

Sunday, 26 October

Sunday, in towns and cities, is regarded somewhat differently in France than in Angleterre. Generally, no shops are open and we have often found petrol stations closed. It is a day more for leisure, for pleasurable activities, sightseeing, visiting museums, etc., a day for recreation and relaxation. Leisurely, was how we intended to spend our day and, appropriately, petit déjeuner is available until 11.00. When we were ready to do so we set off to walk into the centre of Arras again. How nice it was to enjoy this unique atmosphere; the shops were closed and one focused more on the facades of the buildings. Our first stop was at the EGLISE St JEAN BAPTISTE. The first church on this site was constructed in the 12th century; it was demolished in 1564 and rebuilt as the church of Saint-Nicolas-des-Fossés. This was the only church in Arras to survive the Revolution, when it became known as the Temple of Reason. In 1803 it became the Cathédrale St Jean Baptiste and until 1833, when the present cathedral was completed. On 10 July 1915 the church was bombarded and destroyed by fire; two firemen gave their lives, and their names to the street on which the church stands. Reconstructed in 1918–20 in neo-gothic style, it was consecrated in 1927. There are some noteworthy features of this church such as:- a painting by Reubens 'Descent from the Cross', a retable of the 17th century, sculptures and beautiful stained glass windows dating from the 1920s and 1930s and also of the 1950s, notably that of the four evangelists. This is a beautiful and much used church where there is to be a messe at 18.00 today; I took some photographs. In the Place des Héros there were many visitors, but we eventually found a seat in the inviting and very busy, pâtisserie of Pâtissier/Chocolatier, Sebastien Thibaut, where we enjoyed pain-aux-raisins and cups of coffee. Afterwards, we visited the Office de Tourisme in the Hôtel de Ville again, mainly to browse over the many items in the shop and we bought some cards and an interesting book, 'Arras – Pas à pas'. It was approaching the end of the day for the office as we left. We lingered awhile in the Place des Héros for the last time and continued past the Church we had visited earlier, before setting off for our hotel. It had been sunny and warm for a while during the afternoon, but daylight is now fading, for it is the first evening of 'winter time'.

Back at the hotel, we welcomed the evening which we could spend in the friendly atmosphere of the restaurant. It seems that many visitors spend no more than one or two nights here and clearly the waitresses very much appreciate and enjoy having guests for a longer period and creating a friendly relationship. This evening Melody gave us her attention and, before we left, we had a longer conversation with her; she told us that she has served three years of a five year apprenticeship at the hotel and she would like to have a career in the hotel business. At present she works from 14.00 to midnight, when she has a 10 minute walk to her home. We had told her that we planned to spend a few days in Lille after leaving Arras, to which she replied, "Be careful in Lille, it is a big city". What a kind thought! As we said "Goodnight", we thanked her for the attention and concern that both she and Estelle had shown to us and we wished her success in the future. Once again I have no record or recollection of our actual meal, something which I will not have to admit in respect of the three subsequent evenings! In fact, our overriding happy memories of our evenings here have been of the general conviviality and the warm personal friendliness of the staff.

Monday, 27 October

We leave Arras today, but not until this afternoon! It is a sunny morning and we are able to appreciate once more the view from our room, particularly of those two magnificent towers which dominate the city. We have time, also, to enjoy an unhurried further petit déjeuner before preparing to vacate our room by 11.00. Eventually, we took our luggage down to the reception desk, where it was kindly accommodated while we spent another couple of hours in the nearby bar and enjoying a cup of coffee. Our train was due to leave at 16.24 and we must allow ample time to get to the station and to arrange for assistance on the journey. Before we left the hotel we expressed our very sincere thanks to all the staff for the help, kindness and understanding they had showed; our comments were much appreciated. There are no busy roads to negotiate between the hotel and la gare and, once in the foyer, we quickly found some vacant seats. Nearby, there was an enquiry kiosk, periodically manned by a gentleman who from time to time would don his peaked cap, his symbol of authority, and rush off to perform other duties. As soon as there was an opportunity I told him of our situation and our need of assistance; without any formality, he told us to remain in our seats and someone would come to assist us in good time. There was a vacant seat alongside us; soon it was occupied by a young lady, probably a student; when the time came for her to leave, she turned to us and wished us "bonne journée". Next, we had the company of an older man. We exchanged a few comments; regarding our respective nationalities, for instance; I told him that we were English and he said that he was French, but significantly, he added "European". These exchanges were typical of our stay in Arras; everyone had been so friendly; perhaps the presence and the sacrifices of so many British soldiers in bygone years have left a lasting gratitude. While we were waiting for our train I walked across the square for a closer look and a photograph of the monument 'ARRAS – á des Enfants MORTS pour la defense du DROIT'. This stands in front of Hotel Angleterre!

Our visit to Arras has been memorable; apart from the tenuous personal link, it has been a wonderful opportunity to see more and learn more of this ancient city, with such a long and interesting history; a city which saw so much of its treasured past devastated and destroyed in the horrors of the second decade of the 20th century; a city which rose again, a phoenix, from the ashes to recover its previous beauty, as we see it today. Also, we remember the kindness, helpfulness and friendliness of everyone we have come into contact with.

Before we began to think that the time for our train was approaching, a lady, yes, in a peaked cap, arrived with a wheelchair to take us to the appropriate platform. This involved using the lifts which were not large enough for all of us; consequently, I had to be sent ahead with the luggage to be followed by Margaret, in the wheelchair, and our escort; a rather amusing episode! Again, she was a very friendly communicative person and she kindly established us in our seats with our luggage. I do not know where this train originated, but there were not many passengers when we joined, but many boarded at Douai for Lille. It was about 17.00 when we arrived at Lille Flandres, and, as we did so, there again was an SNCF man waiting at the door with a wheelchair. This is a terminus and no lifts are required, but it is a large station. He took us to an exit which was in the direction of Hotel Lille Europe. Yes, as Melody said, this is a big city and it was a very busy time. However, we reached the hotel safely and we were promptly given the key to return to room 512. In this immediate area, we have not found a restaurant providing evening meals; however, immediately underneath the hotel is a cafeteria, Brioche

Doree (it is part of the vast Centre Commercial Euralille) which is open until 19.00. Here, we were able to have a large baguette ham and salad sandwich and a cold drink; it provided an adequate meal and, afterwards, we had only to walk a few yards to the door of our hotel.

Tuesday, 28 October

We have visited Lille many times; even for a day trip from our home in Camerton, soon after Eurostar services were inaugurated in 1994. In the past, we have explored much of the city on foot and we are particularly fond of the area known as, Le Vieux Lille (Old Lille). Where better to spend a few hours, as in its midst stands the cathedral. To limit the amount of walking involved, we first walked the relatively short distance to Lille Flandres where taxis are always available. We asked to be driven to Vieux Lille and the driver set us down, very conveniently, at the junction of Rue de la Monnaie and Rue d'Angleterre. Le VIEUX LILLE is full of history and interest. It holds great charm in the wonderful diversity of the flamboyant architecture of its restored 17th century buildings; the variety of façades, gables and of colours is amazing. Rue de la MONNAIE runs through and forms the heart of the old town, where the city was born many centuries ago. Previously called Rue Saint-Pierre, it took its present name in 1685, when a Hôtel des Monnaies was created in Lille by Louis XIV and installed in the former house of the 'lord of the manor' of Lille, situated in this street.

We slowly walked along the street until we came to a little café; how appropriate – it was time for a cup of coffee. It was at Le Porthos, 53 Rue de la Monnaie and we were served by Juliette. As we continued along the street, we photographed (again) the striking remains of the mill, Saint-Pierre, of 1649. On reaching the end of Rue de la Monnaie, and at the junction with Place du Lion d'Or and Place Louise-de-Bettignies, we came to the building which has attracted our attention whenever we have passed, either on foot or in a vehicle; it is 'Le Lion'. It has a remarkably picturesque façade with a variety of colours and is the office of estate agents; it dates from the late 19th or early 20th century. I had to photograph it again, as one which I took some years ago had been installed on my 'desktop', until, unfortunately, it was lost when the computer was replaced. A little further along Place Louise-de-Bettignies, I photographed another interesting building. Retracing our steps, we joined a passageway from Rue de la Monnaie which leads to the rear of the cathedral. There is a gift shop underneath the building which has an entrance at the side and then is reached by descending a flight of stairs. While standing at the top and wondering if we would find it worthwhile to proceed, a lady noticed us and insisted on activating the goods lift to enable us to reach the shop. It was a kind gesture and we did, indeed, buy a small standing monthly calendar, which has been a focus of interest. Our memories of this cathedral are of when, in 2007, I fell on a step approaching the entrance and had to receive hospital treatment before continuing our visit. Safely inside this time, we were pleased to be able to sit for a while in this magnificent church.

La CATHEDRAL NOTRE-DAME de la TREILLE is not an ancient building. The blessing of the cornerstone took place on 1 July 1854 and construction began on 9 June 1856. Built in the gothic style, the building grew, bit by bit, between 1854 and 1953. With the erection of the translucent marble front wall, the cathedral was finally completed in 1999. The Cathedral contains notable works of art in the form of sculptures, stained glass, frescos and mosaics; we noticed, in particular, the fine statue of Saint Pierre. It is described as a 'living cathedral' as we have witnessed, having attended an office and a concert. Our particular interest today is the organ. When we were here in 2007 a Cavaille-Coll choir organ had been in use since 1869 and we were told about the instrument which was about to be installed; it consists of more than 7,000 pipes and had been donated by Radio France. It is now lofted high in the south transept and the console, with 106 stops, is near the choir. We read that this organ was originally built between 1957 and 1966 for studio 104 Olvier Messiaen at Radio France, Paris, by Danion-Gonzales and has been reconstructed here by Orgelbau Klais of Bonn. It was formally inaugurated and blessed on 1 June 2008. We did not expect to experience the sounds of the organ in the acoustics of this building, but we hoped to be able to purchase a recording. We recognized a gentleman we had seen in 2007, who was, from time to time, at a small kiosk and also acting as a guide and providing explanations to visitors. When I noticed an opportunity, I asked him if we could purchase a CD and a DVD. We are pleased to now have an excellent recording by the Organist of the Cathedral, André Dubois, of music by composers whose lives spanned from 1657 to 1998. We also have a documentary film recording the process of the dismantling, transfer and reconstruction of one of the finest organs in France; it was an immense task, involving 40 tons, 7,600 pipes, 20 km of cables and 28 metres of height. Having completed our visit to the cathedral we hoped that we could find an appropriate eating place nearby. There is a restaurant in the square in front of the Cathedral, but we found that they would not be serving meals until 19.00. However, we were welcome to use the toilets and they willingly ordered a taxi to take us back to our hotel. We were more than happy to resort to another baguette ham and salad sandwich at Brioche Doree.

Wednesday, 29 October

Earlier in this book I wrote about the tradition of the presentation of a weekly religious magazine programme, *Le Jour du Seigneur*, incorporating the live broadcast of la messe, every Sunday morning on the main state television channel, France 2, since October 1949. Back in July, the broadcast from the village of Bouvines was particularly interesting; it marked the 800th anniversary of the BATTLE of BOUVINES.

Early in the 13th century, the wretched King John, in conflict with his barons, planned to invade France determined to recover lands lost in Normandy and Anjou, and thus to regain some of his prestige at home. However, the barons refused John's summons to accompany him and he went without them. He created an army of mercenaries and formed a coalition with some allies, including – Emperor Otto IV of Germany and the Counts of Dammartin and Flanders. John himself went to Poitou, landing at La Rochelle but, despite some initial success, he made little progress. The key confrontation was in the north, in Flanders, where the army was led by Emperor Otto and the English contingent commanded by William of Salisbury, John's half-brother. The armies, comprising about 40,000 men, confronted each other on marshy land near the village of Bouvines on 27 July 1214; it was a hot Sunday afternoon and the battle lasted four to five hours, during which some 2,000 men died; the result was a decisive victory for Philippe Auguste of France. Otto fled, the Count of Flanders and William of Salisbury were captured and the Count of Dammartin surrendered, while John was still in the south. His hopes of re-conquest utterly crushed, John returned to England, defeated, humiliated and deeply in debt, to face the angry barons. Consequently, he was compelled to submit, unconditionally, to the demands of the barons. Hence, on 15 June 1215 he set his seal to Magna Carta – thus forming the basis of English democracy. John died in 1216 and was buried in Worcester Cathedral. Meanwhile, the victory at Bouvines was a very significant event in French history; a 'gift of God', it is said!

It would be interesting to visit Bouvines and we estimated that it may be about 10–15 km. from our hotel. Obviously, the only practical way to reach it would be by taxi. We talked to one of the receptionists, who kindly ascertained an estimate of the cost. It would be quite expensive, but it was our only opportunity and we were already prepared to leave; we decided to go ahead. It was only a matter of minutes before the taxi arrived and we were on our way through the extremely busy environs of Lille and out into pleasant countryside.

Not knowing where exactly it would be best to be taken, we headed for the village church which was easily located. We arranged for the driver to collect us in an hour or so.

L'EGLISE-SAINT PIERRE, a 'mémorial national', was constructed on the site of an 11th century chapel between 1880 and 1886, in neo-gothic style inspired by the architecture of the 13th century. The most notable and remarkable feature of the church are its 21 stained glass windows. Created by master glassmakers at Bar-le-Duc, the windows are eight metres high and 3.2 metres wide. Each window is composed of three parts; at the top is a picture of angels, at the bottom is the coat of arms of the donor and the centre depicts a moment of the battle according to the chronicle of the chaplain of Philippe-Auguste. The cost of 350,000 francs was five times the cost of the church. In addition to these fascinating windows the church contains other information regarding the battle, including a map showing the disposition of the armies at the time. Another feature of the church is the splendid Cavaille-Coll organ and we also noted the statue of St Pierre. Before we left I went outside to photograph the exterior of this 'Monument Historique'. Interestingly, we have learned that the celebrations on 27 July 2014 were attended by descendants of King Philippe-Auguste, including Louis de Bourbon, heir to the throne of France.

Our taxi duly arrived to collect us and, as we left the village, I noticed a sign which may have indicated the direction of the actual site of the battle. However, I could not translate my reaction into French quickly enough to suggest a diversion; in any case it was beginning to rain.

We asked to be taken to the OFFICE de TOURISME in Lille; this is housed in the notable Palais Rihour which was constructed in the 15th century and has been classified as a monument historique since 1875. It was now raining very heavily and we had to hurry into the shelter of the Office. In the circumstances, we decided to book one of the city bus tours, which takes 50 minutes and costs €24. While waiting, we talked to two ladies from the USA, who had travelled from London but, having failed to leave the train the first time at Lille, had been returned from Brussels free of charge! It was still raining as we left on our tour and, unfortunately, the windows soon became steamed up. However, we had excellent pictures on a large screen in the front of the bus, showing the varied places we were passing. Despite the unfortunate weather, it was a very interesting experience and no less so, having taken this excellent tour on a previous occasion!

Back at the Office de Tourisme, surely there must be somewhere nearby where we could have a light meal regardless of the time! Yes, we are in the Place Rihour and here is Le Rihour's – we have eaten here before. Without hesitation, our suggestion of a croque-monsieur received a positive response. We were pleased to be able to relax and to enjoy it, unhurriedly, with cold drinks followed by a cup of coffee. Anxious to make good use of our last available hours in the city, we went for a short walk. We first noted the large monument 'Aux Lillois victimes des guerres' at the side of Palais Rihour; then, to experience the flavour of life and activity this early evening in the busy centre of the city, which has a large student population, we continued into the impressive Place Charles de Gaulle or Grande Place. This has been the living centre of the city since the Middle Ages; its notable features include – the tall column of la Déesse, erected in 1845 to commemorate the siege of 1792, the Vieille Bourse, the bookshop Furet du Nord where we spent a while browsing and, next door, the Grand Hôtel Bellevue where Mozart stayed in 1765. Back in Place Rihour we hoped to find a taxi, but none were evident, except, that is, for a couple of three-wheel 'taxi bikes'. We have never travelled by such means before and so it would be a novel experience. We decided to accept the offer and, with our 'driver' pedalling furiously, weaving through the busy traffic and waving to his friends as we went, we reached our hotel safely; the fare was €5. Well, despite being physically limited there are alternative ways of getting around and, now, we are not too late for a final visit to Brioche Doree for a cup of coffee!

Thursday, 30 October

The final day of this journey; the day of our return! In fact, until leaving Waterloo for Trowbridge at 19.20 we shall be travelling for no more than 27 minutes of the day; however, the times of our trains are the most convenient as they allow a generous three hours in London, to make the transfer and allow time for refreshments, etc. Unfortunately, having to vacate our room by 11.00, we have more than four hours to pass before our train leaves for St Pancras. We are able to store our luggage at the reception and there is an available rest area adjacent to the 'breakfast room'. As on previous days, we had time for interesting conversation with the receptionists. We allowed ample time to proceed to the handicapé centre at Lille Europe. Once there, and having registered our details, we felt completely in the care of Eurostar and we could relax. On the platform, waiting for our train, I told our guide how much we appreciate this service; he seemed a little embarrassed – after all he was only doing his job. Our train was on time at 15.36, the journey very pleasant and as we drew into St Pancras there was a gentleman waiting with a wheelchair.

When our turn came for a taxi we were greeted by a friendly cockney character – "Where are we going then?" he asked. I replied, "Waterloo – do you know where it is?" I promptly added "I'm sure you do". This set the tone of our journey. Our driver asked us where we were going from Waterloo. When I told him, Trowbridge in Wiltshire, he clearly had a picture of a typically English market town. When I told him of the various nationalities living in Trowbridge and that we have public notices on the streets in Polish he was amazed. Then, he boldly stated, "I'm a UKIP man myself," he obviously favours this country's exit from the European Union. An interesting conversation followed in which I said that the founding fathers of the Union had experienced a period of history of ghastly turmoil which we have since been spared and they had the benefit of greater wisdom than most of us; I feel that we have more to lose than to gain by leaving the Union. As we parted company at Waterloo, our driver said that he likes such a conversation; he shook hands and wished us well. Entering the station, it was another world. The usual continuous announcements of train information, was accompanied by an enthusiastic military band; it was an incessant din.

Our first priority was to arrange for assistance when the time came to board our train. Next, we needed some refreshments; we used the lift to reach the upper level; everywhere was so crowded and so busy and it was difficult to move around and control our luggage. Eventually, we found somewhere to sit, not very comfortably, and to purchase something to eat and a drink. We felt we should not move until it was appropriate to check that our help was, in fact, now available. Indeed it was, and a very friendly gentleman helped us to the train and installed us in seats for the handicapped with our luggage. Fortunately, the train had just arrived and was yet to be cleaned of the rubbish left by the previous passengers, for rapidly it began to fill. Soon, passengers were sitting on luggage racks, our luggage was moved to allow sitting on the floor and some were sitting in the doorway; one lady, sitting on the floor, said, "One does not want this kind of journey after a long day's work". The circumstances did not ease for much of the journey, perhaps not until we reached Salisbury. As we approached Trowbridge, we were relieved to hear from the conductor that our request for assistance had been passed on when the crew changed at Salisbury; he came and helped us to leave the train with our luggage. Having booked a taxi during the journey, we were pleased to find a car waiting for us at the station and, after emerging from the taxi at our gate, we were surprised to be told, "I have put your large case outside your door". Yes, another friendly and very helpful driver. We were home before 22.00.

We have successfully accomplished another 'France Journey'. It was an experience we shall not forget, walking when it was practical to do so and using taxis at other times, we have been able to recall past journeys and to visit historic sites for the first time. We are most grateful for the help and assistance we received from so many on so many occasions. I am not sure how many journeys we have made since the 1950s, but they probably represent a total period of some two years. Throughout that time we, as English visitors, have been extended a warm welcome and much respect, courtesy, consideration, kindness and help and not least during these past ten days. We too consider ourselves – European!

THE CRUSADES AND THE KNIGHTS TEMPLARS OF THE 11TH TO 13TH CENTURIES

THE CAUSSE DU LARZAC

During the course of our many expeditions to France we have often driven northwards from the Mediterranean coast in the Department of Herault, across the Languedocienne plain, to the ancient city of Pézenas. Then, formerly, taking the N9, through the villages of Lezignan-la-Cebe, Paulhan, Nebian, passing Clermont-l'Herault, close to the valley of the Lergue to Lodève, before ascending the tortuous route of the Pas de l'Escalette (the ladder pass) to reach the heights of the Causée de Larzac at Le Caylar. We would have left the Larzac by the circuitous descent into the valley of the Tarn and to the ancient town of Millau. However, following the inauguration of the magnificent Viaduc de Millau in 2004, at the northern extent of the Larzac and the completion of the section of Autoroute A75, we have taken this present route to Le Caylar, passing through the Tunnel du Pas de l'Escalette which links the plateau du Larzac with the Lodévois valley. This is a double tube tunnel and is 725 metres long; it was opened in 1994. Finally leaving the Larzac by the Viaduc de Millau, which was designed by the architect Lord Norman Foster and, at 343 metres, is the tallest bridge in the world; when approaching from the south in the early morning sunlight it is a spectacular sight. Both the Viaduc de Millau and the Tunnel du Pas de l'Escalette are amazing engineering achievements.

Our first experience of the Causse du Larzac was on Monday, 17 August 1981. Our impression of this limestone plateau was of a seemingly desolate countryside with huge lumps of rock; the sparse vegetation feeding hundreds of sheep whose milk is used to make Roquefort Cheese. We also realised that it was the site of a number of Commanderies of the Templars and Hospitallers of the Middle Ages. Since that day in 1981 we have traversed the plateau many times and on a number of occasions we have sojourned at Le Caylar to explore the region more deeply and we have often stopped for refreshment at the Aire de Repos. We have visited the five fortified sites of the Knights Templar and Hospitallers – La Cavalerie, La Couvertoirade, Sainte-Eulalie de Cernon, Le Viala du Pas de Jaux and Saint-Jean d'Alcas. Our interest was aroused in the history of the Templars and the Hospitallers and then to that of the Crusades themselves to which they owe their origin. We resolved to learn more.

The Causse du Larzac is the largest and most southern of the Grandes Causses and covers a vast area of 1,000 square kilometres and rises to more than 900 metres. The plateau is uneven with deep hollows of up to 150 metres. Its differing soils providing pastureland for sheep and plains for producing cereals, animal raising and fodder. The area has an annual rainfall of nearly one metre. For many centuries the Larzac has had military associations; beginning with the Templars from the XIIth century to the beginning of the XIVth century. They were followed by the Hospitallers from 1312 to 1789. Since the beginning of the XXth century a military camp has been based at La Cavalerie. A large part of the Larzac was under the control of the Templars for some 200 years. They grouped the scattered populations together at Sainte-Eulalie, La Cavalerie and La Couvertoirade. Following the purchase of the Church at Sainte-Eulalie from the Abbey of Saint-Guilhem-le-Desert and additional purchases and with donations, etc., the Templars became established as the main owner of the Larzac. The Larzac Templars were not soldiers, but mainly agricultural producers. Their role was to supply the soldiers of the Holy Land.

A BACKGROUND TO THE CRUSADES

In the year 324 the tomb of Christ is discovered near Golgotha, Jerusalem, above which Roman Emperor Constantin constructed, in 329, a Basilique du Saint-Sepulchre (Rotonde de l'Anastasis). Subsequently, Jerusalem became the most important centre of Christian Pilgrimage. In 614 it was removed by the Persians who occupied Jerusalem until 629.

The Holy Land (Palestine) was occupied from about 638 by the disciples of the Prophet Mahomet. The Christians were granted, in return for an annual tribute, civil and religious freedom. On the esplanade of the Temple of Salomon, regarded as the place of the ascension of the Prophète, was erected the Dome du Rocher, and the Mosque al-Aqsa was built near the Holy Sepulchre. Thus, Jerusalem became the third holy city of Islam. However, after about 975 relations between Christians and Muslims became strained and in 1009 the Rotonde of the Holy Sepulchre was destroyed by fire by the Calife Fatimide al-Hakim. In 1055 the Turks, pursued from Haute-Asie by the Mongols, took Bagdad and thus severely shook Muslim Middle-East. In 1071, Jerusalem is taken by Fatimides of Egypt and in 1085 Antioch, in Syria, falls to the Byzantines.

From the 7th century, advocating a 'jihad' – a Holy War – Islam had conquered the southern shores of the Mediterranean, crossing the Straits of Gibraltar in 711. The Muslims imposing themselves on Spain and France, until being defeated by the Franks led by Charles Martel, at the Battle of Poitiers in 732. It was a total war between the Cross and the Crescent. This Battle of Poitiers (also known as the Battle of Tours) is a very significant date in French history for it halted the northward advance of Islam into France, Germany and beyond, for centuries to come.

In September 2011, during one of our many sojourns at St Savin we drove westward on the N151 to Chauvigny, then northward following the river Vienne on the D749 until crossing the river into Vouneuil-s-Vienne. From there we were directed by signs to the village of Moussais la Bataille, which lies near the confluence of the Rivers Clain and Vienne. We found the remarkable open-air museum, which overlooks the site of the Battle and which records the event during which Charles Martel, leader of the Frankish and Burgundian forces defeated Abdul Rahman Al Ghafiqi of the invading Umayyad Caliphate Army.

In about the year 1000, two events profoundly shook Christian consciences. In 997 Saint-Jacques de Compostelle was seized by the Muslim, Al-Mansur, who razed the Holy City, but not the tomb of the Apostle Jacques and, in 1009, the destruction of the Holy Sepulchre at Jerusalem by the Calife Al-Hakim.

Western Christians were shocked and, in view of the powerlessness of the Byzantines (of the Roman Empire), the urge for a crusade, a holy war, against the infidels developed during the course of the XIth century, dedicated to the reconquest of the holy places which had been abandoned to the infidels. It culminated in the famous call of Pope Urban II on 27 November 1095 to the Council of Clermont.

THE FIRST CRUSADE (1096–99)

There was a huge and instant response to the Pope's invocation and appeal to mount and support a crusade. Such was the enthusiasm and exalted by the preaching of religious leaders and fanatics that, without waiting for the official planned departure, an 'army' of some 15,000 set off, led by Pierre l'Ermite on a mule. Unfortunately, they were ill-prepared and ill-equipped and, on meeting the Bulgarian and Turkish Armies, Pierre's army was decimated.

It was on 15 August 1096 that four powerful armies left Le Puy-en-Velay. They were:-

1. From Lorraine and Germany led by Godefroy IV de Boulogne. (Also known as Godefroy de Bouillon).
2. Mainly Francais du Nord led by Hugues de Vermandois, brother of Philippe I. Included were the Dukes of Normandy and Brittany and Count Etienne of Blois.
3. From the Midi led by Raymond IV of Toulouse.
4. Comprised of Normands of Sicily led by Bohemond de Tarente.

Le Puy-en-Velay – Un site extraordinaire – Une histoire ancienne!

It is a remarkable city, nestling in a hollow of an amphitheatre of mountains, in a fertile bowl punctuated with volcanic peaks reaching towards the sky. On the side of one of the peaks, is constructed the Cathédrale Notre-Dame du Puy, which dates mainly from the first half of the 12th century. After a long climb, the entrance to the Cathédrale is reached by a flight of sixty steps. High above the Cathédrale and reached by a further climb and steps, stands, on the summit of le rocher Corneille, the imposing statue of Notre-Dame de France. It was a proud moment when we stood alongside the statue and viewed, not only the roof of the cathedral below us, but discovered the magnificent panorama of Le-Puy and its surrounding countryside.

There may have been more than one reason why Le Puy-en-Velay was chosen as the departure point for the First Crusade:-

Firstly, as one of the main leaders was the papal legate, Adhemar de Le Puy.
Secondly, as in the year 950 it had been the starting point of the first of the pilgrimages – Les Chemins de Saint-Jacques de Compostelle – which was led by Bishop Godescalc.

In December 1096 the Army of Godefroy IV de Boulogne reached Constantinople and are joined there by the other Armies in April/May 1097. Crossing the Straits of Bosphore they entered the Muslim world and laid siege to the town of Nicée. On 19 June 1097 the besieged Turks surrendered themselves.

In March 1098 Baudouin de Boulogne (brother of Godefroy) took Edesse and founded the first of the Latin States of the Orient. In spite of serious losses and the policy of the Turks of burning the land, the Christian armies continued their march towards Jerusalem besieging Antioche for seven months before its fall on 29 June 1098.

On 7 June 1099 the armies camped at the foot of the walls of the Holy City and, at the end of a five-week siege, Jerusalem is taken on 15 July 1099. By 'fire and blood' it will be purified! After 15 days of looting and massacres involving thousands of Muslims sheltering in the Mosque of Al-Aqsa – several centuries of Muslim occupation were ended.

On 20 July 1099 Godefroy de Bouillon was proclaimed King of Jerusalem, but he refused the title and the valiant knight died shortly afterwards. His brother, Baudouin, succeeded him and was crowned at Bethlehem on 25 December 1099. During his reign of 18 years there were many warring episodes.

Under the reign of Baudouin I four Latin States of the Orient were established – Jerusalem, Tripoli, Antioche and Edesse.

News of the success of the Crusade quickly spread across the Occident and many Christians took the road to Jerusalem every year.

The main route for the pilgrims was a dangerous one, via Jaffa and the Plaine of Ramleh and the need for armed protection became evident. In addition to the matter of security there was the need to provide accommodation and welcome for the ever-increasing numbers of pilgrims. Two Benedictine monasteries, one for men and one for women, were available. About the year 1050 a hospital, dedicated to St John was founded by Italian merchants near the Holy Sepulcre. From this was formed a new congregation and in 1113 Pope Pascal II approved the Order of the Hospitaliers de Saint Jean-de-Jerusalem. Its main purpose was the accommodation and care of the increasing numbers of pilgrims visiting the Tomb of Christ. The first Master of the Order of Hospitaliers was Raymond du Puy.

THE KNIGHTS TEMPLAR

Following the taking of Jerusalem in 1099, more and more pilgrims journeyed to the Holy Land to venerate the Holy Sepulchre. For the defence of the pilgrims and the protection of their routes, it was probably several knights from northern France, led by Hugues de Payns, who founded in 1119–20, the celebrated Order of the Templars. Certainly, Hugues de Payns became the First Master of the Order of the 'Pauvres Chevaliers du Christ et du Temple de Salomon'. The family of Hugues de Payns (Payns is near Troyes) was linked to that of a monk – St Bernard of Clairvaux – who would play an important role in the foundation of the Order. During the ten following years the Order achieved little success or growth. It may have been due to the difficulty of justifying the principle of armed monks. However, the Concile de Troyes held on 13 January 1129 approved the Order; it had a dramatic impact. The Order would take an essential place in the defence of the Latin States of the Orient.

It was necessary to draw up rules that would accommodate the principle of the monk and the combatant. These rules, mainly the work of Bernard of Clairvaux, (who founded the Cistercian Order) were published in Latin in about 1130 and in French 10 years later. La Regle contained 72 articles being devoted to the religious work of the Templars, the monks pronouncing the vows of poverty, chastity and obedience.

Firstly, privileges afforded to the Templars were confirmed, indeed increased. The Templars will be accountable directly to the Pope and no longer subject to the authority of the bishops. They were given the right to have their own priests and were allowed exemption from the 'dimes' payable in kind to the clergy, priests and bishops. They were also granted the tithes destined to the Order. In addition, they were given the right to have their own churches and cemeteries. From now on the faithful would be able to attend services in the churches of the commanderies, thus increasing their income and depriving parish churches of gifts and alms. The clergy were angered by the increasing donations flowing to the Order of the Temple and at the exorbitant privileges granted to the soldier/monks.

Secondly, the foundation of numerous commanderies, perhaps 1,000, in the Occident, particularly in France; the purpose of which was to produce the food, horses, etc., to meet the needs of the soldiers in the Holy Land.

Clearly, during the period of the second Master, the foundations of a very influential, authoritative, powerful and wealthy Order were laid. With its structure clearly defined and made legitimate by the highest moral and spiritual authority in the Occident, the Temple witnessed a considerable development in the following years.

Hugues de Payns died in 1136 and was succeeded by Robert de Craon.

THE SECOND CRUSADE (1147–49)

Following the defeat, in 1138, by the Turks at Teqoa (near Bethlehem) and the seizing of the first Latin State of Edesse by Zengi, Emir of Mossoul, on 24 December 1144, a Second Crusade was advocated. However, the decree by Pope Eugene III met with little enthusiasm. Louis VII summoned the barons and the bishops to Bourges on 25 December 1145. It was considered that the one preacher who could revive the flame was Bernard of Clairvaux and he preached the Second Crusade on the heights of Vézelay on 31 March 1146. On 27 April 1147 the Pope presided at a general assembly of the Temple in Paris. It is believed that it was on that occasion that the Pope gave the Templars the right to wear a red cross on their white cloaks. This was the first crusade to be led by European kings – Louis VII of France and Conrad III of Germany. Louis VII, with his wife Aliénor d'Aquitaine, led his army via the Balkans. They suffered severe losses in Asia Minor (also Anatolia – most of present-day Turkey) at the hands of the Turks, but wise tactics of the Master of the Temple in France, Evrard des Barres, enabled the army to reach d'Adalia. Louis VII then continued to Antioche, where, without money, he obtained a loan from the Brothers of the Temple. In June 1148 he joined with Conrad III of Germany, whose army had been decimated by the Turks, near Jerusalem, in a joint expedition on Damascus (capital of the Syrian Arab Republic) in July; it was a bitter failure. In fact, this second crusade was a complete fiasco. Conrad III returned to Germany in September 1148 and Louis VII to France, some months later – probably in the spring of 1149.

Robert de Craon died in January 1149. He was Grand Master of the Knights Templar, having succeeded Hugues de Payns in June 1136. He was succeeded by

Edvard des Barres, the hero of the second crusade, who in turn left his post to Andre de Montbard in 1153. Subsequently, Edvard des Barres, faithful to Saint Bernard, became a monk in the Abbey of Clairvaux until his death in about 1175.

We have made two visits to Vézelay and spent much time in its wonderful Abbey Church. We have sat for a contemplative hour or two on the hillside at the rear of the Abbey where Bernard of Clairvaux preached the Second Crusade. We tried to visualise that scene on 31 March 1146 where, we read that the crowd was so great that a large platform was erected on a hill outside the city and that, "his voice rang out across the meadow like a celestial organ". It was a memorable experience.

THE THIRD CRUSADE (1189–92)

Following the failure of the Second Crusade (1147–49) and, in view of the capture of Jerusalem by Saladin in 1187, it was resolved by the leaders of France, Germany and England to recover the Holy Land. The English would be led by Henry II; however, Henry died in the Chateau of Chinon on 6 July 1189 and was succeeded by Richard I – The Lionheart. The French were led by Philip II – Philip Augustus. The elderly German Emperor Frederick Barbarossa led a large army across Anatolia (most of present day Turkey), but unfortunately, he drowned while crossing a river in Asia Minor on 10 June 1190 and did not reach the Holy Land. There was great grief among the German Crusaders and most returned home. After the Crusaders had driven the Muslims from Acre, Philip II and Leopold V, who had succeeded Frederick, left the Holy Land in August 1191. On 2 September 1192 Richard and Saladin agreed the Treaty of Jaffa, which granted the Muslims control over Jerusalem, but allowing unarmed Christian pilgrims and merchants to visit the Holy City. Richard left the Holy Land in October 1192.

The Third Crusade could, therefore, be regarded as largely successful, but it failed to achieve its main aim, the recapture of Jerusalem. This aim was not achieved until the Sixth Crusade in 1229 and then only for a brief period.

It is interesting that, while the inspiration for the Second Crusade occurred at Vézelay, the armies of the Third Crusade actually assembled at and left from Vézelay. They camped their first night about 10 kilometres away at the Château of Bazoches. A nostalgic reminder of, ourselves, driving that short distance to visit the Château and, although it was the official closing time, we were welcomed and allowed a leisurely tour of the home and office of Marshal Vauban, Louis IV's military engineer. That was not all, we were afforded such a friendly conversation with members of the staff while standing on the balcony of the Chateau overlooking the beautiful valley. Afterwards, we visited the little church containing the tomb of Vauban. Memories!!

THE FOURTH CRUSADE (1202–04)

This Crusade was called by Pope Innocent III with the intention of recapturing Jerusalem, by first conquering the powerful Egyptian Ayyubid Sultanate, the strongest Muslim nation at that time. Towards the end of 1202, for financial reasons, the army first sacked Zara. Early in 1203, the Crusaders, en route to Jerusalem, agreed with the Byzantine prince Alexios Angelos to divert to Constantinople and to restore his deposed father as Emperor. On doing so the Crusaders were promised Byzantine financial and military aid. Following clashes outside Constantinople, Alexios was crowned co-Emperor, but in 1204 he was deposed by a popular uprising. Following the murder of Alexios on 8 February, the Crusaders decided on the outright conquest of Constantinople. In April 1204 they captured and ruthlessly plundered the city's enormous wealth. Subsequently, only a handful of Crusaders continued to the Holy Land.

THE FIFTH CRUSADE (1217–21)

In April 1213 Pope Innocent III called all Christendom to join a new crusade to recapture Jerusalem. However, few French knights responded to the call as they were already fighting the Albigensian Crusade against the heretical Cathar sect in southern France. Unfortunately, Pope Innocent died in 1216 and was succeeded by Pope Honorious III. The crusading armies were led by King Andrew II of Hungary and John of Brienne, King of Jerusalem. They landed near Damiette in May 1218 and their aim was to capture Damiette and to force the sultan of Egypt to exchange Jerusalem for Damiette. They laid siege to the city; there was resistance from the unprepared sultan Al-Adil and they were only able to capture the tower outside the city, on 25 August.

In the following months disease killed many of the crusaders; Al-Adil also died and was succeeded by

Al-Kamil. The crusaders received the support of the Templars under Guillaume de Chartres, who died in the fighting, and Damiette is finally taken in November 1219. Meanwhile the walls and fortifications of Jerusalem were demolished to prevent the Christians from being able to defend the city if they captured it. Muslims fled the city, fearing a blood-bath like that of the First Crusade in 1099. The Pope sent his legate, Cardinal Pelage to lead the crusade. John of Brienne wanted to negotiate with the sultan of Egypt, but Pelage wanted total victory. The Christian army remained inactive for about eighteen months and, in July 1221, began to march south towards Cairo. Al-Kamil then allied with other Ayyubids in Syria. The crusader march to Cairo was disastrous; the river Nile ahead was flooded and a dry canal they had previously crossed was flooded, thus blocking the crusaders retreat. With dwindling supplies, a forced retreat began, culminating in a night time attack by Al-Kamil which resulted in many crusader losses and to the surrender of the army under Pelagius. The terms of the surrender meant the relinquishing of Damiette to Al-Kamil in exchange for the release of the crusaders. Al-Kamil agreed to an eight-year agreement with Europe and to return a piece of the True Cross. However, the relic was never returned as Al-Kamil did not, in fact, have it.

THE SIXTH CRUSADE (1228–29)

Seven years after the failure of the Fifth Crusade, it is another attempt to regain Jerusalem; it involved very little fighting and resulted in the Kingdom of Jerusalem regaining some control over Jerusalem for much of the following fifteen years. In 1227 Gregory IX became Pope. The crusade was led by the German Emperor, Frederick II who, in 1225, had married Isabella II of Jerusalem, the daughter of John of Brienne (nominal ruler of the Kingdom of Jerusalem). She died three years after giving birth to a son, Conrad, who becomes the legitimate heir of the crown. However, Frederick usurps the rights of his son and is excommunicated by Pope Gregory. Regardless of these considerations, Frederick, with his army, set sail from Brindisi (Italy) for Saint-Jean-d'Acre, the capital of the Kingdom of Jerusalem. Realising that his army was a mere shadow of the force that had amassed when the crusade had been called, without delay, he began negotiations with the sultan d'Egypte, Al-Kamil. By the Treaty of Jaffa (11 February 1192) he obtains the return of Bethlehem, Nazareth and, especially, of Jerusalem, with the Muslims retaining control of the Temple Mount and their mosques, Omar and Al-Aqsa. The treaty also included a 10-year truce. The Templars were furious; not only did they judge that Jerusalem would be indefensible, but they did not foresee a return to the Order of the ancient 'quartier du Temple'. Moreover, Frederick favoured a new military order, under his control, 'les Chevaliers Teutoniques'; it was a provocative act. Templars and Hospitallers openly manifested their hostility. They did not attend Frederick's crowning ceremony on 18 March 1229 at the Holy Sepulchre. Legally, he was actually only regent for his son, Conrad II of Jerusalem, the only child of Yolande and the grandson of John of Brienne. Frederick left Jerusalem in May 1229. He had demonstrated that a crusade could be successful even without military superiority or papal support.

On the expiration of Frederick's ten-year treaty with Al-Kamil, Pope Gregory IX called for a new crusade to secure the Holy Land for Christendom. This initiated the BARONS' CRUSADE OF 1239, which was led by Theobald I of Navarre and then by Richard of Cornwall. It was a somewhat disorganized affair which received relatively limited support from both Frederick and the Pope. Nevertheless, using diplomacy, it regained more land than even the Sixth Crusade; the Kingdom of Jerusalem returned to its largest size since 1187.

THE SEVENTH CRUSADE (1248–54)

Despite the heroic resistance of the Templars – of the 348 engaged in the fight only 36 survived – the Turks, recaptured Jerusalem for the Sultan of Egypt on 23 August 1244. Once again, the Holy City was in the hands of the Muslims. Once again, the Pope, Innocent IV, called for a crusade. There was little response – there were conflicts in Europe which kept the leaders occupied. However, in December 1244 Louis IX, Saint Louis, King of France, decided to 'take the cross'. In 1248, with a large army and financially well prepared, Louis IX embarked from the newly built port of Aigues-Morte and from Marseille. After a stopover in Cyprus, during the course of the winter of 1248–49, the royal fleet put to sea on the 30 May 1249. Egypt was the objective of the crusade as Louis intended it to be his base from which to attack Jerusalem and where they could find subsistence. They disembarked at Damiette on 6 June, provoking the flight of the Saracens. However, the flooding of the Nile grounded Louis and his army at Damiette for six months. In November Louis marched towards Cairo and his brother, Robert, d'Artois, together with an English contingent led by William Longespee decided to attack the fortress of Mansourah despite its difficult access in the delta of the Nile. They were decisively defeated; Robert and William were killed and only a small handful survived. Louis' main force was attacked and also defeated. However, he did not withdraw to Damietta but remained to besiege Mansourah, which ended in starvation and death for the crusaders.

When, in March 1250, Louis tried to return to Damietta, he was taken captive and his army was annihilated. Louis became ill with dysentery, but was cured by an Arab physician. In May he was ransomed for 800,000 bezants, which was paid to the Sultan of Egypt by the Knights Templar. Damietta was surrendered as a term of the agreement. Louis IX then left Egypt for Acre, one of the few remaining crusader possessions in Syria. In 1254 Louis' money ran out and he was forced to return to France following the death of his mother and regent, Blanche de Castile. Before leaving, he established a French garrison at Acre, the capital of the Kingdom of Jerusalem and it remained thus until 1291. Although his crusade was a failure, Louis IX was considered by many a saint, which gave him greater authority in Europe than the Holy Roman Emperor.

THE EIGHTH CRUSADE (1270)

Despite the abject failure of his previous crusade, during which he failed to reach the Holy Land, Louis IX still pursued crusader aims. He continued to provide financial aid and military support to settlements in the Crusader

States. However, they were being overrun by the campaigns of Baibars, Sultan of Egypt. In 1266, Louis IX informed Pope Clement IV that he intended to go on another crusade. Louis took the cross 24 March 1267. His son-in-law, Theobald II of Navarre, also took the cross. Louis' plan was to disembark on the coast of Outremer (the Crusader States) via Cyprus. However, it was decided to first descend on Tunis – Islam had long been established around the shores of the Mediterranean. Louis' large fleet sailed from Aigues-Mortes on 1 July 1270 and, on the following day, Theobald II and his fleet sailed from Marseille. They arrived on the Tunisian coast on 18 July and were soon confronted with the pestilence of a North African summer and an epidemic of dysentery. Louis' young son, John Tristan who was born in Damiette, died. Shortly afterwards Louis himself died, in penitence, on a bed of ashes on 25 August. His brother, Charles, arrived just after his death. Louis IX is often considered the model of the ideal Christian monarch and he was canonized in 1297. The siege of Tunis was abandoned on 30 October, but in an agreement with the Sultan, the Christians were granted free trade with Tunis and residence for monks and priests in the city was guaranteed.

The day following the crusaders departure from Tunis, Prince Edward of England arrived with an English fleet; they followed the other crusaders to Sicily. The English contingent then continued to Acre in April 1271 to pursue the Ninth Crusade.

THE NINTH CRUSADE (1271–72)

This is regarded as the last major medieval Crusade to the Holy Land. It was the son of Henry III of England,

Edward, who sailed to Acre to achieve several impressive victories over the Sultan, Baibars. He succeeded in capturing Nazareth and, in an agreement with the Sultan, obtained favourable terms for Christians and pilgrims. In 1272 Edward returned home to England and was crowned King Edward I on 19 August 1274.

In the year 1291, pilgrims from Acre were attacked and they retaliated, whereupon, the Mamluk Sultan, Qalawun, besieged the city with the aim of eliminating the last independent Crusader state of the Holy Land. Following the seizure of Acre, the centre of power of the Crusaders moved to Cyprus; the period of the Crusades to the Holy Land was over, 208 years after the beginning of the First Crusade.

THE KNIGHTS TEMPLAR

During the course of 200 years, following its inception in 1120, the Order of the Knights Templar, which, supported by the Pope, had as its initial objective to protect pilgrims travelling to the Holy Land and then as defenders of Christians in the Orient, had become, by the end of the XIIIth century, a very powerful economic and financial institution. They built commanderies and fortresses and appear to have been the major landowners of Europe and the bankers of the Occident. Consequently, it aroused the jealousy of the temporal powers, particularly that of the King of France, Philippe le Bel. Clergy became jealous of the Templars power and independence and success. There were rumours accusing them of being proud, arrogant and mean. From the time of 1305, the rumours grew and there were charges of heresy, idolatry and sodomy. An Act ordered that all Templars in the Kingdom of France be arrested on the 13 October 1307. The Templars admitted to all the charges and in 1312 the Templar Order was abolished. However, their possessions did not fall into the hands of Philippe, but passed to the Order of Hospitallers. The Grand Master, Jacques de Molay and others perished at the stake at the end of an iniquitous trial.

Were the Templars guilty or innocent? This is a question which has been discussed by historians and others for centuries and, no doubt, will continue to be so. For my part I can do no better than repeat the conclusion of the author, Patrick Huchet, in quoting the opinion of the eminent historian, Jean Flori – "L'ordre du Temple n'a pourtant rien d'une société secrète. Il est né de la croisade à laquelle son destin est étroitement lié, il a vécu pour elle, il est mort de son échec." (The Order of the Temple was not a secret society. It was born of the Crusades to which its destiny was closely linked; it had existed for the Crusades and it died following the failure of the Crusades.)

Whatever, it is an intriguing story – so much so that, following our first practical encounter with the story, on the Causse du Larzac, in 1981, we have visited various sites with distinct links with the Crusades, particularly – Le Puy-en-Velay, Aigues-Mortes, Vézelay and all the commanderies on the Larzac. We wished to learn more about these remarkable expeditions, and I had intended to prepare an outline of some of the salient developments of that two-hundred-year period in the history of a very turbulent region. In fact, some ten years ago, while in France, we purchased two books – *Les Templiers de la gloire a la tragédie,* by Patrick Huchet and *Les Templiers* by Michèle Aue and, subsequently, *The Knights Templar* by Robin Griffith-Jones, Master, The Temple Church. It is these publications which have provided me with much information. Still ten years ago in France, I translated the French and prepared a draft of my outline, intending to complete this after returning home. Sadly, Margaret's continuing illnesses prevented me from completing the work. It is with much pleasure that I have now fulfilled my hopes. I hope that the information I have assembled will be of interest to others.

FRANCE – A JOURNEY
RECOLLECTIONS AND REFLECTIONS
THE FINAL INSTALMENT
NORMANDY

SEPTEMBER – OCTOBER 2015 (Tuesday, 15 September – Thursday, 1 October)

It was on 6 October 2011, but only just, that we reached home at the end of the second of two near six-week journeys in France during that year. It had been a long, interesting, enjoyable and memorable journey – a wonderful experience, visiting Burgundy, in particular, and all our friends in France – that is until we reached Cherbourg. To our surprise and disappointment we found that, instead of returning to Poole on the cruise ship *Barfleur* as we had expected, we must travel to Portsmouth on the 'fast-craft' *Normandie Express*. It was a stormy evening and we were warned straightaway to remain seated. As it turned out we had little desire to do otherwise as the little vessel was tossed about by the sea with large waves frequently crashing against the windows. We had never been more relieved to enter into the relative calm of the entrance to Portsmouth harbour. However, the wind and rain certainly extended inland and the drive along the M27, amidst all the traffic, was difficult as we concentrated on remaining on the motorway and not to be enticed onto one of the many slip roads, until reaching the exit for Salisbury. Once heading for the cathedral city we felt a little more secure, although there was little improvement in the weather. The 'final straw' of this journey was saved until we reached the entrance to Green Lane from West Ashton Road; it was closed – closed completely and it was almost midnight! We could see the entrance to our home, but how were we to get there. Feeling like strangers in our own land, we tried one option and then another before finally entering Green Lane from the opposite direction and eventually driving through our gates with a great sigh of relief.

Perhaps 2011 would have been a not inappropriate concluding instalment of our 'France – A Journey', at least by road. Indeed, at that time we did not contemplate a further journey by car. However, we soon had thoughts of returning to the Herault Department in the Region of Languedoc by train, and come the end of the year we had made a reservation for a period in June 2012. Unfortunately, Margaret's continuing ulcer, unrelenting arthritis in her feet and legs, coupled with the onset of memory problems early in the new year, cast constant doubts on the wisdom of attempting such a journey; in particular, we were kept waiting very many months for a planned appointment with a consultant. In the circumstances we eventually cancelled the arrangements made. However, 2012 passed and the situation had changed little – what should we do? We made plans for 2013 similar to those cancelled in the previous year; this time we succeeded in fulfilling our hopes. Then, in 2014, we were grateful to be able to travel to the north-east of France, once again by train.

It is now 2015 and our love of France and its people remains undiminished and there is no better way of visiting the country than independently with one's personal transport; we continued to cherish the prospect of doing so – could it be this year? Unfortunately, Margaret's ulcer, which had remained healed for six months, recurred at Easter and again necessitated weekly visits to the Hospital and, subsequently, thrice weekly dressing. However, the nurse who has been tending the ulcer over a long period helped us to be optimistic and said that she would be willing to provide us with an adequate supply of dressings to enable us to make the regular changes. Also, Margaret's mobility limitations remain a considerable handicap. My eyesight was still an important consideration. Although the consultant to whom I had been referred last year had been reassuring, I was aware that I was not recognising and identifying road signs and obstructions as readily as is desirable; in any case I was due for another test in the middle of this year. Fortunately, after a seemingly thorough examination by the optician, I was not subjected to any further consultation or, particularly, to any comments or reservations regarding driving.

There was now no apparent reason why I should not give serious consideration to once again driving in France. However, it was by no means an easy decision; although I had driven many thousands of miles in France over many years with no difficulties or problems whatsoever, I had had no such experience during the past four years. Most importantly, I had driven so little in this country either, with little desire to do so – driving only in the environs of Trowbridge with the occasional slightly longer journey over familiar routes. In fact, did I now have the confidence to contemplate a journey of perhaps several hundred miles over largely unfamiliar routes? I was concerned of the possibility of failing to observe important road signs, messages and directions, of making errors of judgement, mishaps and of possible breakdowns, etc., and of the likely consequences. The journey would require considerable concentration. We wrestled long and hard with the question – do we plan a further France Journey by car – quite probably our last – or, particularly in view of Margaret's health and our increasing years, do we abandon such a project at this stage. Eventually, we concluded that the latter alternative would leave us with the permanent uncertainty of what we might have been able to achieve – the disappointment of perhaps an opportunity missed. I felt that, for a while at least, we should lift ourselves out of the humdrum routine of daily life to an experience which we could recall and reflect upon long into the future. We began to make positive plans.

We would love to again visit familiar places and friends in the Indre-et-Loire, the Corrèze and the Lot, but that would involve extensive journeys and we must not be too ambitious. In any case the Départements of Manche and Calvados of the Region of Normandy hold so much of interest to us and we could visit friends in and near Bayeux. Fortunately, we find that Brittany Ferries will be operating their cruise ferry service between Poole and Cherbourg, with the *Barfleur*, throughout the year and through the winter. However, the timetable is not as inviting as we would like. The daily sailing from Poole leaves at 08.30; sailings from Cherbourg, from September, are at either 18.30 or 22.15, arriving at Poole at 21.45 and 07.00 respectively. As the year is passing rapidly towards autumn the journey from Poole and a return journey at 18.30 could well involve travelling from and to home during the hours of darkness; this we wish to avoid. The options appear to be to drive to Poole on the previous day and spend a night there and to return on an overnight ferry; this would be our plan.

So far as accommodation is concerned we would like to spend a couple of nights at Valognes, perhaps three nights at Grandcamp-Maisy, four nights at the farm in Vienne-en-Bessin, then four nights in Bayeux, returning to Grandcamp-Maisy for a final night. We then successfully made bookings for just a few weeks in advance as follows: Brittany Ferries – from 16 September to 30 September; Holiday Inn Express, Poole – 15 September; Le Relais du Louvre, Valognes – 16 and 17 September; Hôtel Le Duguesclin, Grandcamp-Maisy – 18, 19 and 20 September; La Ferme des Châtaigniers, Vienne-en-Bessin – 21, 22, 23 and 24 September; Hôtel Campanile, Bayeux – 25, 26, 27 and 28 September; Hôtel Le Duguesclin, Grandcamp-Maisy – 29 September.

Arranging essential travel insurance gave me little encouragement; it was not a straightforward matter, particularly in view of our respective ages, regular treatments and medications, etc. Having virtually completed the process, as I thought, 'online', my screen suddenly disappeared and I had to start again. After finally completing the task a second time, I realised that this time I had failed to refer to Margaret's ulcer condition. I then sent an e-mail explaining my omission. I promptly received a telephone call and I was required to complete the application for a third time. The outcome was that the cost of covering Margaret's various conditions became prohibitive and I finally accepted full cover for myself alone. This is what I had hoped for in the first place – as I explained to Staysure, I particularly required cover for the possibility that I could suffer an accident and be unable to drive, for instance. Having completed these formal arrangements, we could now relax and look forward to the day of departure? Most certainly not! There is little time left and there are all the personal arrangements to complete. I have to arrange for the car to receive a reassuring check and also to be cleaned and washed and, importantly, to arrange to temporarily extend breakdown cover to apply in France. We must ensure that the numerous essential items, particularly medications, dressings etc., are taken with us and, having the benefit of the facilities the car provides, such items as might be useful. No doubt there will be occasions when some additional revitalization might be welcome in the car, if not elsewhere, and I filled a large cool box with a varied and plentiful supply of cereal bars, biscuits, bottles of fruit shoot, water, etc. One piece of equipment which we most certainly wish to have with us is Margaret's three-wheel walker as, hopefully, there will be opportunities for its increased use.

Tuesday, 15 September

I had already placed in the car much of our 'luggage', etc., and, this morning, we are well advanced towards being ready to leave. Finally, after a lunch of sandwiches, purchased the previous day, we left home at 14.05, feeling reasonably well prepared for the journey, but with some apprehension! Heading eastwards in West Ashton Road for the first time for a number of years we soon encountered the new roundabout; then on to the busy A350 before passing slowly (that was familiar) through Westbury; the fast moving traffic along the A36 section (the Warminster bypass) became more intimidating and we were relieved to resume on the A350 towards Crockerton. Although there was quite a high volume of traffic, village names such as Longbridge Deverill and East Knoyle give this road a more rural flavour. It is attractive countryside, but I must not take my eyes off the road ahead.

Following my examination by the Consultant Ophthalmologist last year he wrote to the optician saying that there are 'corneal guttata' and I was finding that my Marciac Jazz cap (a souvenir of a visit to the town of Marciac in the Gers Department and the Region of Midi-Pyrénées, where the world famous jazz festival is held for two weeks in August of every year) was being very effective in combatting the effects of the problem by excluding the background light (the sky) and assisting in focussing on the surfaces. Soon we reach Shaftesbury and we remember to take the Salisbury direction and then, almost immediately, the road through the village of Melbury Abbas with its severe speed restrictions. The route across Cranborne Chase affords excellent views; it is not a main road, but it is fairly straight and many motorists are impatient and driving uncomfortably fast.

At the outskirts of Blandford Forum we rejoin the very busy A350. From now on the route requires much attention and care, particularly the speed restrictions through the villages of Charlton Marshall, Spetisbury and Sturminster Marshall. At the roundabout link with the A31 it is important to take the correct exit, for Poole, and at the junction with the A35 to join the B3068 through Hamworthy. We are now on the last part of this journey and it is fairly familiar. However, we were suddenly alarmed to notice an illuminated sign which said 'Poole Bridge Closed'; we were not able to read the entire message – probably containing directions for an alternative route – and we were very concerned; we are not familiar with this area and we had no idea what alternative route to the hotel was available and how we could then reach the ferry terminal in the morning. Soon we passed a second sign, but again we failed to read more. As we continued, we thought we must find a convenient place to turn around so that we could take a careful look at these signs, but we found nowhere. However, quite suddenly there was the bridge ahead of us and vehicles were moving over it – what a relief! What we had not been able to read was the dates of closure!

We were now in the area of Poole which Paul had guided me through on the internet two or three weeks earlier. Although I still had a general idea of the directions we should take – follow West Quay Road; get in the right-hand lane to return in the opposite direction along West Street keeping in the left-hand lane, then turning left into the Quay – I did not recognise the surrounding buildings as my attention was focussed so much on the moving traffic, but we did reach the Quay successfully. We found it difficult to read the street names, but we probably entered Ballard Road correctly, continuing in the direction of the hotel. However, we felt we had gone too far as we were now entering a more residential area; we stopped to ask a gentleman the way to the Holiday Inn Express. We were pleased to hear that we were then only about 200 yards from the hotel, although we could not see it. He kindly directed us to a car park where we could turn round and then, if we turned to the left a short distance ahead, we would find the hotel. In a matter of a few minutes, there it was standing at our left at the intriguing address of Walking Fields Lane! We parked in a 'disabled' parking place near the entrance, which we learned afterwards we were welcome to use. We had arrived! The journey had been completed successfully with a good degree of attention and care and, consequently, with no particular difficulties. It was 16.30 and the journey had taken two hours and 25 minutes; the distance travelled so far is 55 miles. In August 2011 the journey to the ferry port took 1 hour 30 minutes!

I was anxious to report our arrival and to complete the check-in formalities and to know that the arrangements had been completed satisfactorily. This is a very modern hotel; I had read that both English and Polish is spoken here and the smart and very polite young man who welcomed me could well have been Polish, for English was certainly not his native tongue. While I had the opportunity, I enquired if he could offer directions for driving to the ferry terminal in the morning. He gave me a sheet of directions, but he pointed out that it was for travelling from the port to the hotel. When I enquired if there were any one-way streets on that route, there was clearly some uncertainty – perhaps we shall discover! How curious to be given instructions for finding the hotel (from the ferry-port) when one is already there! I had mentioned when booking that facilities for the handicapped would be appreciated and we were allocated a very comfortable room conveniently on the ground floor. This was very helpful for the purpose of transferring our luggage from and to the car. The hotel does offer a 'restaurant' and, although we had had some lunch at home, something to eat would now be appreciated. The menu was somewhat limited, but we chose to have a crepe – after all we should be in France tomorrow! After a long delay we were advised that crepes were not available. We turned to the menu again and chose 'apple crumble'; after a while we were told that that was available, but it was some time before we were served; however, it was satisfactory and enjoyable.

There was another couple on a nearby table and they, particularly the husband, joined in conversation with us. They had had a particularly difficult time. They were on their way to their home in Jersey after returning their daughter to her University in Winchester, but they had been delayed for two days in Poole. On one day their crossing had been cancelled because of weather conditions and on the other it was cancelled because of technical problems; they were now hoping to leave at 05.30 in the morning. Although they had been able to be accommodated here for tonight, on the previous night they had had to go into Bournemouth to find a room. Surprisingly, the husband said to me, "What do you think of Jeremy Corbyn's election – I think it is terrible – I was a Labour Party supporter, but not now". What a note on which to end such a day – a day which had been reasonably successful for, with much diligence, we had accomplished the first stage of our journey; we must not prolong it unduly for tomorrow is to be another challenging day and it begins early! (Today 55 miles)

<u>Wednesday, 16 September</u>

Our room at the Holiday Inn Express was quite acceptable with comfortable beds and we enjoyed a restful, but short, night. Of course, our sole purpose of being here is to catch the ferry for Cherbourg which sails at 08.30 and we are advised to arrive at the port no less than 45 minutes before the scheduled departure time; we decided that we should aim to be there by 07.30! The early morning routine is a very slow process these days and we felt we should set our alarm for no later than 06.00. We had been informed that breakfast would be available from 06.30; however, my attention was now focussed entirely on leaving the hotel and, as the minutes passed alarmingly quickly and, in view of the tardy service we had experienced in the restaurant during the previous evening, we decided to forgo the breakfast which we had already paid for. I am not sure exactly what time we left the hotel, but it was later than we had planned. When handing in the key of our room I hurriedly asked the receptionist which way we should go from here.

However, it was by now a very busy time in Poole with much traffic. We had not driven very far when I felt unsure that we were going in the right direction. We interrupted a lady who was hurriedly making her way to her work; even so, she kindly gave us some further directions; at one point we found ourselves in what appeared to be the rear entrance of commercial premises, perhaps a supermarket. Gradually, we moved forward with the general traffic in, hopefully, the right direction. It was certainly a relief when we recognised that bridge ahead of us; after that we knew we had to turn left towards the ferry port. As we entered territory we recognised we were intercepted by a Brittany Ferries man who would point us in the right direction. As he looked inside the car he must have spotted the walking stick and he asked if we required any assistance – would we be able to negotiate the stairs. We responded that we thought we could manage.

However, on reaching the border control and Brittany Ferries check-point I asked what help was available. I was told that I should have requested assistance when making the booking; however, the lady kindly enquired if it was still possible to implement the appropriate procedure; I was pleased to see the thumbs-up signal. We had a label stuck on the windscreen and I was told to keep my hazard lights switched on and follow the directions. As the boarding continued we were set aside until we were perhaps the final car. We were then invited to drive on to deck five and we were positioned just outside the entrance to the staircase and the lift. That was indeed most helpful and, taking no more than we were likely to need, we made our way, by lift, to deck seven without too much difficulty.

During the preceding days we had been led to believe that the weather today would be rather unpleasant, with references to the tail-end of a hurricane reaching the English Channel by Wednesday! There were a number of empty seats and we chose a reasonably comfortable one by a window and conveniently near the cafeteria. This was a very significant stage in our adventure; perhaps we could now relax for a while, that is providing the sea did not make us feel too unwelcome. After some minutes into the crossing we were pleasantly surprised to realise that the ship remained fairly steady; we felt sufficiently confident to walk the short distance to the cafeteria for the breakfast we had left behind in the hotel. We bought Fruit and Fibre cereals, etc., and the assistant, seeing that we were going to have difficulty in carrying what we had purchased, immediately abandoned her duties and, as well as carrying our tray, assisted Margaret to a convenient table. What a helpful spontaneous gesture! However, sitting in the chair at the table was not going to be the most comfortable way of spending a large part of the four and a quarter hour journey.

As we entered the lift after leaving the car I had noticed the large area of reclining seats on deck five and I ventured to the enquiry office from the cafeteria to ask if it was necessary to book those seats; I was surprised to hear that they were, in fact, free and we were welcome to use them. Returning to Margaret, we summoned up enough energy and courage to make our way to the lift using available fixtures for support as the ship was now rolling somewhat more. Even at the lift it was difficult to control our movements until, suddenly a gentleman left his seat to come and give us his support. Leaving the lift at deck five was less difficult, but we were relieved to sink into the nearest available reclining seats; there we stayed until the end of the voyage. On reaching Cherbourg we were advised, with apologies, that the ship would dock at 14.00 hours – 15 minutes late because of weather conditions in the Channel. In fact, the crossing had certainly not been as stormy as we had anticipated. Bringing the ship to a standstill and linking it to the port facilities requires no little skill on the part of the captain and members of the crew, for it has a gross tonnage in excess of 20,000 and the sea is by no means calm; yet the manoeuvre was accomplished almost imperceptibly.

We were now pleased to be just a few steps from the door to the car deck and there was our car, with ample space around it, waiting for us. Being, probably, the last car to board, we were now perhaps the last vehicle to disembark. Most other vehicles have now disappeared ahead of us and, as we left the cosiness of the car deck and drove onto the expansive port area, there is some feeling of loneliness; however, it was not to last for long, for we are now in France! I remember that we must go to the left to leave the port and, ahead of us, we noticed a small group by a kiosk – it was the border control point. After a friendly welcome, a brief look at our passports and a glance inside the car we were allowed to begin our journey – it was all very informal. Soon we reach the roundabout and the direction sign for Caen.

Driving on the right-hand side and giving way to traffic from the left just comes quite naturally again. This excellent new road is the eastern bypass of Cherbourg; it must be close on 10 miles of mainly dual carriageway – through Tourlaville – then climbing up the N13 to reach the roundabout junction with the direct route from the centre of Cherbourg, at the top of the hill. Here we take the exit for Caen. There had not been a great volume of traffic, nevertheless, I had driven cautiously, keeping in the right-hand lane and resisting being enticed into any of the slip-roads. Soon after the junction we had to begin to keep a very watchful eye for signs for the exit for Valognes for it is no more than a further 10 miles. Fortunately, we spotted the advanced sign for the junction and so we were prepared for it. The N13 is not an autoroute, but it has most of the characteristics of a motorway with, naturally, fast moving traffic – it is the main route to Caen and beyond. It had not been an easy journey from the ferry port as, apart from the need to be very watchful of traffic, road signs, etc., the weather conditions added to the difficulty with heavy storms alternating with bright sunshine.

It was with some relief, therefore, that we entered into a much more relaxed kind of road system. Now, we must find Le Relais du Louvre; I had printed a street plan, but we did not find it particularly useful – the latitude and longitude references were of no practical help; so we drove around for a while asking a couple of people for directions. The address of the hotel is 28 Rue des Religieuses and so we assumed it would be somewhere near the church. Of course, this is a building which is not normally difficult to locate in any town or village. Having found the church, we drove down one of the ancient streets leading from it. Margaret thought she had seen a reference to a hotel, but we had now gone some distance beyond it and we are in a one-way street. We found a way to enter the street again and this time drove very slowly and, yes, it was

Le Relais that she had seen. There was a direction to a guest's car park through an arch in the buildings. I made several attempts to position the car in line with the arch; while doing so I was obstructing other cars, but no one expressed any irritation or impatience – yes, this is France. I could see that the 'car park' was quite small and the access was very narrow. Eventually, I abandoned the attempt; in any case, if I managed to get in I would probably have difficulty getting out. There was, in fact, space for one car immediately in front of the entrance. It would be partially on the pavement, but other vehicles were parked similarly. I made use of this space with relief to me and to other drivers! It was now about 15.30 and we had travelled a mere 20 miles from the ferry port.

I was pleased to find that the door was not locked and I was even more pleased and relieved to find that our reservation was confirmed. Madame then offered to take me to our room. However, I was somewhat less pleased as she led me up the stairs – a spiral staircase of 17 steps. How was Margaret going to be able to negotiate such an access, not once, but many times; how was I going to be able to carry all our necessary luggage up – and then down – such a staircase. The room had the necessary facilities, but the bed was rather small. Had we made an unwise choice? I mentioned that I had parked the car outside the entrance, not knowing what parking regulations apply; the reply was reassuring – pas de problème – and I decided there and then that the car would remain there throughout our stay. I took the opportunity of asking if the restaurant would be open in the evening and I was pleased to hear that it would be open at 19.00, but I was told there would be one menu only – pork!

Fortunately, we had ample time in which to establish ourselves and eventually, and with some difficulty, Margaret reached our room and after many journeys I felt that we had all that we would need at least for the remainder of this day. There was now time for a welcome hour's rest. We made our way down to the restaurant shortly after seven o'clock, and we were pleasantly surprised. After passing through the kitchen, the dining room is quite large; it is on a slightly lower level than the street outside, which is viewed through large windows; this image is projected to the opposite side of the room by the use of large mirrors; indeed, it has 'the charm of bygone times'. We learned that, in fact, Le RELAIS du LOUVRE is an historic building – a 17th century Coaching Inn; it incorporates a tower at the rear which accommodates the spiral staircase; the 'car park' is a cobbled courtyard adjacent to former stables. A notable guest of the 19th century was the writer Jules Barbey d'Aurevilly. Perhaps we were a little surprised by our meal for it was excellent and the service was good. There were a number of other diners present and it was a very friendly and pleasant atmosphere. We were happy to spend a couple of hours there before deciding it was time to summon up the energy and courage to make the ascent to our room. Well, concerns and worries there certainly have been, but with appropriate application we have successfully reached the end of the second day of this adventure. We feel reasonably pleased with our progress. (Today – 20 miles)

Thursday, 17 September

The first sounds we are aware of are those of the occasional vehicle travelling along the street, rue des Religieuses, below our window – we had had a good night. Petit déjeuner did not disappoint; it was generous and nicely presented. The ascent and descent of the ancient spiral staircase is a laborious and stressful process, but with much care and attention we have avoided any mishaps – myself, going first and backwards, when descending, but following when ascending, hopefully available to offer any necessary assistance!! However, we feel privileged to spend some time in this old part of the town. From our window we can appreciate the great variety of designs, styles and heights of the buildings opposite; there is certainly no uniformity. Fortunately, this part of this street did not suffer the degree of destruction which was inflicted upon so many others in June 1944.

Many times have we driven down the N13 heading south and hoping that one day we would visit this nearby ancient and historic town. In the first century the Romans established the town of Alauna and the ruins of hot baths and the site of the theatre are still visible. It was abandoned in the third century and the inhabitants resettled nearby, at VALOGNES. Although destroyed by Viking invaders in the 10th century, as Normans, they rebuilt the town and castle and, none other than William the Conqueror spent part of his youth here. When Edward III invaded France early in the Hundred Years' War, which began in 1338, one of the first towns he took was Valognes; he spent one night here before destroying it. The château suffered sieges and occupation during the War, but survived to be finally demolished in 1689. However, the rebuilt town continued to grow and with the establishment of various administrations it took on a role of 'capital' of the Cotentin region. At the same time it attracted many distinguished families who constructed aristocratic mansions; social life among the nobility was very strong and the town became known as the Versailles of Normandy. Some of these town houses remain to this day.

Following the Revolution in 1789, Valognes lost much of its status and prestige, but survived and its recovery was assisted by the arrival of the railway in 1858. However, much of the town centre, including the parish church and many of the grand town houses, was destroyed in the course of the bombardments of 6, 7 and 8 June 1944 and following days, by the United States Air Force; the purpose of which was to prevent or disrupt the movement of German reinforcements. Sadly, so much of Valognes' heritage was destroyed by its liberators in a matter of hours; its citizens who survived, having lost their homes, faced many months without water, electricity, coal, food and clothing – a life of misery, of cold and of mud! In time, temporary barracks and other facilities were erected, but it took some 20 years to rebuild Valognes! In 1992 its rich heritage earned it the title of 'Ville d'Art et d'Histoire'. The population of the town now is about 8,000.

It seems that the existence of a church was recorded in a charter at the time of William the Conqueror, but Christianity was probably established in this area, centuries earlier. After the Hundred Years' War, the church was rebuilt on the ruins of the roman chapel. It was constructed in the flamboyant Gothic style and was decorated with additions during the 16th and 17th centuries to become a most beautiful church; its cherished Renaissance dome was early 17th century work; from 1574 the square tower contained five bells and in 1866 the spire was raised to a height of 47 metres. An old drawing shows what a splendid building it was; in utter contrast, a photograph after the bombardments of June 1944 depicts a 'horrible carcass'. However, after the war the CHURCH of SAINT MALO was rebuilt; the choir was reconstructed in its original style on what remained of the original building, but the nave was rebuilt in a boldly contemporary style. This church, "symbolises both the permanence of faith throughout the ages and its constant adaptation to its times."

It was a dry morning, if somewhat 'maussade', and we decided to explore some of the town, aided by the three-wheel walker. First, I took some photographs of this street and then, walking slowly along the Rue des Religieuses, we noted some of its interesting features; a warning above No 20 – 'Attention à votre tête!'; the Ecole Sainte-Marie – the ancient Hôtel du Mesnildot de la Grille (XVII–XVIII Siècle), which became a school in 1895, but was requisitioned by the Germans from 1940 and became an internment camp for 300 prisoners – gypsies and homosexuals; the little Pont Sainte Marie over a little river – perhaps it is the Merderet or one of its tributaries – which reveals an interesting view of the backs of ancient houses. At the end of the Rue des Religieuses we join the Rue de l'Officialité where we are at the chevet of l'Eglise Saint-Malo. Some photographs! We continued to the right of the church, avoiding many steps to the left, into the Place Vicq d'Azir. (Félix Vicq-d'Azyr was born here in 1746.) Since leaving the Ecole Sainte-Marie we are now in a vast area which was heavily bombed and largely destroyed.

Our attention was soon drawn to one of those attractive pavement cafes, on the upper side of the Place – Le Versailles Normand – some refreshment would be welcome! It was an opportunity to make use of the toilet facilities and, recognising Margaret's difficulty in negotiating the steps at the entrance, our waiter immediately came to her assistance. We had noticed a nearby road leading up to the Place du Château and we decided to explore. Of course, there is no château, but a very large surface car park. Before the war it was the site of livestock markets, fairs and public festivities. During the war the Germans constructed an underground telephone exchange here, but after the bombardments the square was the site of a provisional church, of prefabricated commercial facilities and of barracks for the homeless survivors. In the corner and raised above the level of the roads is the Office de Tourisme; we found that the office was closed, but it would be open later.

We decided to wait, despite it being a somewhat exposed and bleak location; there were no conventional seats, but some substantial concrete barrier pillars, standing about two feet high, were useful to rest on! When the staff eventually arrived, we were glad we had waited, as they were very helpful and provided us with much information about the history, etc., of the town.

It was now time to make our way back to l'Eglise Saint-Malo. The entrance is through a long porch and the supporting pillars each bear the figure of a prophet. Once inside, we noticed a remarkable memorial – to an American airman who, although wounded on 6 June, he insisted upon flying and was killed on 8 June over Valognes; it is dedicated to him and to his comrades who made the, "sacrifice supreme pour liberer la France". An expression of forgiveness, also? Always ready to take the opportunity to sit for a while, we chose a pew which gave us a good view of this beautiful church; it is difficult to believe that it is only a little more than 50 years old. We noted the rather slender pillars. The organ certainly attracted our attention; the instrument is in an elevated position at the rear of the church, but the console is on the floor.

I was reading how the choir had been restored to its original style – I must take a closer look to see how the remains had been incorporated in the new. As I went step by step focussing on the structure rather than on the floor, I suddenly experienced the sensation of first one foot, then the other, meeting no resistance – I could not prevent myself falling on the hard floor. It was not a very dignified entry – first, I realised that my glasses were on the floor and I was very relieved to find that they were intact for, unfortunately, I had not brought a spare pair with me – I gradually struggled to regain my feet and was pleased to realise that I did not appear to have suffered any particular damage. Slowly I returned to the pew, where Margaret had heard my exclamation and was anxious to attract some attention, but there was no one else in the church. Then, suddenly, the door opened and a lady carrying a music case came in. Margaret immediately tried to explain to her what had happened; she was very concerned and she looked at my left knee which had been grazed – it seemed to be sound! During our ensuing conversation she told us about her health; I'm not now sure whether she had recently had a major operation or was waiting to undergo one but, as she said, her situation is "very grave".

As suggested by the music case, our friend was, indeed, the organist and she was quite excited when I told her that I too had been an organist many years ago. With that news she was particularly pleased to proceed with the purpose for which she had come and, of course, it gave us much pleasure to hear the sounds of the organ. We enjoyed the music for some while, until I felt that we should continue our tour of the town; however, before leaving, I must thank her for the 'recital' and for the concerns she had shown. Taking the most direct route to the organ I attempted to walk between the pews; it was not very wise for, suddenly, I somehow missed my footing and went crashing to the floor again. This time I had not only severely knocked my right thigh and shoulder, but scraped skin off the back of my right hand. Once again, Madame, l'organiste, came to assess the damage. She enquired where we were spending the night and she strongly recommended that I should either see a doctor or visit a pharmacie; we had to agree, as my hand needed a dressing.

We left the church rather hurriedly and were pleased to see the pharmacie sign not far distant. As soon as I asked the young lady assistant for some plasters she invited me to the rear of the counter, where she proceeded to clean the wound, apply an antiseptic solution and carefully applied an appropriate dressing. When I asked how much I had to pay for this attention, she emphasised that the treatment was free. I was extremely grateful for the concern and care she had exercised.

As the afternoon was now passing we did not consider attempting any further walking, but a return to Le Versailles Normand for a cup of coffee would be a good idea. We were received by the same waiter; he was sorry to hear of our misfortune and gave us his sympathetic attention. After some while of viewing the scene and activity of the Place and, not least, some relaxation, we set off on the fairly short distance to Le Relais. As we approached the hotel we were surprised to meet Madame, l'organiste. She had called at the hotel to enquire how I was, but, of course, they knew nothing about our experiences; she was, therefore, very pleased to see us. We found it difficult to find the words to express our gratitude for the concern she had shown – what a gesture! The three-wheel walker had been exceptionally helpful today; however, after returning it to the car we now had to resort entirely to our 'unreliable' and unwilling feet to reach our room. There was still reasonable time for rest before making our way to the restaurant at 19.00. Again, there was no choice of menu, but the meal was excellent and the company very friendly. I am not a connoisseur of food and rarely remember particular menus; the test for me is the degree of satisfaction and enjoyment. Well, the day had not been wholly as we had hoped; however, we had explored the centre of Valognes and visited its church, we had learned something of its past, of life during the years of occupation and about its dreadful suffering at the hands of its liberators in 1944 and, once again, we had experienced much human compassion.

<u>Friday, 18 September</u>

So much has been written about D-Day and the beginning of the Battle of Normandy with regard to the military operations; however, we have learned less about the consequences on the many towns and villages affected and the experiences and plight of the civilian population. After four years of brutal oppression they were then inflicted with death and destruction and, for those who survived, a long period of great hardship and deprivation – in the course of their liberation. We have long hoped to learn more of the experiences of those towns and villages and of their inhabitants. It has, therefore, been an opportunity and a great privilege to spend some time here in historic Valognes, just one of the many towns which suffered such experiences. Perhaps it was appropriate that our visit to Valognes should not be made without some particular personal experience and 'suffering' – certainly, thus it became even more memorable! Following yesterday's falls, thoughts of the wisdom of continuing the journey inevitably occurred; however, the prospect of cancelling all the remaining arrangements we had made, not least of having to arrange an early return to England, quickly nullified such thoughts. We would continue, certainly for the time being, from day to day.

Friday did not dawn with the promise of a lovely day; on the contrary it was maussade et humide.

However, we have petit déjeuner to enjoy – a pleasant interlude before preparing to leave Le Relais. Before we leave we have one important task; after all her diligent care and attention during many months and her approval of us making this journey, we must not disregard the advice and instructions of Nurse Anna-Marie for dressing the ulcer and she had provided us with ample dressings, etc. However, it was not an easy exercise in the restricted facilities and poor light of an ancient inn and, at least once, the 'spider' dressing was more inclined to stick to itself than to the surround of the wound, until I felt the job had been done satisfactorily. Returning all our various items of 'luggage' to the car was a slow and careful process; having completed it successfully, we had a short chat with le propriétaire and we thanked him for the opportunity of un séjour at this ancient hotel. It was 11.50 and raining steadily as we sat in the car studying the map and considering which direction we should take. Our destination for tonight is little more than one hour's journey by the most direct and quickest route, via the N13, but in spite of the poor weather, we wished to explore a little of this area of the Cotentin Peninsula.

The COTENTIN PENINSULA is wholly in the Department of Manche of the Region of Normandy; it is that huge piece of granite thrusting out into the English Channel. In fact, at one time the Marais, or marshlands, at its southern boundary, almost created an island. For many, ourselves included, its port of Cherbourg provides a very convenient and quick route to Brittany and far beyond and it often does not receive the attention it deserves.

We decided to continue along the Rue des Religieuses (we had no choice – it was a one-way street) and then head north-eastwards towards Quettehou. Unfortunately, we first took a right turn assuming that the opposite direction would lead us back into the town and we soon had no choice but to join the N13 which sweeps round to the south of Valognes; however, it was not for long and we escaped at the first opportunity – the exit for Montebourg. Here, it was not difficult to find the D42 towards Quinéville and then we joined the D14, the coastal road to Quettehou. Just a couple of miles further, on the D1, we are in St-Vaast-la-Hougue on the coast. Then we drove some distance towards Barfleur in the north-eastern corner of the Peninsular before returning to Quettehou. It was now time to begin travelling in the direction of our destination for tonight. We continued on the D14, past the junction for Montbourg – at the village of Fontenay-sur-Mer we could have visited the gardens of the Château de Courcy, but the weather was still rather inclement. At St-Marcouf – a reminder of the rural and peaceful nature of this countryside – cows grazing in the adjacent field and, then, two or three on the road itself! At Ravenoville the D15 takes us very conveniently into Ste-Mère-Eglise. Here, it was time to pause, visit the church again and have something to eat – it was now 13.45.

Once again we are making a journey in our Saab 9-5 Auto Estate. We purchased this car in June 2004, having owned a very satisfactory Saab 9000 during the previous 10 years. On noticing its registration (Y304 UGF), Margaret commented that it suggested that this car would be Useful for Going to France. We noted from the Registration Document, that it had previously been owned by Great Percy Productions Ltd – John Smithson. Quite remarkably, and barely one month later, we read an article in Le Monde headed 'John Smithson, un producteur Britannique à Marseille'. It revealed that Darlow Smithson Productions had produced many documentaries for the BBC, Channel Four and Channel Five, but they had now decided to work with producers in France in producing documentaries for TF1, France 2 and Arte for instance and had, consequently, moved to Marseille. Perhaps, therefore, this car was destined to spend the subsequent period of its life traversing the roads of France! For us, 'UGF' has been more than useful; its size, its comfort – at times in temperatures of 30+ – and its reliability has served us well and has taken us safely over many thousands of memorable miles in France.

After well over 60 years of driving the physical aspect of managing and controlling the vehicle – it is an automatic – requires little effort and comes very naturally; however, for a number of years I have had little enthusiasm for doing so, without a very good reason and, exceptionally, when we have been in France! Remarkably, this quite short tour today has again recaptured for us the pleasure and the joy of motoring, which we had not experienced for the past four years.

Here, there is not spectacular scenery, nor exceptionally beautiful countryside views; it is not hilly and barely undulating; a rather ordinary paysage consisting of pastureland, of trees, of hedges, farmsteads and occasional dwellings and, of course, livestock. However, the adequately well signed roads are comfortably negotiated and one is able to leisurely observe the features of the landscape and associate with the quiet peace and calm of the countryside. Why? – because there is such a welcome sparseness of moving vehicles; one is not continuously distracted by having to pay constant attention to the movement, and anticipating the intentions, of other vehicles. Here are the 'quiet roads' we long for! This is France!

However, at times in centuries past this land has seen much activity – in the 11th century William the Conqueror's army preparing for the invasion of England – in the 14th century Edward III passed this way with his army, on foot and on horseback, beginning his invasion of France and the Hundred Years' War – in the 20th century it was occupied by the hostile German Army, much more mobile, to be removed some four years later by the Americans. Indeed, this journey has taken us through a region which encompasses much interest and historic significance from far back in the Middle Ages to the present day.

It was at SAINT-VAAST-LA-HOUGUE – we 'met' St Vaast in Arras last year – on 12 July 1346 that Edward III landed with an army of 12,000 men and proceeded to victory in that most decisive of battles, Crécy, on 26 August 1346. Its fortifications were constructed by Louis XIV's great military engineer, Marshal Vauban, and are a UNESCO World Heritage Site. In the 19th century its jetty and harbour were developed and it was the first harbour to be freed from German occupation in 1944. Today Saint-Vaast-la-Hougue has a population of about 2,000 and is known for its oyster farming and fishing; its large marina accommodates some 700 yachts.

In the year 1066, BARFLEUR was an embarkation port for William the Conqueror's army heading for England and the Battle of Hastings. A significant event in English history of the period occurred nearby in the year 1120. Prince William, the only legitimate son of Henry I, died when the White Ship sank outside the harbour. A period of civil war followed in England, known as the Anarchy, as Henry attempted to install his daughter, Matilda, as his successor. However, on his death in 1135, his nephew, Stephen, like Matilda a grandchild of William the Conqueror, seized the throne. When Stephen died in 1154, the crown passed to Matilda's son Henry II. The new king's father was Geoffrey of Anjou, who habitually wore a sprig of broom (planta genista) in his cap, a name which was adopted by the new dynasty. Thus, began the Plantagenat Dynasty which continued for more than 300 years until the death of Richard III in 1485. Barfleur today is a village of about 650 inhabitants; it is twinned with Lyme Regis and, of course, it has given its name to the Brittany Ferries cruise ship we are travelling on.

Immediately following his arrival in Normandy, on 12 July 1346, Edward III knighted his 16-year-old son, the Black Prince, in the church of QUETTEHOU; there is a plaque in the church commemorating this occasion. Quettehou dates from the period of the Viking invasions of the, perhaps, ninth century. Its name derives from that of chief Ketil who settled on the top of a hill and, in time, Ketil's hill became known as Quettehou. The population of the village is approximately 1,500.

The small town of MONTEBOURG (population 2,000) suffered a similar degree of destruction in June 1944 as Valognes. In their excellent *Battlefield Guide of Normandy* Major and Mrs Holt recount the experience of a 12-year-old girl who was living in Montebourg on D-Day, as she recorded it. Her father was the local doctor, but at Easter he was taken ill and was sent to a sanatorium in the Alps. On 5 June her mother received a telephone call to say that he was dying. Her mother called the ten children still living at home together to brief them as to how they were to look after each other in her absence. Each older child was given direct responsibility for a younger one. She was given responsibility for her seven months old brother. At about five o'clock in the morning of 6 June the replacement doctor was called out to tend wounded soldiers – Allied soldiers – the invasion had started. For a while they stayed in their own home, but it was terrifying. Bombs were falling and there were fires everywhere. A vehicle full of ammunition was hit by a bomb and exploded near their home. They were very frightened. They bundled as much as they could, including cans of milk and – most precious of all – a tiny burnous (a hooded woollen cape) which was kept in a pillowcase, into the baby's pram and took refuge in a nearby abbey. As the battle came to the very courtyard and there was fierce fighting they managed to get to a nearby farm, but it was already full of refugees. They had lost all their possessions – except the little 'burnous' still in its pillowcase. The first Allied soldier she met was an American, which surprised her as she had always expected to be liberated by the British. A poignant commentary of the experiences of a child of the Battle of Normandy!

RAVENOVILLE consists of Ravenoville Bourg and, about one and a quarter miles to the east, Ravenoville Plage; the population is about 250. Near St-Marcouf, are two prominent structures, the CRISBECQ BATTERIE and the AZEVILLE BATTERIE, which formed part of Hitler's Atlantic Wall. This defensive system was constructed by the Todt Organisation using forced labour (slaves) recruited from the occupied countries of Europe. Despite one of these batteries being camouflaged to resemble ancient Norman cottages, with their obvious massive strength and extensive underground network, will they be allowed to remain and ultimately fall into a category similar to that of the fortifications built by Vauban in the seventeenth century? Prior to the war, Fritz Todt was involved in the construction of autobahns and also the Siegfried Line!

We have visited STE-MERE-EGLISE a number of times during the past thirty-five years and we have always found a large number of visitor cars in the spacious car park alongside the village church. Today was no exception, but we were able to park for a modest two euros. This town (present population about 2,500) had, remarkably, passed four years of relatively peaceful occupation; there had been occasional air raids and on the night of 5/6 June a house near the church was set on fire; it was not subjected to the kind of bombardment inflicted on many others. At about 01.40 on the morning of the sixth, some 13,000 American parachutists began to descend on to this area from about 900 aircraft and at 04.30 of that morning Ste-Mere-Eglise became the first town to be liberated. However, for one unfortunate soldier, JOHN STEELE, his parachute became hitched in the tower of the church; he hung there, pretending to be dead, until freed by the Germans; his life was spared and he was taken prisoner, but he soon escaped. In the succeeding years, until his death in 1969, John Steele often visited the town. Today, the experience of this one man is commemorated by his effigy suspended from the tower and by the nearby Auberge John Steele; there are also relevant stained glass windows in the church. Now, more than seventy years after the events, people still flock to this place. Although, during the 24-hours following l'aube du jour-J, some 2,500 French civilians perished at the hands of their liberators in such places as Valonges, Montebourg, Caen, Lisieux, Condé-sur-Noireau, Vire, Flers and Argentan and much of their heritage devastated par une pluie de feu et d'acier, there was, inevitably sorrow, but also such great relief, joy and deep and lasting gratitude felt by the liberated population, expressed by the creation of so many permanent memorials in the form of street names, etc. Here, we have Rue Eisenhower, for example, and, before we left Ste-Mere-Eglise, we enjoyed some welcome refreshment in La Libération!

It is now 16.00 and we must continue and complete our journey for today – to Grandcamp-Maisy. After returning to Ravenoville by the D15, we did not feel that we should spend the time to drive along the D421 to Utah Beach, and we turned right, re-joining the D14. We passed through the villages of Foucarville and St-Germain de Varreville each with a population of about 100. After Ste-Marie-du-Mont the D13 takes us to the N13, which here becomes the E46 as it skirts the bottom of the Marais and the Baie des Veys, a large estuary where four rivers (le Douve, la Taute, la Vire and l'Aure) discharge into the sea. It is a fast section of road, but soon after passing from Manche into the Department of Calvados, we are relieved to be at the exit for ISIGNY-SUR-MER. In no time we are passing close by that symbol of the lush fertile meadows of this area of Normandie – the impressive premises of the Isigny Sainte-Mère Cooperative. Milk processing began here at the beginning of the 19th century and the present Cooperative was formed by the merger, in 1980, of two cooperatives originating in 1909 and 1932. Apart from milk, its products of butter, cream, cheese and skimmed milk are known all over the world and more than half is exported. Isigny is no longer on the coast, but in past times coal from Littry was exported from its port and, following the D-Day landings, Dutch coasters used the port to bring supplies and equipment ashore from large supply ships out at sea. In June 1944 the town suffered much damage, but was mainly rebuilt. Oysters are cultivated nearby in the bay. The town has a population of about 2,750 and is twinned with Kingsbridge.

It is about five to six miles to Grandcamp-Maisy on the D514. After Osmanville we pass, on our left, the access to the MAISY BATTERY. Now here's a fascinating site and experience – built with Russian, Czech and Polish forced labour, it was part of Hitler's Atlantic Wall; surprisingly, it did not appear on D-Day maps! After the war it was buried by the Americans, concealed by nature and lay unknown for some 60 years; that is until a British historian, Gary Sterne, acquired, by chance, an old map, which led to his discovery of the site in 2004. He bought the land and subsequent excavations revealed a vast complex, of buildings, gun platforms, two miles of trenches and even an underground hospital. It was opened to the public in 2007.

GRANDCAMP-MAISY (the two communes merged in 1972) is a fishing port with a population of about 1,800. Grandcamp is of very ancient origin being mentioned in records of 1082. It was heavily bombarded on 6 June 1944 causing enormous damage and suffering; it was liberated at 17.00 hours on 8 June and became a principal port for the supply of materials for the armies. As we approach the sea and bear left into the harbour we recognize the distinctive memorial to the two French bomber squadrons – Guyenne and Tunisie – which were attached to RAF Bomber Command on D-Day, for it incorporates a striking silhouette of one of their Halifax bombers.

Now we can see our hotel, Le Duguesclin, but – and I had forgotten this – there is a 'no entry' sign preventing us from reaching it. We must return past the harbour, turn left and continue through this little town until taking another left turn which takes us to the other end of the sea-front road – Quai Crampon. It was now 17.30 and, after parking outside the hotel, I found the door open, but no immediate signs of activity within. After operating the 'attention bell' a gentleman arrived and I was relieved to know that our reservation had been correctly recorded. I was advised that we could park in the private car park at the rear and that our room would be in the separate building at the far side of the car park – I was given the code for gaining access to the building and the key to the room. The vehicle entrance is narrow, but there was sufficient room in the car park.

Taking some of our luggage, we set off in search of our room. First, up one flight of stairs, then another, until, on the second floor, we found our room. After all the strenuous exertions in negotiating the 17 step spiral staircase at Le Relais, we were not greatly pleased to find that we now have to overcome 34 steps every time we will have to ascend or descend this staircase, while there is probably half of that number leading up to the restaurant level of the hotel itself. However, in our building, at least the staircase is wide, enabling side by side assistance, with a fixed hand-rail and we will be able to progress at our own speed! The room itself is satisfactory and comfortable with a view of the rear of the hotel and of the car park below! Having established ourselves we are looking forward to a meal and a pleasant evening in the restaurant. At about 19.00 we began to make our way down the staircase, into the car park and climbed the somewhat more narrow stairs and then individual steps of the hotel and into the restaurant.

We have stayed at this hotel before and, as we entered the large and long room it was very familiar. It is a lovely setting, on the first floor well above the road level, its many and large windows providing a wonderful view of a large expanse of the sea. We were warmly welcomed and invited to take a seat alongside one of the windows. We noticed that, in the centre of the restaurant, a number of tables had been arranged together across the width of the room to form a single large table. Obviously, this was to be the scene of the celebration of a special event. Gradually, the guests, of at least three generations, began to arrive, greeting one another in that warm and affectionate manner in the way they do in this country. Soon it became evident that the occasion was the celebration of the birthday of the senior member of the family – the father. There was much animated and lively conversation – clearly a happy and joyful gathering. However, the group was not obtrusive, rather, the atmosphere it created permeated throughout the restaurant. How nice it was to be associated in this way with a French family occasion. Towards the end of their celebrations, fireworks attracted the attention of us all.

Yes, we did have a meal. So far as I recall it consisted of entrecôte, vegetables, including chips in a basket, accompanied with a small glass of wine and followed by une glace. There were quite a few other couples and groups in the restaurant all, no doubt, enjoying their own special occasion. In particular, we were conscious of a couple immediately behind me talking together quite a lot during the evening. Guests were beginning to leave and we too decided that, after perhaps about three hours, we should, at least, begin to make our way back to our room. As we did so, we felt it would be courteous to wish the couple behind us 'bonne nuit'. They were delighted that we did so and thus began quite a long conversation.

They were so pleased to know that we were English and that we love France and, as we have often experienced, were so interested to know that we have visited their country many times. The gentleman told us that he was previously in Paris, but emphasized, with pride, that he originates from Alsace. (Alsace is the small cultural and historical region in the far east of the country and borders Germany and Switzerland. Now, from 2016, it is part of the Region of Grand Est) On the other hand, his wife is proud of her Norman background. We were all somewhat reluctant to bring our conversation to an end, but we succeeded in doing so with a final 'bonne nuit'. While talking to this couple another couple sitting quietly in the corner were provided with a firework display – they too had something to celebrate!

By now more guests had left and we too, slowly made our way cautiously and carefully down the stairs, across the car park and successfully negotiated the entrance to our building, to climb the 34 steps to the comfort of our room. What a varied and enjoyable day it has been – awaking in an ancient inn to a maussade (gloomy) outlook, then a thoroughly pleasant and interesting drive, revealing so much history and reviving many memories, and ending in the light and warmth of the restaurant welcome and in the presence of a happy family gathering, followed by a most interesting and friendly personal conversation. (Today – 70 miles)

A demain!

Saturday, 19 September

'Tis le week-end here in France (and in England too!) – one of the words which have found their way into the French vocabulary. However, these two days, particularly Sunday, are experienced somewhat differently in France.

For instance, there is a welcome absence of heavy goods vehicles on the roads – they are prohibited and we have often seen lorries parked on waste land during weekends. Many petrol stations will be closed, particularly on Sunday and on D (departmental) roads and some N (national) roads. Many restaurants and hotels are closed, certainly during part of the weekend – we recall a number of occasions when, with the code of access provided, we have been welcome to spend a night in a seemingly otherwise empty hotel, accepting that there would be no service of food available! Also, here there is no widespread 'Sunday shopping'.

In France it is, rather, a time for re-creation – for relaxation, for leisure and pleasure; for visiting places of interest – on one weekend in September of every year (Les Journées du Patrimoine) all sites of historic and cultural interest are open to the public free of charge; it is a time for walking, for cycling – we have often seen families with young children cycling on the quiet roads. The contrasts are emphasized in the nature of television programmes too. On Sunday mornings the main state television channel – France 2 – broadcasts a programme entitled *Le Jour du Seigneur,* which, every week includes a live presentation of la messe. I have already explained that it was introduced in October 1949 and has continued to this day.

So, how are we going to spend this weekend in France? Well, from our window we see that it is a clear and sunny morning, and, in fact, we have a very minute view of the sea, just visible between the buildings which separate us from it. However, on reaching the restaurant and returning to the table we had occupied during the previous evening, we have a splendid panorama – a wide expanse of calm sea and to our left the eastern coast of the Cotentin peninsular and, in the distance, will be one of the D-Day landing beaches – Utah Beach. The atmosphere this morning is somewhat different, relaxed and informal, compared with that of the evening meal. Petit déjeuner is available in a buffet style over quite a long period during the weekend, although a member of staff is available to advise and assist if help is needed, such as how to operate the orange crushing machine and kindly carrying drinks, etc., to our table.

After leisurely enjoying our breakfast, we returned to our room and decided that we would spend our day in Grandcamp Maisy. Making use of the three-wheel walker, we walked the very short distance towards the harbour's seaward entrance, where a seat beckoned. It was not a particularly comfortable seat, solidly constructed in concrete to withstand the ravages of coastal storms rather than to resist vandalism, I would think. However, it was such a lovely day and such a peaceful, serene and tranquil setting that we spent a considerable time here. For much of the time the silence was only disturbed by the splashing of the water against the harbour walls as a boat silently made its way out to the open sea.

Then, a number of tiny yachts with distinctive coloured emblems began to assemble some distance from the shore, making an attractive sight – perhaps it was some kind of competition! After a while I returned to the car to fetch some welcome refreshments. Midst this heavenly tranquillity one could not begin to imagine the scene that morning of 6 June 1944 – the hundreds of warships at sea, the hundreds of aircraft flying overhead, the incessant noise of gunfire and of bombs – simply a hell on earth. It must have been terrifying for those civilians who were not able to escape and many did not survive. Of course, for us at home these events prompted immense interest, excitement and optimism. Perhaps we could look forward to the end of the war, the restrictions, the rationing, the tyranny and destruction – that Europe could live in PEACE as ONE

Eventually, we felt we should seek rather more physical exertion and we walked past the harbour on our right and the several fish restaurants on our left and turned left into Rue Aristide Briand in the direction of Centre Ville. This road is closed on market day (Tuesday?), but it is a pleasant walk today with very little traffic. Soon we spot the familiar sign of a Pharmacie (Pharmacie Besnard, 72 Rue Aristide Briand) and I immediately thought it may be an opportunity to purchase some dressings for my injured hand. Fortunately, it was open and on explaining the circumstances to the young lady she immediately decided that she should examine the wound. She did so with great care and exclaimed "it is still bleeding". However, having cleaned and treated the wound she was happy to renew the dressing and I purchased a supply of dressings for future use. Again, there was no charge for the excellent attention I had received.

As the street broadens out, it reveals a village-like scene. Although of a character of bygone years, many buildings are of an elegantly smart and clean complexion.

No doubt much rebuilding was carried out after 1945 and, in any case, these properties, sheltered and facing inland, have not become 'weathered' like those looking out to sea. It is as if the houses have been set back to accommodate this striking profusion of trees of different sizes, of shrubs and of varied plants providing a splendid display of colour – on window sills, in tubs, on railings and on lamp standards, indeed, everywhere, it seems. What an attractive prospect. It is all the more remarkable considering that not far behind these houses enclosing such colour and warmth, are the buildings of a more austere appearance facing the varying weather and climatic conditions of the English Channel! We did not fail to notice one particular building – it was 'La P'tite Frincale Crêperie'. How opportune – a crêpe would be most welcome at this time. It was open and we were welcome.

We enjoyed the refreshment and, particularly, the opportunity to sit for a while and, not least, the inevitable conversation. Rather reluctantly we resumed our walk which soon took us to re-join the Quai Crampon towards its eastern end. Although it was now late afternoon, the sun was maintaining a comfortable temperature as we walked slowly towards our hotel, while appreciating the totally different scenery than that which we had just left behind. On approaching Le Duguesclin, our thoughts soon turned to the prospect of our evening meal.

We have not only sojourned at Le DUGUESCLIN in the past, but we have driven along the sea front road on a number of occasions, always casting an envious eye up at the restaurant windows. Also, it was the first hotel at which we sought accommodation on our first family holiday in France – on 17 July 1979; unfortunately, there was only one room available! Perhaps it is not surprising, therefore, that we have had an interest in the history of this hotel.

In June 2010, when driving along the N88, midway between Mende and Langogne, over the higher regions of the Department of Lozère, in the deep south, in the Region of Auvergne (after 2016 – new Region of Occitanie) we passed close by Châteauneuf-de-Randon and we noticed on our map a reference to a 'Tour des Anglais'. We did not feel that we had sufficient time to make a worthwhile short detour, but we subsequently learned that the Battle of Châteauneuf-de-Randon took place in 1380, during the Hundred Years War. The English garrison commanded by De Ros was besieged by the French under, one Bertrand du Guesclin; the English surrendered on 4 July 1380. Is there a link with the hotel we know on the coast of Normandy?

With grateful thanks for information provided by Monsieur, le propriétaire, we now know that Bertrand du Guesclin was born at la Motte Broons near Dinan in Brittany in 1320. He was a distinguished warrior who became connétable – supreme commander of the French armies. He was the complete chevalier, a popular hero who incarnated one of the first patriotic manifestations of the kingdom of France. Bertrand du Guesclin came to Normandy and established his camp at Maisy; moreover, vestiges of his tower can still be seen. The Comte de Bayeux and Bertrand du Guesclin maintained a relationship which explains his sojourn at Maisy.

Bertrand du Guesclin was engaged in several campaigns, but he contracted an illness during the siege of Châteauneuf-de-Randon and died on 13 July 1380; he was buried at Châteauneuf-de-Randon. (I have also read that his remains were interred in the tomb of the Kings of France at the Cathédrale de Saint-Denis in Paris and his heart at the Basilica of Saint-Sauveur at Dinan, but we have never visited these churches.) Apparently, everywhere he established a base, an establishment carries his name; this hotel has that distinction.

At the beginning of the 20th century Le Duguesclin was a Maison de Maître. In 1928 it became a Hôtel-Restaurant-Dancing and in 1932 it appeared in the Guide Michelin for the first time.

The three-wheel walker has been a great asset today, but we must now hasten to return it to the car; then make a brief visit to our room before negotiating the many steps leading to our window table in the restaurant, with its splendid grandstand view of la mer. Splendid it is, indeed, at this time, as day slowly and reluctantly succumbs to night – the period of crépuscule (twilight). We enjoyed our meal last evening and felt that we could do little better than to repeat the order – except that we would advance to un filet de boeuf (French), which together with frites in a basket and mixed vegetables, followed by une glace, all accompanied by a small glass of red wine, completed an excellent repas. We did not have the celebratory atmosphere, the excitement, of yesterday, but it was certainly pleasant and friendly. As soon as we began to leave the restaurant Monsieur approached; he took Margaret's arm to help her down the stairs, across the car-park and saw us safely inside our building. What a kind spontaneous gesture! Today has not been a particularly eventful one, more relaxed and somewhat restful, yet nonetheless memorable. (Mileage - Nil)

Sunday, 20 September

Dimanche – the second day of 'le week-end' and how different it is than that which is familiar en Angleterre. Again, it is a beautiful morning with the promise of a lovely day ahead. It is surely an opportunity to explore a little of an area we have not visited, the Parc Natural Régional des Marais du Cotentin et du Bessin.

Here, petit déjeuner is not to be regarded as a routine episode, but as an overture to a new day, a setting and atmosphere to be absorbed and appreciated and nourishment to be enjoyed, to be prepared in mind and body for the new day. As we left the restaurant, Madame came to us to say that they had realised that it was difficult for Margaret to frequently ascend and descend the flights of stairs in the detached building and, consequently, they would like to offer us a room in the hotel building. Although the charges for such rooms were higher, we would not be required to pay an additional sum. All we need do was, gather our belongings together in our room and a member of the staff would transfer them to room seven during the day. We expressed our appreciation for this gesture.

Although, at this time, we don't wish to give thought to our return journey to Poole, it has occurred to me that we should have made advance arrangements for the same service of personal assistance as we received on the outward crossing and that I should have contacted Brittany Ferries to do so. Madame offered me the use of her telephone and, in fact, established contact with the company offices in Cherbourg for me. I was then able to talk to a very helpful lady who, having established the relevant details, assured me that the full service for the disabled would be available for us on our arrival at the port. It was a great relief and comfort to know that we could look forward to this excellent service.

How irritating it is, how annoying, when one of those vital components of personal clothing fails to function when its services are urgently required, when it chooses to abandon its roots. I was not equipped to deal with such an event and, somehow, I will have to continue without it! That was not the only misfortune this morning, for shortly afterwards a shoelace broke – for this, I was prepared. Fortunately, these events did not delay us greatly, but because of the slow process of preparing ourselves and making other arrangements, etc., it was 12.50 when we left the hotel.

We set off from the car park by an exit which leads directly on to Rue Aristide Briand and then joined the D514 for Isigny-sur-Mer, from here the D5, the D11 and the D8 led us into St-JEAN-de-DAYE. We are familiar with this village of about 600 inhabitants, having driven through many times on the N174 towards St Lo, en route from Cherbourg to Vire. However, today we wondered if there might be a possibility of having something to eat here. We stopped, first on one side of the road, then the other, but there was little sign of life and all the premises appeared to be closed – until we left the car to look through the door of what might be a bar or a salon de thé; we could see two or three people sitting at a table. We ventured inside and asked if they could offer us some refreshment – the choice would be very limited, perhaps no more than un gateau – that, with a drink, would be very welcome, merci! It was evident that the premises were shortly to close and we thanked Madame for the hospitality.

Nearby is the CHATEAU de la RIVIERE, a building with an interesting history. Constructed from the 11th century, it was the possession of the grandson of Odon, Bishop of Bayeux (half-brother of William the Conqueror). It ceased to be inhabited in 1818. In 1944 it was seriously damaged by the Germans after using it for the storage of 'ammunitions'. However, it was subsequently acquired and used by several owners, but is now a sanctuary for cigognes (storks) and there is no access to the interior. It is now classified as 'ruinè'. In fact, some years ago we spent a night in this ancient building – a night which is remembered because the roof leaked and we had to move the bed to avoid getting wet!

Our Michelin map tells us that there is a 'viewpoint' in the region of the village of Graignes-Mesnil-Angot – a good place for a general view of the marais, we thought, and so we left St-Jean-de-Daye in a westward direction. We have since learned that, in 1944, there was an airfield in this area, operated by the US Army Air Force. It seems that the runway was the straight stretch of the road D389 towards Mesnil-Véneron. Perhaps we drove along that 'runway', but I cannot be certain! As we approached Graignes-Mesnil-Angot (merged in 2007) we were guided by a sign to the 'Memorial'. We did not know of the wartime events in the village of Graignes or the significance of the Memorial. As the road reached its highest point, there, above us, were the remains of a church and a cimetière all securely enclosed and surrounded by a substantial stone wall; but where is the 'view-point'?

We continued, but immediately the road began to descend; it was narrow and there was no immediate opportunity to turn around. Why not carry on and make a short circular tour of the marais? This we did; however, being on the same level, it was difficult to comprehend the extent and vastness of this natural region. When we reached the Memorial for the second time we did not hesitate to park the car; we climbed the steps to enter the large cemetery. On the inside of the perimeter wall there is a continuous pathway loosely surfaced in fairly large gravel; it is a long distance to walk round and Margaret found it increasingly uncomfortable to do so on the uneven surface; however, being about halfway round, we had little choice but to continue. We are very glad we did so, as we eventually came to a gateway in the wall with access to an excellent viewing platform. Although I did so, Margaret did not feel able to climb down the short, but uneven, bank and up into the platform; however, she had a good view from inside the wall. Whereas, for the first part of this 'walk' we were looking down on to a typical rural scene of a farmstead, etc., here, before us, were spectacular views of the vast PARC REGIONAL DES MARAIS DU COTENTIN et du BESSIN – a peaceful expanse (1,480 square kilometres) of wetland, moors and hedgerows, full of birds and extending across the base of the peninsular; it is a protected nature park. We spent some time in the cemetery, contemplating on the scene – the tombstones, the memorials and the remains of the church. Well, we had found the viewpoint but, unfortunately, we left without being aware of the events which gave rise to the Memorial.

The BATTLE OF GRAIGNES is not very prominent in the history of the Normandy Campaign; however, it was a gruesome episode which left a permanent scar on the village. In the very early hours of Tuesday, 6 June 1944, 12 planeloads of American paratroopers were dropped some 15 miles from their drop zone, near Ste-Mère-Eglise, and thus scattered over the flooded marshes near Graignes. Many drowned by the weight of their equipment, but those who survived, scattered and isolated, identified in the moonlight, that most recognisable of village buildings – the parish church. Gradually, more and more reached this focal point and 48 hours later 14 officers and 168 men had struggled into the village. Commanded by Major Charles Johnson and being far inside enemy territory, they decided to establish themselves and to defend the village. On the morning of 7 June the Mayor, Alphonse Voydie, called a meeting which was attended by almost every man, woman and child of the village; it was unanimously agreed to assist the Americans, despite the inevitable consequences if caught – execution. Villagers searched the marshes to recover considerable quantities of weapons and equipment and to provide much needed food for the soldiers. From 8 June there were sporadic skirmishes with the enemy, mainly reconnaissance patrols, and several Germans were killed. However, during the course of the afternoon of Sunday, 11 June, Graignes was subject to a heavy bombardment and, in the evening, a final assault by some 2,000 men of the 17th SS Panzer Division. The Americans, with Major Johnson now dead, could hold out no longer – the battle had been lost. However, 150 paratroopers escaped and some civilians also. Subsequently, the Germans ransacked the village and carried out a merciless massacre of a number of American prisoners and many villagers, including the parish priest; they then destroyed most of the village, including the eight centuries old church.

Graignes is the third village we have visited which suffered an indiscriminate and brutal massacre and ruthless destruction following D-Day. The others are Oradour-sur-Glane, Haute-Vienne, near Saint-Junien (10 June 1944) and Maillé, Indre-et-Loire, near Chinon (25 August 1944).

We returned to Grandcamp-Maisy via Saint-Jean-de-Daye and Isigny-sur-Mer and reached Le Duguesclin at 17.40. We were pleased to remember that we had far fewer stairs to climb to reach our new room (No 7) and we managed well. Our belongings had been transferred as promised and we are now on the floor above the restaurant and we have a sea view – splendid! As 19.00 approached we made our way down to the restaurant; we spent little time studying the menu as we could not resist the opportunity to enjoy an identical meal to that which we had yesterday and at 'our' table. A fitting end to an interesting day! (58 miles)

Monday, 21 September

We are nearing the end of our stay at Le Duguesclin, but it will be a leisurely departure as it is a fairly short distance to the next destination on our journey; also, we will be spending another night here next week when returning to Cherbourg. In contrast to the past two days the weather this morning is somewhat overcast; however, it does not greatly detract from the panorama from the restaurant windows as we enjoy our petit déjeuner. In fact, it was 11.50 when we eventually left the hotel.

We soon re-joined the D514 which hugs the coast of Calvados; we passed the turning for the famous Pointe du Hoc, but at the little commune of Vierville-sur-Mer (population about 250) we drove down to the beach road – D517 – of OMAHA BEACH. We soon found a convenient spot to park and we sat in the car at this historic site for a considerable time. Nearby, and at the western end of Omaha Beach, is the National Guard Memorial. On D-Day Omaha was divided into two sections, DOG, where we are and EASY to the east. The plans were that an Infantry Regiment and supporting forces, of the United States 29th Division would establish a foothold on DOG and proceed to clear the area beyond the N13 and to Isigny to the west. A similar force of the 1st Division would embark on EASY and advance eastwards to link up with the British Army at Port-en-Bessin. By the end of 6 June it was expected that a bridgehead some 16 miles wide and five miles deep would have been established. In fact, by nightfall on that first day the bridgehead was barely the length of the beach and less than one mile deep. In unexpected storm conditions many soldiers failed to reach the beach; those who did so had to climb the cliff-like slopes overlooking the beach, negotiate the barbed wire and overcome the German defences. They suffered very heavy losses in doing so and for many of the young Americans their D-Day was very brief. Many were from a Pals Battalion and a small American town of 3,000 inhabitants lost 23 men on D-Day, including three sets of brothers. It was here on DOG Green that the heaviest casualties, perhaps of the entire invasion coastline, were suffered; it features in the film '*Saving Private Ryan*'.

Eventually, and slowly, we drove eastwards – the beach on our left and, on our right, attractive dwellings positioned on the low sea-facing cliffs – a peaceful scene now! At the end of Dog Green, Les Moulins, we parked in the spacious car park to view the impressive memorials and the fascinating sail-like structures and pillars rising out of the sand and of which I would like to know more. There are information panels which include a poem by Jean, which ends:

> *To those brave men*
> *A ship of iron,*
> *time – defying in our thoughts*
> *on each side, Hope and Fraternity*
> *and, central, Liberty dearly bought.*
> *In the whole, a breath of history*
> *murmurs, "Hold fast our Liberty".*

So far as I am aware, it was in this area that the second artificial harbour was erected, but it was severely damaged by a violent storm on 19 June and, unlike that at Arromanches, it could not be repaired – apparently vestiges are still visible at low tide.

We did not continue into EASY Red – we recall driving along the pebbles of this section of Omaha with George and Samuel some years ago and of climbing the cliffs to reach certain memorials – of course, we brought home some souvenir pebbles! Instead, we continued to re-join the D514 at St-Laurent-sur-Mer (population 250).

It is just a short distance to Colleville-sur-Mer and the site of the NORMANDY AMERICAN CEMETERY. Situated high above Omaha Beach, where many of them died, it contains the graves of 9,387 soldiers and the names of 1,557, who have no known grave. We have visited this cemetery several times and one cannot pass by without recalling its grandeur and its emotional solemnity, its inspirational design, its expansive layout and, always, its immaculate presentation. In the car park there is a message for the visitor:

> *Look how many of them there were*
> *Look how young they were*
> *They died for your freedom*
> *Hold back your tears and be silent.*

Soon, we reach PORT-en-BESSIN, a pretty little harbour-village – Françoise Sagan described it as 'le petit Saint-Tropez Normand'. It was an important harbour in past centuries – at the time of the Romans and Normans – and Vauban built a tower here in 1694. It was an important harbour too and a key target for the Allies in 1944. However, it would have been suicidal to attack the heavily defended port from the sea. Therefore, on 6 June 1944 No 47 Royal Marine Commando, 420 mainly young men of 18 to 22 years of age, landed at Le Hamel east of Arromanches; they lost 76 men, as well as weapons, in reaching the shore, but the remainder, carrying some 90lb of weapons, etc., each, worked and fought their way some ten miles westward along the coast to attack Port-en-Bessin from inland. Towards the end of the next day they discovered an undefended pathway to the German port defences and in commando style, shouting and firing, they stormed the enemy bunker – the Germans surrendered. By nightfall on 7 June they had liberated the village – they had achieved their objective. This must have been one of the greatest feats of endurance, bravery and suffering of the entire Normandy Campaign. They had created a link between the British 50th Division on GOLD BEACH and the US First Division on OMAHA BEACH and, remarkably, within a week the port was handling more than 1,000 tons of vital supplies each day. Importantly, it was a vital stage in establishing PLUTO (Pipe Line Under The Ocean), the facility for supplying the armies with vital supplies of petrol from England. It is said that the idea of PLUTO was that of Lord Louis Moutbatten! Port-en-Bessin is now one of the most important and modern fishing ports of France. Since the 1940s the population has surprisingly risen and then fallen – 1946 – 1,314; 1975 – 2,388; 2008 – 2,080. In the past we have looked at the details of apartments being constructed here! Port-en-Bessin is well worth a visit!

Only about five kilometres further along the D514, through Commes, we come to Longues-sur-Mer and, at the traffic lights at the crossroads, we turn left to drive the short distance to the site of the Longues (le Chaos) Battery – another section of Hitler's Atlantic Wall. This is not our first visit here and we decided not to attempt to walk to the actual battery, but we parked the car as there is a boutique and a convenient toilet nearby!

Back to the D514, then, as we leave Tracy-sur-Mer we meet the roundabout at the junction with the D516 for Bayeux. Turning left and descending gently, still on the D514, the familiar and nostalgic sight of the remains of the Mulberry Harbour emerges – it is Arromanches. Bearing right we continue to the car park on our left, where we have parked so many, many times – the first occasion being on 17 July 1979 – and on our right is the bureau de poste and the parking spaces for coaches. It is now 15.20 and we can think of nothing better at present than a visit to our favourite restaurant – Brasserie Au 6 Juin. The free car park is parallel with, and open to, the Boulevard Gilbert Longues which leads down to the sea front – on the opposite side is the convenient little supermarket and then l'école maternelle, where we have often watched the young children in their supervised activities. Leaving the car park, with the aid of the three-wheel walker, and crossing the road from the right, we join the pavement which, we are pleased to find, has been resurfaced since we were last here. There are then, on our right, one or two private dwellings, a small car repair workshop and a small military memorabilia store. Next is a favourite patisserie, before the wheelchair side entrance to the restaurant. AU 6

JUIN is a popular meeting and eating place of the many visitors of different nationalities who constantly visit Arromanches; the staff are efficient and friendly and it generates a wonderful atmosphere and we have enjoyed many hours here absorbing the animated conversation of the different languages and also, when at a window table, observing the seemingly endless stream of visitors along the pedestrianised rue Marechal Joffre. Often, we have exchanged comments and sometimes joined in conversation with visitors at nearby tables. It is an entire experience. I do not recall what we had to eat on this occasion, but quite probably it was ham, egg and chips or something of that nature.

The Maison Jeanne family enterprise was established in 1963 and in past years we have found a senior lady at the till, however, today we have not seen her and a very courteous and friendly gentleman is accepting the payments. Has the business changed hands, or perhaps our lady has retired! It is now 17.35; we have enjoyed our meal and the couple of hours in which to revive and enhance our memories of this special place. Incidentally, the background of the chosen name of the restaurant is explained on a small leaflet which is presented with the receipt!

ARROMANCHES is now a small tourist town of about 600 inhabitants – in June 1944 it was the site of one of the two artificial harbours, codenamed Mulberry, and it is proudly referred to as Port Winston. However, Arromanches was not attacked from the sea, but was liberated on the afternoon of D-Day by men of the Royal Hampshire Regiment, commanded by General

Sir Alexander Stanier, who had landed further east on Gold Beach and descended upon the German defenders from the heights of St Come. Consequently, there was very little damage to the buildings in the town, but six civilians died. Despite a severe storm on 19 June, which lasted three days, during the first 100 days of its operation the Mulberry Harbour had handled 2.5 million men, 500,000 vehicles and four million tons of materials. The conception and creation of the artificial harbour was an ingenious and incredible enterprise. Arromanches possesses two excellent museums – le Musee du Débarquement, on the sea front, and le Cinema Circulaire 360*, up the hill at Come.

Over many years we have visited Arromanches very many times – with its easily accessible and free car park, the short pleasant walk down into the busy traffic free Rue Marechal Joffre offering restaurants, refreshment bars and shops, leading into the attractive compact open sea front with a further car park and many memorials, all enclosed by inviting hotels, restaurants and shops and, on its eastern side, the excellent museum; on the beach and out at sea are the permanent reminders of that momentous event in 1944 and, not least, its respectful and reverential atmosphere. Arromanches has long been a favourite place of ours.

Returning to the car park is an easy walk and we leave Arromanches in the direction of Ryes. On leaving Ryes we remember to take a left turn on to the D127, then to cross the D112 by the grain store, to turn right (towards Bayeux) on to D12 and, after a few hundred yards, to take the left turn signed for Vienne-en-Bessin.

Soon we see the welcome sign 'Ferme des Châtaigniers' on our left. This access to the farm and to a number of private dwellings, we would describe as 'single track and not made up'. However, there is an easy entrance into an adequate parking area surrounded by the farm buildings and property. This is a journey of five miles and we rarely meet more than two or three other vehicles; in fact, later in the evening we are likely to see more rabbits than cars on the road! Although it is now raining, we are pleased to arrive at this peaceful Normandy haven again and we look forward to meeting the owner, Fabienne. Unfortunately, Fabienne is nowhere to be seen! However, we do not have to wait long before Fabienne arrives, explaining that she has joined a choir in Bayeux – perhaps we shall hear more about this! We receive the usual warm and friendly welcome and Fabienne assists us up the concrete staircase, along the passageway, with its unforgettable view of her fields and cows, and into the room, with its typical ceiling beams, which we have occupied in past years and which overlooks the parking area, etc. We feel at home! (32 miles)

Tuesday, 22 September

Ten to fifteen years ago we visited a number of gites in this Calvados Department with a view, in particular, to finding accommodation which would be suitable for us to give our grandsons an experience of France and French life. We found nothing better than a living farm, in a small village but, at the same time, adjacent to open farmland – we found la Ferme des Châtaigniers and we met Fabienne and her, then, very young daughter, Amandine. In addition, it was only five miles from one of the notable sites of the D-Day landings – Arromanches. The property offered not only a gite, but also chambre d'hôte. Since that time, we have enjoyed memorable weeks here with George and Samuel and made many visits ourselves. Now, we could not make what may well be our last visit to Normandy and France without spending a few days here in Vienne-en-Bessin.

LA FERME des CHATAIGNIERS comprises a number of stone built buildings of a type traditional of the Bessin and which I believe are about 200 years old. The farm lands of 60 hectares (about 150 acres) are used for the breeding of (at present 24) Charolaise beef cattle and the production of, in addition to meat, wheat and maize.

The BESSIN is an extensive, peaceful and undulating region of rich pastures and marshlands with historical origins. It corresponds to the territory of the ancient tribe of Gaul, the Bajocasses, who gave their name to its chief town, Bayeux. The Bessin corresponds to the diocese of Bayeux, prior to the revolution. One of the features of the Bessin is the bocage, the hedgerow farmland which the allied armies had such difficulty in conquering in 1944.

Fabienne is very kind as she tolerates our late arrival for petit déjeuner – normally after other guests have left – for there is always a good selection of confitures on the turntable, cartons of juice and yoghurts still available, although we may have to wait for fresh coffee to be made. This morning we relax and linger at the large solid table in this spacious room with inviting bookcases and also with windows on each side and which is underneath our room. When Fabienne is free she joins us and we have the opportunity of a long and interesting conversation. She well remembers the visits of George and Samuel and is interested to hear of their progress. We are pleased to learn of Amandine's progress at College (?), of her clarinet playing and to learn that she is now studying English and Chinese! Not surprisingly, we took the opportunity of asking if she has any recollections of personal family memories of the events of the 6 June 1944.

Yes, she does, and she told us that on that night/day her Dad was at Longues-sur-Mer and only two kilometres from the sea. He has described the experience as, "The night was like day" and "The sea was black". Fabienne also recalls her aunt telling her of sitting on the knees of liberating British soldiers – no doubt there are photographs! That was a very interesting conversation and we still haven't heard more about the choir, but we must not take up more of her time this morning. Fabienne has many responsibilities, the management of the farm – she has an assistant – and the gite and chambre d'hôte; there are also rabbits, cats and a dog to be looked after and, not least, the care of her father who is about the same age as myself and who now lives with her. Our priority now is to renew the dressings on Margaret's ankle and my hand.

Early rain had cleared when we eventually set off from la ferme and we head, as we have so often done, across the open plains of Bessin in the direction of Arromanches. There is only one village between Vienne-en-Bessin and Aromanches – Ryes. RYES is a commune of about 500 inhabitants; in 1060 it was referred to as Rigia, when it was the seat of Hubert, a vassal of the Duke of Normandy. From 1899 until 1932 a 60cm gauge railroad between Courseulles and Bayeux passed through Ryes with a branch from Ryes to Arromanches. Much of the church of Saint Martin is of the Roman style and dates from the early 12th century. It was classified as a Monument Historique in 1840.

We cannot resist pulling in at the entrance to this church to read again of the remarkable episode in the life of one of the outstanding characters of all history. He was born in 1027 and from the time that he succeeded his father, at the age of eight, William, Duke of Normandy faced opposition, in particular, from his uncles and cousins on the grounds of his illegitimacy. Early in 1047 and aged about 20 he was in Valonges, (where we were last week) when he had word of a plot to assassinate him. In the middle of a winter's night he fled southwards on horseback in an attempt to reach the safety of his castle at Falaise. It must have been a difficult, uncertain and perilous journey. His route took him through Asnelles and brought him here to Ryes – it became known as 'la Sente au Batard' (William the bastard's pathway). At Ryes he visited his friend Hubert, who had a fresh horse saddled for him and provided an escort to accompany him on the rest of his journey. He reached Falaise successfully and, subsequently, became WILLIAM the CONQUEROR and KING of ENGLAND. If the young William had not survived this determined plot, how differently our history would have been written!

When we have been in Normandy together, George and Samuel always welcomed the opportunity of visiting a salon de thé pour une tasse de thé. One day in the centre of Bayeux we were passing such an establishment – it was also a patisserie – and we decided to go in. It was quite small and there was only one other customer, a gentleman. As we discussed how to arrange four chairs around a table, he did not hesitate to speak to us – in English. Almost his first words were, "What part of England do you come from?". When we are asked such a question, particularly in France, we do not respond by saying Trowbridge or Radstock, but invariably the name of Bath is instantly recognised. Yes, he knew Bath. We then mentioned Radstock which, to our surprise, he also knew and, indeed, Midsomer Norton. In fact, he was quite familiar with our area, for his two sons, now in their forties, were educated at Downside School.

This was an introduction to a most interesting and friendly conversation. Our friend introduced himself as CHARLES HARGROVE. He told us that he had lived in Leeds, but he did not speak of that city with any great affection. He told us too that he now lives in France with a home in Paris and another nearby in, I suspect, Asnelles. His wife is French and her father was a contemporary of eminent French composers such as, I believe, Gabriel Faure. We learned that he had landed in France on D-Day, 6 June 1944. After the war he had been *The Times* correspondent in Paris. We gathered that, currently, he is active in French public life. It had been a most interesting meeting and conversation and a privilege to meet, so informally, such a distinguished yet friendly gentleman. We left the Salon de Thé at the same time and, being so absorbed in the conversation, I almost forget to pay for the cups of tea we had enjoyed.

As we were returning to the street, our friend, for that is what he had become, said, "By the way I have written a book – *A Gentleman of the Times* – but it is in French" and he added that we might be able to buy a copy at the nearby bookshop. We hastened to the shop but, unfortunately, they did not have a copy in stock. Needless to say, soon after our return home we were pleased to acquire a copy. Since that chance meeting we have seen Charles Hargrove on the television taking part in D-Day anniversary celebrations in Ste-Mere-Eglise and we have been interested to read more about his life and, sadly, of his death towards the end of 2014.

Charles Hargrove was born in Genoa in 1922 of a French mother and an English father. He was educated in Paris and became trilingual in English, French and Italian before gaining a degree at Cambridge. On enlisting in the army his language skills were to be of great value. In the early morning of 6 June 1944 he landed at Asnelles on 'Jig' sector of Gold Beach with 231st Infantry Brigade (known as the Malta Brigade) and alongside No 47 Royal Marine Commando. In the face of very fierce German defending he drove his jeep through shallow water on to the inhospitable and dangerous beach; he was transporting the brigade commander, Brigadier Alexander Stanier and Maurice Schumann, a close aide of Charles de Gaulle, who had become known as the 'Voice of France' for his BBC radio broadcasts. Maurice Schumann subsequently became French foreign minister. After his distinguished wartime service, Charles Hargrove married a French girl and they eventually made their home in Paris and Asnelles, where he was made an honorary citizen. He had had a distinguished journalistic career, as a foreign correspondent for *The Times* for 34 years, serving in Paris, Bonn, Berlin and Tokyo. Charles Hargrove wrote several books; in addition to *A Gentleman of the Times* he wrote two on Queen Elizabeth II. Unfortunately, his health had deteriorated following an attack in his Paris apartment in 2013, but he was still able to take part in the D-Day celebrations at Asnelles on 6 June 2014 when he dined with President Hollande.

Charles Hargrove, soldier, journalist and author: born Genoa 30 May 1922; OBE; Commandeur de la Legion d'Honneur; married; died Paris 19 September 2014.

On hearing the news of the death of Charles Hargrove, we resolved to visit his grave; today seemed to be a suitable opportunity! After a short visit to Arromanches, we re-joined the D514, climbed up and over St-Come before descending towards the beach at La Hamel, a hamlet of Asnelles. ASNELLES has a population of about 600 – the latin origin of its name apparently means 'little donkeys'. The village was severely damaged on 6 June 1944, but there were no civilian casualties. We decided we should head for the parish church and, from the D514 which becomes the Ave. de la Libération, we turned into Rue de Débarquement leading to Rue de l'Eglise Saint Martin. There was a convenient parking area nearby and just across the road there were quite steep steps up into the cimetière. As we entered and approached the church we soon became conscious of a very strong and unpleasant wind blowing in from the sea. However, despite the weather conditions, often using, unwisely I'm sure, old and unstable tomb stones for support, we searched the cemetery, but we could find no evidence of any recent inhumations. We were very disappointed – there must be another cemetery! The church itself was not open, but I took the opportunity of recording the following historical information displayed on the door.

ASNELLES – Le patrimoine religieux

The construction of Saint Martin's church dates back to the end of the 12th century. The building was modified in the 16th century and enlarged in the 19th century. The Romanesque style tower was built in 1856. The base of the spire shows the symbols of the Four Evangelists: the eagle, the man, the lion and the ox.

In the Middle Ages Sainte-Honorine chapel was built in a neighbouring field. The inhabitants of Asnelles and the surrounding area came in pilgrimage, to invoke the saint who cured fevers caused by the coastal marshes. It was destroyed by the protestants in the 16th Century.

The tithe barn, situated behind the church, was built in the 14th century. Farmers put a tenth of their harvest there, for the benefit of the abbey Saint Julien de Tours, the chief collector, for the Asnelles parish priest. Thus the abbots of Tours were authorised to display their coat of arms on the church; an escutcheon with an azure field, and a cross and four fleur de lys in silver.

There was nothing more we could do today and we returned to Arromanches, where we were pleased to find ourselves in the warmth and comfort of the restaurant Au 6 Juin. We had an enjoyable meal spending a couple of hours in the usual convivial atmosphere, leaving at, I see, 20.18 and returning by the very familiar route via Ryes to 'home' at la Ferme des Châtaigniers. (18 miles)

<u>Wednesday, 23 September</u>

Petit déjeuner chez la ferme – and an opportunity to relate to Fabienne the story of our meeting, about ten years ago, with Charles Hargrove; our interest in his life and our disappointment in not being able to visit his grave yesterday. "I will see what I can find out about it for you," said Fabienne. Soon, she returned after consulting the internet and was able to confirm that he is indeed buried at Asnelles, but in the current cimetière and she gave us directions for finding it. We will make a further foray to Asnelles today.

However, it would be sensible to first purchase some petrol. How habits quickly become established – whenever we have been in this area we have always purchased fuel at one particular petrol station and we will do so again today. On leaving the access road to la ferme we turn left until reaching the road from Creully, D126, then, turning right towards Bayeux. After passing the quarry on our left we arrive at the city's ring road. Driving clockwise, we pass, first, la gare and then the Campanile Hotel on our left before the road surface and layout prompts us to slow down in recognition and respect of, on our left, the Bayeux Commonwealth

War Graves Commission Cemetery containing 4,648 graves; on our right is the Memorial to the Missing, recording 1,805 names. Continuing on the ring road and as it bears to the right the exit for Cherbourg is on our left. Soon we approach our immediate destination the Esso du Bessin. There are several petrol stations on the ring road, but this is the one we have patronized in the past. It does not present a spacious and grand appearance. In fact, the situation of the pumps does not make for particularly easy access and positioning – more of an intimate situation. The shop itself, although well stocked, is quite small and compact, but the service is friendly and we are greeted courteously in a way that suggests that we are recognised; perhaps we or the car are remembered and perhaps this is a family business. In any case we like this petrol station. For this record we purchased 53 litres of petrol which cost €71.02; the time was 13.15.

Now we must set off on our second foray to Asnelles. Continuing on the ring road we soon reach the exit to Arromanches – a very pleasant journey of about five miles passing La Rosiere. From Arromanches, it's once again up and over St-Come and down to Asnelles. but today we leave the D514 (now Avenue de la Libération) at the right turn into Rue de Southampton; shortly, another right turn into Chemin du Magasin, then bearing left we are in a parking area and ahead of us is the entrance to the Cimetière De Cavigny. As we walk in we find a ceremony is taking place just inside. However, we were able to ask some bystanders if they could direct us to the grave of Charles Hargrove and they indicated that it was in the far corner of the cemetery. As we made our way respectfully past the tombs we realised that, ahead of us, were two standards, one bearing the Tricolour and the other, the Union Jack We were first attracted to an established and impressive tomb – it was that of 'Maurice Schumann 1911– - 1998 Compagnon de la Libération' and 'Lucie Schumann 1929–2014'. Nearby, and beneath the furling Union Jack, was a somewhat insignificant grave with no more than two small trays and a single bowl of small plants standing above the level of the untended surrounding turf. No doubt it is intended to install a more appropriate and lasting memorial. Nevertheless, we are in no doubt that this is the resting place of Charles Hargrove. Gradually and slowly we retired from the surprisingly unkempt grave in the quiet extremity of the cemetery, but casting our eyes back as we did so – to the colourful concentration of tombstones, standing and lying, lovingly bedecked with plants, flowers and personal mementos and, at the rear, the flags of our two countries standing tall – for a final memory before passing through the gates and returning to our car. This is a very peaceful location with just a few dwellings some distance away across the field.

On all our journeys Margaret has maintained a daily record of varied and invaluable information and she has done so again on this journey. Sometimes it is relatively trivial, but it often revives the memory of a particular place or experience. Today, she has noted that while sitting in the car after leaving the cemetery, "We ate potato crisps at last" and that we left at 4.30pm.

We note that a section of the 'Sente au Batard' is close by the Cimetière. However, we returned along the

Rue de Southampton and continued on to the Boulevard de la Mer where we lingered in contemplation, viewing the beach and sea – 'la belle plage entre mer et campagne'. It was not a beautiful beach on 6 June 1944 as tens of thousands of British soldiers poured on to the enemy occupied and defended territory. One of the first being Charles Hargrove – now he lies just a short distance from that very spot on which he drove ashore. One cannot fail to recognise the measure of gratitude permanently bestowed by the liberated on their liberators by the naming of streets – Libération, Débarquementt, Southampton, The Dorset Regiment, The Devonshire Regiment and Major Martin. At 17.30 we continued, but paused again on the heights of St-Come to comprehend the vast extent of the vestiges of the Mulberry Harbour and to appreciate the seemingly advantageous position of the German defenders and the vulnerability of the attacking forces on D-Day.

From St-Come it is only a matter of minutes to the car park on Boulevard Gilbert Longues in Arromanches and in no time we are once again welcomed in the Au 6 Juin. After an enjoyable meal and a pleasant evening we left at 20.15 but, before returning to the car, we could not resist a short late evening stroll along to the sea front. The five mile drive to Vienne-en-Bessin is a unique experience. It is now late evening and darkness has fallen; after leaving Arromanches there is no sign of personal human activity – only animals assert their presence – and the roads are not just quiet, they are virtually devoid of vehicles; after Ryes, crossing the wide open plain – there is no bocage here – we feel very much alone, but not insecure. We reached 'home' at 21.00. (24 miles)

Thursday, 24 September

After petit déjeuner we spent more time in conversation with Fabienne – unfortunately our French has been neglected – and we were pleased to have the opportunity of taking some photographs – with the assistance of her 'farmhand'.

Once again it is time for the respective dressings to be renewed!

It was in April 2004 that we, and George and Samuel, spent our first week in the gite. One day we walked to the village church of Vienne-en-Bessin; we were not able to go inside but we spent some time in the adjacent cemetery and the boys were intrigued by the inscriptions on certain tombstones – the following, for instance – "A LA MEMOIRS DEM PAUL MORICE, DOCTEUR MEDECIN, 1818–1875, PRIEZ POUR LUI". Perhaps he was the village doctor!

It was well into the afternoon (14.40) when we left la ferme, but we decided that we would first make a brief visit to the church. L'EGLISE SAINT-PIERRE de Vienne-en-Bessin was constructed from the 11th Century and has been classified as a monument historique since 1974. A very interesting feature is the fishbone masonry of the nave, a building method used in Normandy until the 12th Century. Unfortunately, we were again not able to see the inside of the church, but here is a copy of the historical record displayed on the outside.

Eglise Saint-Pierre -XI- XVIII Centuries

The estate belonged to the monks of Jumieges until the Scandinavian invasions and Duke William the Bastard gave the church to Saint-Pierre-de-Preaux (Eure). The 11th century building is famous for its fine gateway-belfry. The Romanesque nave exhibits opus spicatum or fishbone masonry an ancient construction technique often used in Normandy until the early 12th century. The cornice is supported by a magnificent collection of sculpted brackets. Most of the openings are 18th century modifications, but a magnificent embellished Romanesque doorway remains. The choir, sacristy the north and chapel to the south, were rebuilt in the 18th century.

We have driven along the D514 through the village of Longues-sur-Mer many times and, several times, have visited the famous Batterie, but otherwise we have not stopped in the village. It was the home of Fabienne's dad and he was there in June 1944. The Batterie was a prime target for the RAF – I understand that, unfortunately, many bombs fell on the village instead of on the gun emplacements. Leaving Vienne-en-Bessin for Ryes where the D127 quickly takes us to Longues-sur-Mer. We are attracted by the signs to L'ABBAYE-SAINTE-MARIE – a Monument Historique. We were particularly interested to read that the Abbey's Foundation Charter was dated 1168 and was confirmed by Henry II and that in 1932 the American Senator, Charles Dewey, bought the Abbey site. We parked at the side of the road alongside the site where we had good views of the various buildings and, although Margaret decided not to do so, I walked into the site for a closer view of the exterior of the buildings and the activities going on. We recorded the following information.

Sainte-Marie Abbey

The Longues Abbey, dedicated to the Holy Virgin, was created by Hugues Wac, wealthy lord of the Bessin. Henry II Plantagenet King of England and Duke of Normandy confirmed the founding charter dated 1168, a short time later. The estate of the first Benedictine monks from Hambaye Abbey (Manche) was enriched with donations from local lords. When the Archbishop of Rouen, Eudes Rigault, visited in 1257, the community numbered twenty-two monks, possessed four priories and the patronage of some twenty parish churches across the Bessin. The 16th century was even more of a disaster than the Hundred Years' War. Conferment of abbey revenues in 1526 deprived the monks of a regular abbot and the community became obsolete.

Protestants ransacked the abbey in 1562, during the Wars of Religion. The decline continued and in 1760, the community counted only five members. After a lengthy procedure, the Bishop of Bayeux succeeded in having the abbey closed in 1782. The revenues (24,000 pounds) were then shared between the last abbot having benefited from conferment, who was also the Bishop of Lectoure (Gers), Louis Emmanuel de Cugnac, and the Bayeux seminary. Sold during the Revolution, the remaining buildings were saved from ruin by the American senator Charles Dewey who, in 1932, bought the whole complex and began work to safeguard the buildings. The Abbey, fortunately spared by the destruction in 1944, is undergoing renovation and its owners have opened it and its recreated gardens to visitors.

Well, it is only about five kilometres to Arromanches, but if we set off now we must be sure of a window table Au 6 Juin. Yes, a window seat it is and we are able to observe all the activity both within and outside in the street. We had an enjoyable meal and as the time passed we entered into a long and interesting conversation with a couple at a nearby table. They were Lynn and Arthur, who were in Arromanches on their way home to Chichester after a cycling holiday in France. We did not leave the restaurant until 21.20, but were home safely at 21.50. (19 miles)

THE PREPARATION OF THE RECORD OF THIS JOURNEY HAS BEEN SPREAD OVER A LONG PERIOD, MAINLY BECAUSE OF THE ATTENTION TO THE CARING NEEDS OF MARGARET. IT IS NOW NOVEMBER 2017 AND AT THIS POINT, SADLY, SHE PASSED AWAY AT HOME ON 18 NOVEMBER 2017. ALTHOUGH SHE HAD BEEN ABLE TO READ THE EARLIER DAILY RECORDS, SHE WAS NOT WELL ENOUGH TO READ THE MORE RECENT ONES. HOWEVER, IT WAS HER CLEAR WISH THAT I SHOULD CONTINUE TO FINISH THE RECORD OF THIS JOURNEY, AND INDEED OF EARLIER JOURNEYS,

MAKING USE OF HER DETAILED DAILY DIARIES.

Margaret was taken from us as I was in the stage of reliving and recording our final journey in France and, it so happened, at the time we were in Normandy, at La Ferme des Châtaigniers, the home of a special friend, Fabienne. At this point I must resume my 'recollections and reflections'.

<u>Friday, 25 September</u>

We awake at la ferme for the last time – it is our final day here and we shall be in no hurry to leave. As usual we have no difficulty in spending excessive time enjoying our petit déjeuner and absorbing this, for us, unique situation and atmosphere. After a while Fabienne joins us and, during the course of the conversation, she decides that her dad may be able to join us also. Soon she returns with son père and clearly the thoughts of Monsieur turn immediately to the events of 6 June 1944. He proceeded to give us a vividly descriptive account of a British bomb exploding just 50 metres from him, how it extracted the air from his lungs – clearly a frightening and unforgettable experience. We already know that he described the scene as "The night was like day" and "The sea was black". We were so pleased to have this meeting, to learn personally of the memories and emotions of an innocent civilian as the mighty allied armies descended on the shores of France on the most momentous day in European history. We must now hasten to leave Vienne, but not before expressing our sincere thanks to Fabienne for the warm welcome and help. Our four days here have cost a modest €188. We finally leave La Ferme, with a fond farewell, at 13.30 and, as we are not likely to return, we promise to keep in touch.

Without any consideration we proceeded to drive directly to Arromanches. After parking in the usual park we take the three-wheel walker and passing Au 6 Juin, we continue along Rue Marechal Joffre until we find that to continue beyond the refreshment bar we have to step down to a lower level. It was obviously going to be a very difficult manoeuvre for Margaret to achieve – getting both her feet and the walker together on to the lower level. Suddenly, an English gentleman left his ice-cream and his wife and came to our assistance; with the walker on the lower level he simply lifted Margaret down to join it. What a kind spontaneous gesture! After which he told us that he was born in 1952, that he had worked in a residential home and, I think, that they came from Portsmouth. It would now be sensible to have a meal at this time and we returned to Au 6 Juin. Our visits to the restaurant earlier in the week have been later in the day and we have remarked on the absence of the familiar 'senior lady' at the till of past years. However, we realised with great joy that today she is at – for us – her usual station. We chose to have a croque-madam today – it was very enjoyable. We left the restaurant at 17.50 and Arromanches at 18.15 to drive to Bayeux. Our 'home' for the next four nights is the Campanile Hotel which we reached at 18.40. We were allocated Room 8 on the ground floor and facing inwards towards the restaurant and not, as we always hope, a room overlooking the meadow with views of the railway on the right and, to the left, a view of the splendid cathedral spires. However, we are familiar with this hotel and we shall be happy here. I must, of course, add the recorded observation that it had been 'a lovely day'. (18 miles)

Saturday, 26 September

There is one feature of the Campanile Hotel which we do not welcome – its petit déjeuner timetable. On weekdays it is available from, perhaps, 7.00 to 9.00. However, this is the week-end when breakfast is available until 10 o'clock. It is a very different regime than that we enjoyed with Fabienne!

When we read, in the directory of 'Special Places to Stay', of a property at St Germain-du-Pert of, "The solid beauty of the old fortified farmhouse and the serenity of the Marais lapping at the lawn", "of a luminous landscape of marshes and fields, watch storks nesting, the heron fishing in the pond", we could not resist making a reservation. On our initial arrival, quite late in the evening, I am not sure whether it was Paulette or Herve who led us up the 28 steps of the rope-handled stone spiral staircase to our room; unforgettably, there on the wall was a painting of the scene of the Battle of Bosworth! When, as we left after a later visit our hosts told us that we were, in fact, their final guests, that they were retiring to live in Bayeux; they added that if we were able to visit them in their new home we would be very welcome. We accepted their invitation and we have made a number of visits and, with great pleasure, taken George and Samuel with us on some occasions.

Paulette and Herve know we are in Normandy at the present time and, on telephoning them, we are pleased to find that they would welcome us this afternoon. The Campanile is adjacent to the ring road at its western end and the home of Paulette and Herve is in a quiet street near the opposite end of the ring road. Equipped with the essential dictionary and atlas, we reached them at about 15.00 to a warm welcome. Although we have communicated electronically, we have not, in fact, met since the year 2011 and we soon find that our versatility and familiarity in the French language had clearly diminished. However, with mutual contributions and accompanied by lovely refreshments, we are able to create meaningful conversation. Paulette and Herve are always pleased to tell us of the places they have visited during their latest tour in France and of family members they have visited in different parts of the country. They are particularly pleased when, quite often, we can say that we have also visited those same sites. We mentioned that tomorrow, Sunday, we might plan a short drive around some of the pleasant villages of the Normandy countryside; wherewith Herve suggested that we might find a visit to Colombieres interesting. We have so many interests in common – family, travel, etc; we had had an enjoyable and rewarding afternoon, having, we think, acquitted ourselves quite well. Paulette and Herve were concerned for Margaret and her great difficulty in walking as we left them at about 17.30. Margaret's comment on the afternoon was that it was a "Wonderful visit".

We returned directly to the Campanile for a meal in the restaurant of ribeye steak and chips followed by fruit salad. It was not an inspiring meal! (6 miles)

Sunday, 27 September

There is always a very wide range of choices invitingly laid out for petit déjeuner at Campanile – it is a pity that the timetable does not appear to encourage wider selection to be enjoyed more leisurely. However, we are always content with the basic menu of cereals, croissants, bread, etc. Fortunately, we succeeded in reaching the restaurant soon after nine o'clock; nevertheless, we have not finished eating when staff begin clearing the restaurant and laying out the tables for lunch.

It is a lovely morning and the view from our parked car towards la Cathédrale is accompanied by the bells calling worshippers to morning messe – we wish we could join them, but it is not practicable. We must prepare ourselves for an afternoon drive and, hopefully, before staff arrive to carry out the daily service of our room – they are usually quite accommodating!

Our first family holiday in France – in July 1979 – was not as well prepared for as the present journey. We had not made any reservations and we were unable to find accommodation, first at Grandcamp Maisy, then in two other towns until reaching Le Molay Littry, where there were rooms for all four of us in the Hotel du Commerce.

The Campanile is situated at the junction of the ring road and the D5, the road for Le Molay Littry. Where better could we begin our nostalgic drive? We left the Hotel at 13.30 and, about 14km later, parked in the centre of Le MOLAY LITTRY. It is an attractive little town with a population of about 3,000, colourfully dressed with shrubs and flower beds and, being Sunday, no shops are open and it is virtually deserted. We are close to the 'Hotel' which is now described as a 'Cafe de Commerce'; also, overlooking, is the clock which regularly interrupted our sleep during that hot July 1979 night. Back in the 17th century it was a centre of coal mining and a wealthy town. There is an excellent mine museum nearby which we have visited. Outside the town the beautiful Château du Molay stands in 45 acres of magnificent wooded grounds – it was built in 1758 by Jacques-Jean le Coulteux du Molay, a wealthy young banker, and his wife Geneviéve-Sophie.

Taking the D10 and D13 we continue to BALLEROY (population about 900) where the rising road skirts the town's large car park. There was one other car and a couple enjoying a picnic. We sat for some while appreciating the scene, particularly the splendid building ahead of us – it is l'Hôtel de Ville and we admired the impressive War Memorial. The nearby Château de Balleroy dates from 1626 and was in the Balleroy family until 1970. From our earlier visit we recall that an annual Hot Air Balloon Festival took place at the Château. However, this was discontinued after 1999, but since 2007, by public demand, a festival has again been held at the village stadium.

We returned to L'Embranchement on the D13 and continued on that same road towards Cerisy-la-Forêt. Le FORET DE CERISY is a national nature reserve extending over more than 5,000 acres and comprising of mainly beech woodland; it is rich in fauna and flora.

We cannot simply drive through the forest without more intimately savouring and absorbing its special features. It reminds us of our home at Camerton in the early days when there was a beech wood adjacent to us – in fact, we named our house 'The Beeches'. As soon as we see an opportunity to do so we drive off the road a very short distance into a small open area where, on one side and in front and behind us, we are seemingly quite deep in the forest. Now, we can open doors and windows and breath the fresh air and appreciate the distinctive and pleasing smells of the forest. What an appropriate time to enjoy a couple of Mr Kipling's Trifle Bakewells! In fact, we ate the boxful!!

Eventually, we drive on, leaving the forest and, at the same time, the Department of Calvados. CERISY-LA-FORET is in the Manche Department; it has a population of about 900. There are ruins of an oppidum nearby and the Romans built a fort here. When Christianity arrived early in the 6th century, Vigor built a monastery dedicated to St Peter and St Paul on a former Druid holy site. The Vikings invaded in the 9th century and destroyed the monastery. Under the Normans, Cerisy became an important market town; they built the Abbey of Saint-Vigor de Cerisy on the site of the former monastery – it consisted of 48 parishes, including Sherborne and Peterborough in England.

It would make a more interesting journey to continue on a somewhat circular route, heading now towards the coast and visiting Colombières in doing so. The first lords of COLOMBIERES (present population about 200) were three brothers – Guillaume, Raoul and Baudoin

– friends of Guillaume le Conquérant. Subsequently, the town passed into the hands of the powerful Bacon du Molay family. During the course of the Hundred Years War the village and the château were ruined. On 9 June 1944 Colombières was liberated, following which General Omar Bradley established his headquarters in the château.

Our approach to le CHATEAU DE COLOMBIERES was well assisted by the direction signs. However, as we approached we found the gate closed. We left the car outside and we walked the quite long distance to the Château. At the door we were very courteously greeted by a very polite and friendly gentleman; we paid the entrance fee and we were invited inside. Almost straightaway our host explained that he had noticed that it had been difficult for Margaret to walk the distance from our parked car. He said that if we would like him to do so and that we would give him the keys, he would drive the car to just outside the door. He mentioned that it was a Saab car!!! We were very grateful for his offer and he invited us to sit in the stately dining room while he did so. Afterwards, we were invited into the medieval kitchen, with many pans hanging on the wall, and the chapel. The oldest parts of the present Château date from the end of the 14th century. After 1750 the Château came into the ownership of the Girardin family to which the present owners are linked.

We are very pleased to have been prompted to visit this Classified Historical Monument and privileged to be welcomed by Le Comte Charles on behalf of himself and the Comtesse de Maupeou d'Ableiges and their children. As we expressed our thanks and said au revoir to the Count he told us that we had the distinction of being their last visitors for the season. Even so we lingered for quite a while to savour the exterior of this exceptional location and to photograph our Saab standing proudly near the entrance to the Château, before driving off in the direction of Trevieres. With our thoughts still focussed on what we had left behind we twice took a wrong turning in Trevieres before finding Formigny and eventually linking up with the D514 at St. Laurent. Thenceforth we find the coast road to Arromanches very familiar. We had hoped that we might arrive in time to buy some food at our favourite patisserie – unfortunately, it had already closed. Never mind, we still have an assortment of nourishment bars and varied cartons of drinks in our 'larder'. We drive on to Bayeux arriving at the Campanile at 19.40. We have had a splendid journey of more than six hours, visiting places familiar and new, enjoying driving many miles along the peaceful roads of rural Normandy passing typical shuttered old houses. Now to enjoy our 'meal' accompanied with a welcome cup of coffee. (60 miles)

Monday, 28 September

After petit déjeuner our first priority is to renew our respective dressings. Margaret's comment on the weather is that it was "Il fait très beau mais il fait du vent"

It is 14.15 when we leave the Campanile, but this being our last day in Bayeux, we feel that we would like to make a final visit to its magnificent Cathédrale. The entrance on the north side is that most familiar to us, but we do not know of any parking facility nearby; it is in the medieval area of the city with pavements difficult to negotiate and, once inside la Cathédrale, there are many steps to descend. Consequently, the three-wheel walker will not be of practical help. Margaret will have to rely on her walking stick – and me – for support. We drive towards the entrance and we find some cars parked (and one or two spaces) in a small square – I think it may be Place Aux Bois – but I could not find any facility for purchasing a ticket – perhaps it's free. However, a visit to a nearby pharmacy revealed that there is a ticket machine, quite small and inconspicuous, hidden behind one of the cars. We can now happily leave the car and begin to walk down the ancient Rue des Chanoines. There is a narrow pavement, but the surface is very uneven and cars are parked indiscriminately. Nevertheless, I seized an opportunity of taking a photograph of the two spires soaring majestically above the city. It was a difficult exercise for us both, but eventually we reach the Cathedral entrance and with great care and caution we descend the steps safely. It was with relief and a feeling of accomplishment that we sat and relaxed for a while.

NOTRE DAME CATHEDRAL BAYEUX is the title of an excellent book produced by François Neveux, who is also the Cathedral Organist. It tells us that, "Construction of Bayeux Cathedral began in the Roman period, under Bishop Hugues, to continue under William the Conqueror's brother, Bishop Odo (11th century). Following serious fire damage during the 12th century, the Cathedral was rebuilt in Gothic style in the 13th century. Construction of the central tower began in the 15th century, under Bishop Louis d'Harcourt, to be completed only in the 19th century following major work by Eugène Flachet; this is one of France's finest cathedrals and an indisputable masterpiece of Norman Gothic art".

As we sat and observed this wonderful building we took more photographs including, of course, the organ and we reminisced on earlier visits. We recall Samuel expressing his wish to "light a candle for Mr Mills" (our late neighbour at Trowbridge). On one Sunday morning in 2008 we visited shortly after the office had finished. Exceptionally, it had been the occasion of the celebration of the installation by Bishop Pierre Pican of a new archiprêtre, Laurent Berthout. There was a distinct atmosphere of excitement and hope. We were welcomed by a gentleman who also offered us a glass of wine. Regrettably. we did not accept his offer and I have never been sure why we declined the invitation. Eventually, we began to move around a little and independently. Soon I noticed Margaret in conversation with another elderly lady visitor. They were both using a walking stick and it became obvious that this was the subject of their conversation. As we converged, our new friend suggested that the three of us should sit down and we had an interesting conversation. Madame was, I think, 91 and Bayeux has been her lifelong home. She didn't hesitate to express her gratitude that on 7 June 1944 the British mercifully liberated her beloved city without causing any damage. She asked if I was there and I had to explain that I was too young to be involved. She was very interested to know from what part of England we came from.

Of course, London was familiar and the West Country conveyed something to her. She appeared to have a recognition of Cornwall and perhaps in relation to a wedding. Eventually she decided that she should leave. Perhaps this is part of her daily routine of physical exercise and spiritual renewal. We then spent some time in the shop and, in addition to the book I have mentioned, we chose a selection of CDs of organ music played by Francois Neveux playing the Cavaille-Coll organ and also with trumpeters and a vocalist. (Sadly, after returning home and into the increasingly demanding routine associated with her general health, the CDs remained unopened – Margaret never heard the music she had chosen.) Before leaving the Cathédrale we had to note this Memorial

"TO THE GLORY OF GOD AND TO THE MEMORY OF ONE MILLION DEAD OF THE BRITISH EMPIRE WHO FELL IN THE GREAT WAR, 1914–1918, AND OF WHOM THE GREATER PART REST IN FRANCE".

A monumental fact!

Eventually, we began to climb the steps towards the door and then, out into the street, make our way carefully and cautiously back to our car. Our last day in Bayeux means that it is our final evening meal at Au 6 Juin in Arromanches. Once again we spent an enjoyable couple of hours here as we have done so many times in past years. We enjoyed our meal and it was 19.53 when we left to return to our room at the Campanile. Another memorable day! (17 miles)

Tuesday, 29 September

Campanile Hotels are widespread in France; with their distinctive design and prominent locations they are readily recognised and easily found; all facilities, services and standards are identical. Although lacking a little of the personal attention and concern found in privately owned hotels, Logis de France for instance, they often provide very convenient accommodation. We have used them on a number of occasions, particularly that on the outskirts of Vire, in the south of Calvados, for our first night on many France journeys. We are pleased to have spent the last four nights here in Bayeux Campanile, but the time has come for us to leave for the very last time – it is 11.45!

Before leaving Bayeux we return to Esso du Bessin to purchase petrol for our journey home – 35 litres for €46.91. It is now noon and we will make a final visit to Arromanches – at 12.30. Just one last walk down Boulevard Gilbert Longues and into Rue Marechal Joffre where we visited la Presse to buy one or two items, including a copy of that excellent daily regional newspaper 'Ouest France' and two large table mats displaying historical information of 1944; then on to the sea front where, surprisingly, we found the sea very angry, which was a challenge to one brave lady. At 14.15 we reluctantly drove away from Arromanches. We travelled leisurely along the D514 until St Laurent-s-Mer where we decided to make a detour.

In the course of an identical journey on 6 October 2011 we reached this point only to find that the road ahead was closed and we had to make a detour via Formigny. It revealed to us the site of the Battle of Formigny but, we did not have sufficient time to visit the whole area. Today our time is not limited.

The BATTLE of FORMIGNY was fought on 15 April 1450 between the English and French and ended in a decisive French victory. It was the penultimate battle of the Hundred Years' War. The opposing monarchs at this time were Henry VI of England and Charles VII of France. The final battle of the war was fought at Castillon in Gascony in 1453 − another decisive French victory.

When we reached the area of the Battle we found the Office de Tourisme open and a very helpful lady explained the various features of the site and directed us to interesting leaflets, etc. She advised us to visit the little chapel, dedicated to Saint-Louis, which we did. It was constructed in 1486 by the Comte de Clermont (also Charles I de Bourbon), commander of one of the French armies, to commemorate the victory. It is situated at the side of the road and Margaret was able to have a good view from the car. It appears to be in good condition, but I read that the bell tower is in danger of collapsing and there are appeals for donations; I was not able to go inside. Back near the Office we parked near the magnificent statue, created by the Norman sculptor, Arthur Le Duc; it was inaugurated in 1903 and is entered in the Inventory of Historic Monuments. It incorporates three bronze statues, one of which represents France pointing its sword at England symbolising France's victory. The re-conquest of Normandy was finally achieved in the summer of 1450. Across to the other side of this rather busy road we were able to park alongside another memorial – to those who fell in the Great War – 'FORMIGNY A SES ENFANTS 1914–1918'. We are disappointed that in the course of moving from one position to another and being engrossed in what we had discovered we somehow failed to see the little Memorial which marks the actual battlefield. Nevertheless, it was a most interesting diversion!

We left Formigny to rejoin the D514 at St Laurent-s-Mer; we left the road and drove towards Pointe du Hoc, but it is not now possible to drive beyond the official car parks and, as we have visited the site several times in the past, we promptly returned to the D514. The approach to Grandcamp-Maisy from the east, where the road forks to the sea front, is unforgettable; there, salient, soaring, shining, sparkling is the spectacular "STATUE DE LA PAIX – WORLD PEACE STATUE" by Yao Yuan (Wen Yuan Yan) – "AU PEUPLE DE NORMANDIE". In this attractive garden there is a particular memorial:

"In memory of Leonard G. Lomell DSO CO D. 2nd Ranger BN. WWII US ARMY RANGER. HALL OF FAME and the 225 American soldiers who, on 6 June 1944 assaulted and destroyed the 5 German guns at Pointe du Hoc. By the morning of 8 June, only 90 were still able to bear arms. They gave proof of their great courage. We will never forget them."

As we neared the sea front we noticed a variety of temporary makeshift barriers which were, or had been, positioned at a number of accesses to the sea front.

However, we found we could now drive on to the Quai Crampon and as we continued towards Le Duguesclin we were amazed to find so much debris across the road. There must have been a severe storm, but we had not experienced any of it. At the hotel entrance I was barely able to stay on my feet, the wind was so strong and when I eventually reached the door, it was locked! We drove on past the harbour, turning left into rue Aristide Briand then along the narrow route to the rear of the hotel – relieved, we parked the car. I climbed the stairs and found a lady at the desk. When I enquired what had happened, she said that it was une grande marée (a spring tide). It was a new experience for us! I returned to the car to accompany Margaret up to our room.

Even here we have not escaped the exceptional weather conditions, for the very strong wind was making an unbearable noise in forcing its way through the not tightly closed window. We could not tolerate that throughout the night! I called for the assistance of Monsieur who promptly applied sufficient physical strength to improve matters considerably. After an hour's relaxation we felt ready to make our way to the restaurant for we were looking forward to another enjoyable meal. Sitting at the table we occupied last week (I am sure) we did not hesitate to once again choose un filet de boeuf, with frites and mixed vegetables which, together with profiteroles and a small glass of wine, made an excellent and fitting final evening meal in France. On returning to our room we were pleased to find that the very strong wind had abated a little and was not likely to interrupt our night's sleep. (36 miles)

Wednesday, 30 September

Morning – and we have had a comfortable night. It was not inappropriate that we should spend our final night at Le Duguesclin, the hotel at which we hoped to spend our first night together in France some 36 years ago. We enjoyed a very leisurely petit déjeuner, appreciating for the last time the splendid 'sea view'. After thanking and saying au revoir to les propriétaires, we finally left the hotel at noon.

It is only about 50 miles to the ferry port of Cherbourg and our sailing time is not until 22.15 – we do not need to take the most direct route, via the N13. Instead, for the first part of the journey, we will take the road we used to use. Again, it's the D514, first to Osmanville and then Isigny-s-Mer, but continuing on the old road (D197A) to Carentan where we pass again the entrance to le gare. From Carentan we drive along the D913 to Vierville and Ste-Marie-du-Mont. STE-MARIE-du-MONT (pop. 800) was in the forefront of the actions on D-Day, being close to Utah Beach. Thousands of American soldiers were dropped in the area, scattered and finding themselves isolated in hostile territory, many were able to make use of their click-clack devices and congregate using the distinctive shape of the church steeple as a focal point. We are able to park near this same church and photograph it. The Church of Our Lady of the Assumption dates from the 11th century and has been a Listed Monument since 1840. In this same position we are close to the impressive war memorial and also the Hotel de Ville – it is evident that the village is eagerly looking forward to the privilege of being a 'GRAND DEPART du TOUR de FRANCE 2016' – 275 days from today.

As we sat in the car we could see a direction sign – it conveniently took us along minor roads into Ste-Mere-Eglise. We parked at the church again and walked the short distance to La Libération for our lunch of croque-monsieur and Kit Kats. There is a useful toilet here – it has minimal space, situated under the stairs, but it is quite satisfactory. We could not leave this historic village without a final visit to the church; we spent some time inside in quiet contemplation. I looked at the organ (again) and I meant to record the inscription, but I think the instrument was donated by the British (?) Army. Close to the entrance is the figure of SAINTE ANTOINE de PADUA with child. We have found the figure of this saint in so many churches and he has been a favourite of Margaret; I had to take a photograph.

Sainte Antoine (1195–1231) was a Portuguese Franciscan priest who died in Padua, Italy. He was a powerful preacher, with a great knowledge of the scriptures; he had an undying love and devotion to the poor and the sick and he was one of the most quickly canonized saints in church history. He was proclaimed a Doctor of the Church in 1946. We returned to our car and after surveying the scene of the church and its effigy of John Steele, we set off at four o'clock to now join the N13 and drive directly to the ferry port. After entering the bypass of Cherbourg I have to be particularly attentive on the descent as there are roads leading off to the right and we must ensure that we remain in the direction of the ferry-port. Often there are other vehicles and by their nature and appearance it is certain that they are heading for the same destination. However, the road is very quiet today, but we successfully reach the entrance to the Brittany Ferries terminal – it is now five o'clock.

We look forward to our first experience of an overnight crossing on this route. *BARFLEUR* was built in Finland and entered service in 1992. It has 72 four-berth cabins and 295 reclining seats.

Boarding for *Barfleur* will not begin for several hours and we find a convenient place to park near the refreshment hall; that is where we spend much of the time enjoying a snack and a drink in the company of a number of other travellers. Before the official time for boarding I moved our car to a position in front of the entrance gates and, in good time, we returned to the car to be among the first to pass through the ticket and passport check-point. However, when we reach the boarding queue we are held back to be, perhaps, the last vehicle to drive on board. The reason being that we had to be positioned with sufficient space for a member of the crew to assist Margaret from the car into a wheelchair. We were then taken to our outside large two-berth cabin with ensuite facilities – No 8104. It was very compact, but comfortable and we soon established ourselves for the night. As the ship sailed at 22.15 we were a little disappointed to realise that, although we had an outside cabin, the superstructure of the ship obscured our view as we left Cherbourg and France for the last time. Also, we soon realised that with the ship moving we had to be exceptionally careful when moving about, particularly in getting in and out of the bathroom. Clearly the beds were the best and safest place to be and we quickly settled down for the 'night'. Our arrival time at Poole was 07.00 and we had not been given any advice that we should be ready to disembark at that time. In fact, before that time members of the crew were knocking on the door wishing to prepare the cabin for the next voyage. We were by no means ready to leave; it was a very hurried process and we had no time for breakfast. Soon a member of the crew returned with a wheelchair and he checked that together we were taking all our belongings with us. In no time we were back to our car. We had had a satisfactory night, but we should have observed the time reminders which were broadcast and prepared to leave the cabin much earlier. However, the assistance we had received was invaluable. (55 miles)

Thursday, 1 October

Driving off the ship at seven o'clock in the morning was an unfamiliar experience and we did not feel fully alert. However, there was a long delay at the customs checkpoint and we had time to collect our thoughts. As we left the port at 07.10 and began to drive through the urban area, already with a considerable volume of traffic, we felt we had been plunged into a different world. Nevertheless, we successfully found our way through Hamworthy to Blandford. By now, the sun was very bright and quite low in the sky and with the considerable volume of traffic I was finding it difficult to read all the road signs correctly. Suddenly I realised we were heading towards the centre of Blandford. I am not familiar with the town and it took us quite a while to return to the A350 in the direction of Shaftesbury. Henceforth, we succeeded in negotiating the route successfully, but it was with relief that we reached Green Lane at 9.15. (53 miles)

Our total mileage for the journey was 541.

Despite her physical condition and the progressive nature of her dementia, Margaret determinedly maintained a record of this journey as she had done for so many journeys in the past; I have since appreciated that it required a considerable effort for her to do so.

We had serious misgivings regarding the wisdom of undertaking this journey; however, it was an entire success and gave us much interest, pleasure, satisfaction and a feeling of accomplishment. We have no regrets!

Above all, we have been moved by the numerous instances of recognition and concern of our physical limitations and difficulties and we have been immensely grateful for all the help and support given to us on so many occasions. Those sixteen days left us with a permanent memory of so much kindness and goodwill.

This is, indeed, the end of our *'France – A Journey'* and we are immensely grateful to have been able to accomplish this final stage at the ages of 82 and 85.

Please turn over for dedication...

A DEDICATION

I dedicate these pieces to Margaret, who supported and encouraged me in all my endeavours throughout some 60 years. She was my inspiration and she always welcomed and read whatever I had written. It was her wish and hope that they should culminate in the form of a book. What better way to spend my final years, than to fulfil her wishes? I am pleased that she was able to read several of the pieces, but I have prepared those relating to the Crusades, the Great War and the autobiography since she left us in November 2017. For 60 years of Love, Care and Devotion, I thank You and may God Bless You.

At the National Memorial Arboretum in May 2017

Lightning Source UK Ltd.
Milton Keynes UK
UKHW020242060819
347431UK00001B/1/P